THE DOOR
WHEREIN I WENT

Quintin McGarel Hogg was born in 1907, son of the first Viscount Hailsham, and after being educated at Eton became a Fellow of All Souls College, Oxford. He first trained as a philosopher but rejected that as a profession in favour of law, becoming a Barrister of Lincoln's Inn in 1932, a Bencher in 1956 and Treasurer in 1975. He also became a Q.C. in 1953.

He was a Member of Parliament 1938-50, and a member of the House of Lords 1950-63. In that year he disclaimed the title of second Viscount Hailsham, re-entering the House of Commons until 1970, when he was created a Life Peer.

Lord Hailsham has led a very distinguished legal and political career, having been Leader of both Houses of Parliament, Lord Privy Seal and Lord Chancellor. He has also headed the Conservative Party organization. He has twice been Minister of Education and as the first Minister of Science so distinguished himself as to be elected a Fellow of the Royal Society.

He is the author of numerous books, many of them on legal or political topics.

The Law of Arbitration (1935)
One Year's Work (1944)
The Law and the Employer's Liability (1944)
The Times We Live In (1944)
Making Peace (1945)
The Left Was Never Right (1945)
The Purpose of Parliament (1946)
The Case for Conservatism (1947)
The Law Relating to Monopolies, Restrictive Trade
    Practices and Resale Price Maintenance (1956)
The Conservative Case (1959)
Interdependence (1961)
Science and Politics (1963)
The Devil's Own Song (1968)

LORD HAILSHAM

THE DOOR WHEREIN I WENT

COLLINS
Fount Paperbacks

First published by William Collins Sons &
Co Ltd, Glasgow, 1975
First issued by Fount Paperbacks 1978

© Lord Hailsham 1975

Made and printed in Great Britain by
William Collins Sons & Co Ltd, Glasgow

TO MY WIFE

Contents

1

The door wherein I went

This is a book largely about philosophy and religion. As I only have a first degree in philosophy acquired laboriously nearly forty-five years ago and none in theology, it may well be asked why I am writing it. I do not deceive myself into thinking that I am a particularly good man. I have had no blinding revelations to describe, and no sudden religious conversion. I am one of those condemned to live this life in the discipline of darkness, and therefore in doubt, in faith but without certainty.

It is more conventional, and perhaps more profitable, for ageing politicians to publish a volume of autobiography or reminiscences. At least I am sure that this, for me at least, would be a mistake. I have been trained to a profession which is taught that it is wrong to give other people away, and I am sure that it would be foolish to give myself away even if I had such entertaining memories as David Niven, or such exciting adventures as Winston Churchill to recall. Any autobiography I wrote would thus inevitably be lacking alike in spice and candour.

Moreover, and I must confess this at once, I have always wished to write a book of this kind after I had reached an age when I had leisure to do so, and it is now clear to me that it must be written soon, or else it will never be written at all. It seems to me that I have one gift which makes me the richer for its possession, and others of my contemporaries the poorer for its lack, and I would like to share it with all who can do so. It is that I have genuine and coherent and related views about life and its meaning which give me sense and direction in all I do, consolation in misfortune, and courage when tempted to despair. These views would not do these things for me at all if I did not believe them to be true. Their utility and their relevance have not been sought or contrived for their own sake, but derive solely from my conviction about their truth, so far as abstract convictions of this kind can ever be described as accurate and true.

I do not claim any credit for this. Indeed, at first blush, I think it requires a little justification. For very little of it is original. I was brought up as a member of the Church of England by Christians who, though by no means saints, believed and practised their religion. I owe many of my political convictions, and certainly my adhesion to the Conservative Party, to my father, and my lifelong devotion to the law and the legal profession also to him. At the end of the day, I find myself surprised rather than self-satisfied that, after so many doubts and difficulties, after so much discussion and argument, and a life full of incident, it looks as if I am leaving by the door wherein I went. My world is a coherent whole, but is a possession which I have inherited, not one which I have built for myself by my own brains, or my own brilliance. I think it is the better for this, but one sobering doubt remains. Amongst all the various opinions open to men, and the almost infinite number of permutations amongst them, and in an age of almost incredible confusion and change, the mathematical chances against my being right in all my views or even a significant proportion of them would seem to be almost astronomical. But the same, I suppose, would be true of any set of opinions, original or selective, coherent or syncretistic. Despite their largely inherited character, at least these are my own, and I desire to give some account of them before I die.

Come to think of it, I believe I would have to set them down even if they never had a reader other than myself. It is not, I think, either mawkish or unhealthy at the age of 68 to begin to prepare one's soul for death. We do not think enough about death nowadays. But we never quite forget about it, since we know that, at the end of the corridor, Azrael awaits us all. The beginning of such a self-examination must be an enquiry about one's own beliefs. Mine are here.

2

The Unknown God

I am quite sure that the centre of all my life, the thing which gives coherence to the rest of it, and purpose to the whole, is my belief in God. I had better explain first of all what I mean by this, and why I think it reasonable to hold this belief. But this involves a series of quite separate enquiries, some of them autobiographical, some expository. I want first of all to explain that I do not regard the belief which I am trying to describe as necessarily corresponding to the childhood picture of a heavenly father, looking down from the sky, pardoning or punishing our offences, and granting or refusing our petitions. It is not so much that I regard this view as false, for there is a sense in which I shall be saying that I think it true, or rather the nearest approach to truth of which we are capable. But I do regard it as totally inadequate. What I am first of all saying is something which I believe about reality. No doubt the human personality is the thing in our experience which gives us more than anything a clue to the existence and nature of the divine. It could hardly be otherwise, since the human personality is to my mind by far the most sophisticated and interesting thing we know. But the idea of God is infinitely more mysterious and baffling than that. What I am trying to say is something about the Universe itself. I am trying to say that it is not self-explanatory and that however much we learn about physical nature or human history it cannot, in principle, become self-explanatory. It is not simply that we shall never know enough about the present state of the Universe to give it the coherence and sense which I believe it has. It is that in principle it cannot be known or understood in this way. I believe, in fact, that this is implicit in all the theories of the modern scientists. Some hold that the world began with a 'big bang'. According to this view, at some infinitely distant moment of past time, a solid object of infinitely heavy density exploded in some fashion and its fragmented parts are even now disappearing and parting from one another at incredibly high and probably accelerating speeds and will continue to do so till the end of time, whatever time may mean. Others hold the view that the present state of the universe is based on the continuous creation of new matter constantly appearing, quite literally, out of nothing. I do not seek, in my ignorance, to speculate which of these two theories is the more, or less, plausible. I only say that each postulates a universe which is not self-explanatory. The first cannot answer the question what happens before the big bang; the second cannot answer the question what brings the new matter into being. These questions are not merely unanswered. They are in principle unanswerable. But they only lie at the beginning of the list of unanswerable conundrums which the human intellect is bound to ask. Take, for instance, the speed of light, one hundred and eighty-six thousand miles per second (or whatever the right figure is, for it does not matter what and I am not going to look it up). We are assured by the scientists that it follows from the theory of relativity that nothing faster can possibly exist in principle. This is by no means self-evident. But when we ask the scientist why he asserts this, what he says in effect is that, since everything which is observed usually requires light in order that it may be observed it is not possible in principle to observe anything which goes any faster than light. The underlying hypothesis of this is, that only that which is observable exists, and that what is not in principle observable is not in fact in existence. I am inclined to think that this is true of the physical universe, though I am told now that a new generation of scientists is beginning to make observations and measurements which can best be explained on the hypothesis that certain movements take place which are in fact faster than the speed of light. I do not think that this affects the nature of the argument. For, whilst I accept that it may be true that the field of science, its terms of reference as it were, are circumscribed by the proposition that only that exists which can be measured or observed, the proposition itself is one which cannot itself be measured and cannot itself be observed, and is therefore one which cannot be true of all being and if it is asserted as such becomes immediately self-contradictory. In the last resort, unless one accepts from the outset the fact that the universe is not self-explanatory, the position of the scientist is as intellectually indefensible as that of the savage who believed that the world was supported on a giant tortoise. 'And by what is the giant tortoise supported?' asked his questioner. 'By an enormous elephant,' was the answer. 'And by what is the elephant supported?' Puzzlement, followed by: 'Don't ask silly questions.' The philosopher, however, is, I believe, bound to ask the questions, if only to show that the hypothesis, although it may be sound, is not in principle an explanation of all that is. A rather clever man once told me that philosophy is about those questions which children insist on asking and adults insist are silly and should not be asked.

But, of course, this is not the only kind of thing which has to be explained. Quite apart from the observable phenomena of nature there is the existence of life, the origin of which remains as obscure, or perhaps more so, than any of the facts of the inanimate universe. When I was a boy it was seriously being propounded that life on this planet was brought here, say on a meteorite, from an extra-terrestrial source. This, of course, may or may not be true. But it no more explains the origin of life than the existence of a strange bird in my garden is explained on the hypothesis that it flew in from next door. Nowadays it is more popular to explain the origin of life from an evolutionary chemical development of the heavier atoms and molecules assumed to exist in the primeval oceans, and this of course may also be true. But in so far as life includes consciousness, which in its higher forms it undoubtedly does, the theory no more explains what requires explanation than the fact that my body contains carbon, hydrogen and oxygen atoms explains either the existence of the French language or my ability to talk it. In other words, the world is not self-explanatory if only because there is consciousness in it.

But the problem becomes more baffling still if we ask ourselves the questions we are bound to ask about some of the human experiences which we describe by the generic term 'value judgements', that is, judgements we make about things, people, or actions, by way of praise or blame, saying 'good' or 'evil', 'just', 'righteous', 'beautiful', 'ugly', 'cruel', 'right', 'wrong', or 'true' and 'false'. This must involve a universe in which some kinds of experience or reality transcend the bounds of what one can describe as verifiable, measurable, or observable. We know that the universe contains these judgements and the people who make them. I am not, at the moment, seeking to dispute with those who claim that these are merely emotional noises amounting to no more than statements of like and dislike, pleasure or pain, although, as will emerge at a much later period of the discussion, I believe that such people are talking nonsense. The fact is that the universe which contains such judgements or emotions and the people who make or feel them is not self-explanatory, and that any explanation that we seek of such experiences must account for them, and be itself above and outside them. In a paradoxical sense, aware that, at this stage, I am doing no more than apply a label to an unknown, I choose to call this unknown, and in a sense unknowable, factor, God. My belief in It, or Him, whatever It or He may be, is grounded in my scepticism and not in my credulity. Our ancestors said the same thing when they spoke of God as the first cause. But in one sense this phrase is too restricted, and in another it is misleading. The next question is how, if this 'God' is unknown and, in a sense, unknowable, you can claim to find such value in belief in Him, and how indeed you can know Him at all. This requires a separate enquiry, into the nature of knowledge itself.

3

The Tree of Knowledge

I have not always been a Christian, nor even believed in God. At the age of 23, when I sat down to write my Logic paper in Greats, the school at Oxford of Ancient Philosophy, and History, I certainly had no such beliefs, and had not possessed them for years. I possessed, I think, a kind of belief in duty, a sort of categorical imperative imposing obligations of honesty, courage and kindness, though not, I am almost sure, of chastity. But this was based on no sort of religious belief, nor any rational idea about the universe. There had been no exact moment when my belief in religion had failed, but the point at which I realized acutely that it had wholly disappeared was the day upon which my mother died.

I was at Eton, and I was 17 years of age. It happened that I was in bed with influenza. My brother, Edward Marjoribanks, came into the room, unexpected and unannounced. 'I have bad news for you,' he said, 'Mother died this morning.' She had died of a stroke, and I had not expected it. Nothing quite so awful, indeed nothing really awful at all, had happened to me before, for mine had been a fairly protected childhood. In the afternoon the headmaster came in to comfort me. He was a gentleman, and a Christian. He sought to console me with talk about the after life. I was discourteous. I suddenly realized that I did not believe a word of what he was saying, and I told him so. I said that I believed that when we died we were nothing. 'Like the animals,' I said, for good measure. He was angry and went away.

I did not openly break with the Church. There was my father to consider, and I loved him. Moreover there were other relatives and friends who would have been upset at my apostasy had they known of it. So I drifted in a world in which there was no God, doing more or less as I liked, but devoted to my scholarship, my work, and my ambitions. I did not cease to mourn my mother. But I was not un-happy, and when I had got to Oxford, the excitements of the social life, the Union, of which I became President, undergraduate politics, and the schools carried me along without a great deal of time for reflection. I had lost my religion, but I was wholly absorbed in the world and I was not aware that anything serious was missing.

So imagine me sitting down to a three-hour paper, on what was described as 'Logic'. It was in fact the most general philosophical paper of all and most of it was about the theory of knowledge. Looking back on it I realize now that the generation to which I belonged was a remarkable one. We were almost the last generation of Oxford undergraduates to study Greats before the works of Wittgenstein rose over the scene like a chariot of fire. Gilbert Ryle was my tutor, but he had not yet written his book about the ghost in the machine. Freddie Ayer was my younger contemporary, but I do not suppose he had then begun the studies which have since made him famous. Professor Joachim was still lecturing in New College on objective idealism. The English books on philosophy which we were told to read included Bosanquet and F. H. Bradley, whose style made a greater impact on me than his opinions. Even now, in my political speeches, I sometimes borrow his splendid prose: as, for instance: 'It ill becomes the parents of a monster to blame it for following the laws of its being.' Ayer, and Hampshire, Berlin, Austin and Dummett were creatures of the future. I had studied Plato and Aristotle, particularly Plato's Republic and Aristotle's Nicomachean Ethics, each of which I must have read sixteen times at least. I had read, and attended lectures on, Descartes and the English empiricists, Locke, Berkeley and Hume. I had read, in translation, Kant's *Critique of Pure Reason*, and Norman Kempe's book on its teachings. I knew, broadly speaking, of Hegel and his writings, without having studied them, and I knew of Broad, Russell, Cook Wilson, and went to the lectures of Professor Prichard, whose essay in *Mind*, 'Is Moral Philosophy founded on a mistake?' seemed to me the last word in destructive criticism.

The logic paper lasted three hours, and we were supposed in that time to write answers to three, or perhaps four, questions out of about eleven or twelve. I scribbled hard in my illegible hand, and when time came to show up my answers I found that I had answered no more than two questions and part of a third. I was in despair. I passionately desired a first class, like my brother Edward, and if this sort of progress was all that I could make, I thought I had not a chance. Yet I had filled three whole manuscript books of the paper provided for candidates.

A very odd thing had happened to me in this examination. I had entered it, as I believed, exceptionally well prepared, and there were few of the questions I could not have attempted except the one or two designed for candidates interested particularly in music or the arts. But the strange thing was that I had only attempted to answer two of the questions about which I thought I knew so much. Most of the time I had spent in attempting to answer a question about which I knew nothing, and about which in fact I knew rather less than this. It was a question about mysticism, which I was ignorant enough to equate with belief in God. It was this strange episode in my intellectual history which, I believe, proved the turning-point in the slow recovery of my Christian faith.

I must now explain why the question interested me so much, and why the attempt to answer it proved such a milestone in my intellectual life. The fact is that, for a very long time, Western philosophers had been preoccupied with the question how can we be sure of anything. At the end of the Middle Ages men believed on the whole that we knew everything that we did know by a process of deductive reasoning, and the various modes in which these deductions could logically be made were all catalogued and labelled by the various modes of the syllogism. It was, of course, all nonsense, but argumentation about it formed a beautiful and coherent system of study based on Aristotle's *Organon*, which had been rediscovered after having been first lost for centuries and for a time known only through Latin and Arabic translations. The syllogism, however, must have a premise, or premises, and so long as it was believed that both the Bible and the Church were infallible and inspired sources of revealed truth, it did not seem altogether absurd to demonstrate a wide range of propositions by deriving them from scriptural or patristic texts or from other sources of apparently reliable information.

But suppose that the Bible or the Church be not an infallible source of knowledge, at least on secular subjects, where do matters

stand then? How can we be sure of anything except our own existence, whatever that may mean? The answer is that the question is an
unreal one because we not only do not, but in principle cannot,
discover anything new or important by purely deductive reasoning,
since so-called deductive reasoning is really no more than an analysis
or rearrangement of things already known by some other means.
It is, at best, a method of demonstration and argument, a means of
conveying to, or convincing others of, the truths we know, or
believe we know, and not a means of discovering truth at all. But
the fact is that this was not immediately apparent and, to a great
number of people who have not reflected at all deeply about philosophical problems, it is not immediately apparent today. And so a
variety of solutions came to be proposed. We can be sure of our own
existence, and so can, as it were, work outwards from that. *Cogito
ergo sum.* We can be sure of our sense data, and so discover new facts
from the variety of our visual and other sensory experiences. But
what are these, and how do we know that they are real, and, if we
can know this, how can we establish the nature of the reality to
which they correspond? The English empiricists proposed answers
to all these questions, increasingly ingenious, but all in vain. By the
time of Hume it became apparent that all this had failed, and that
on these lines all that was really intellectually respectable was a
universal scepticism. I feel myself that there was less superficiality
than is generally alleged in Johnson's refutation of Berkeley's theory
of subjective idealism. 'Sir, I refute it thus' (kicking a stone). For if
this is indeed the conclusion, it is surely true that common sense
does refute it thus, even when it does not trouble fully to understand
it.

Bacon, one of three Lord Chancellors - the other two being
Haldane and Thomas More - to be considerable philosophers,
achieved a European reputation by pointing out that the nascent
natural science of his time achieved its already substantial discoveries
by a process other than deduction. Following Aristotle, he called it
induction (ἐπαγώγη), but, realizing that he was breaking new
ground, he called his work the *Novum Organum*, the new *Organon*,
thus directly challenging the great original which, since its rediscovery, had so long dominated European thought. The new
doctrine derived its label from the fact that, as Bacon pointed out,

science evolved its discoveries by generalizing from specific observations instead of deriving particular truths by deduction from more
general principles. Unfortunately it was soon replied that the mere
enumeration of the recurrence of specific events failed to provide a
logical justification for the kind of prediction about the occurrence
of future events which is both the basis and the chief glory of modern
science. 'It ought to cause you increasing surprise,' as H. W. B. Joseph
of New College used to tell his pupils when they tried to convince him
that Newton had been able to infer the law of gravity by watching
apples repeatedly fall to the ground. The uniformity of natural laws,
due to the operation of cause and effect, cannot be inferred from any
number of past occurrences unless the observer of these already has a
belief in the existence of general laws of this kind and, since this
belief can only itself be based on past experiences, the inference on
which it depends must derive from some insight into the actual
nature of things which does not depend simply on the enumeration
of particular instances, however frequent, or however widespread,
any more than it depends upon deduction from general principles,
separately given and established by some other means.

The first philosopher who correctly diagnosed this basic sickness
of Western philosophy was the Prussian Protestant Immanuel Kant,
who labelled the problem that of discovering the justification for
'synthetic *a priori* propositions'. In the end he related the solution
of the conundrum to the existence of God by means of the 'categorical imperative' he divined in moral judgements about right and
wrong. In this, I believe, he saw a good deal further than he knew,
and certainly a great deal further than he said, but, first, it is necessary to see a little further into the history of the philosophy of
thought than was achieved in the middle of the eighteenth century.

It is significant that, outside the small group of Western philosophers whose evolving thought I have been trying to describe, the
question which I have asked has not often been discussed. The
Eastern philosophers, of whom, at the time of my logic paper so
long ago in 1930, I had scarcely heard, have not thought of the
problem as a problem at all. It was specifically the constantly increasing and rapidly accelerating increase in the body of knowledge
as the result of what is broadly called natural science that finally
forced the question on human consciousness. So long as the general

corpus of knowledge remains more or less constant there can be no real bother about the nature or the routes by which we can expect to acquire it. In fact, we can learn it from books or from teachers, although we may convince ourselves that we come by it in some other way, and the tests which we have to apply are really tests by which we can judge the general reliability of the authors and the extent to which their views can be verified or justified logically. But, in a dynamic situation, with knowledge growing exponentially all the time, and new facts and new theories pouring in faster than we can digest them, we are really forced to ask ourselves what we can be said to know, how we can be said to know it, and what are the processes of thought by which this vast influx of new ideas and new facts can be assimilated, arranged systematically, and accepted or rejected as true or false.

It was about this time that the system known as objective idealism came into being. Whether, in a sense, Kant can be described as its first exponent need not be discussed here. Although it is incredible, and although I had already found it so by the time I was writing my logic paper, it is, I still think, one of the most marvellously subtle constructions of the human intellect. More than this, it was the point at which Eastern and Western philosophy most closely converged, and I believe at one point it has unravelled an important clue. Knowledge grows. It evolves like a species. It grows like a plant. It is like a tree. Whatever the relation between appearance and reality, between sense datum and the physical world, the inner structure of knowledge, following its own laws, laying down its own principles, develops like a living thing. This is because, if not itself a living thing, the subjects in which it grows are in fact living beings. The earlier objective idealists wrote before Darwin or, if not before Darwin wrote, at least before Darwin had been fully understood and assimilated. Thus Hegel developed the theory of knowledge into something which has come to be called a dialectic, thesis, antithesis, synthesis, a theory still embalmed, like a fly in amber, in the writings of Karl Marx, who claimed to have 'stood Hegel on his head'. There is nothing so simple as this about it. Like Topsy, knowledge grows. The process of verification, of elimination of possible alternatives, and rejection of hypotheses which do not fit subsequent experiments is infinitely complex, and its relation to reality different in kind from that conceived of by the objective idealists. But none of this could exist, knowledge could not exist, beliefs could not exist, falsity and lies could not exist, if there did not also exist a power in the human intellect to spark directly across the gap which forever exists between knower and the object known. This means that it is for ever false that that only is significant or true which is capable of proof or disproof by experiment. Indeed, if anyone sets up the proposition that that only is true or significant which is capable of proof or disproof by experiment, he is guilty of self-contradiction, since the proposition which he has just asserted is itself a proposition incapable of such proof or disproof.

All this, or something like it, unrolled from my pen as I wrote my answer on mysticism, which, in my ignorance, I thought meant the same thing as belief in the existence of God, and, as I wrote, it seemed to me that a new world was opening before me. If this was indeed the truth about knowledge, of course nothing was as yet proved by this truth about anything. But the way was open. The road was clear which I had thought completely blocked by heaps of stone. If there was no reason why an intelligent man should believe in God, there was clearly no reason why he should not. If there was no reason why he should attach any particular content to the value judgements of right and wrong, beauty and ugliness, justice and injustice, truth and falsity, there was equally no reason why human experiences of each, the existence of which is undeniable, should be downgraded to the status of the purely subjective, nor any reason why all human experiences of the same subject matter should be given an equal value, the saint's insights made no better than those of the criminal's, the philistine's equated with the aesthete's, that of the tone deaf lumped with the musician, even though, unlike the judgements of science, they be incapable of verification.

Years later, when I was Minister for Science, I thought I acquired a certain confirmation of the viewpoint I have just expressed. It happened that I was in a position to talk, on more or less intimate terms, with a number of eminent persons who, in various disciplines, had made significant contributions to knowledge in the field of natural science and to read the descriptions of their discoveries by several others. Incidentally, the difference between those who are admittedly first class in their own field, and those who are not, lies very often precisely in this, that the first are able to give a coherent account, in lucid terms, of what they are trying to do, and what they believe, whilst the others are not. This is not always true, for Darwin, a genius if ever there was one, was once described by a contemporary as having processes of thought which he was as incapable of describing 'as an aboriginal'.

But as I spoke with them I found that with those who were able to describe the process of discovery there was always an element akin, at the moment of discovery, to aesthetic appreciation, which sometimes reflected itself in the language which they used either in describing their own invention or discovery or in praising those of others. A theory, afterwards verified, is described as 'elegant' or 'simple'. There is, at it were, as there was for Archimedes, a moment of Eureka. There is a sudden illumination, when facts, which up to that moment have to be arranged in a meaningless or unduly complicated pattern, assume a simpler, and more elegant, shape. It was precisely this which in the end, and when it was confirmed by observation of the stellar parallax, made the theory of Copernicus more acceptable than that of Ptolemaic astronomy. There is an element in all true knowledge in which the mind of the knower leaps like a spark across a void to an intimate and direct contact with reality itself.

My enunciation of this opinion in my logic paper made no immediate difference to my life. I was not better, indeed for a time I suppose I became marginally worse, than I was before. But life was never quite the same again, for it had become clear to me, and whatever doubts or difficulties I may have had, the clearness of that vision has never wholly left me, that it is possible rationally to believe in things which a man may neither touch nor see, in objective values which are neither verifiable nor mere emotive noises. At this stage I was not a Christian. I was not even a theist. But my scepticism had become so deep that it had undermined even my unbelief.

4

Natural Law

My formal education began at the age of five before the First World War, when I was sent to a pre-prep school in Rosary Gardens. It continued through governess, private school, college at Eton, Christ Church, private tuition and a correspondence course at the law, until I was called to the Bar in 1932 and finally began to earn my own living. By that time, if one accepts the educational assumptions on which all this was based, I must have been one of the best educated young men in the country. But what were these assumptions and what were they worth? If I am to give any account of my intellectual and spiritual furniture today, I must put down something about them. But, before I do so, I must emphasize one lasting result which has remained with me all my life, and carried me through my days of irreligion without lapsing into any but a few of the irregularities revealed, for instance, in Evelyn Waugh's diaries. Indeed, until I read of them long afterwards I remained unaware that most of it was going on. I claim no credit for this, for the characteristic I am about to describe is not a virtue. But it saved me a lot of bother and, it may be, my widowed father a lot of heartache. I was, and am, a slave to my work. I acquired, and have retained, an almost unlimited capacity to absorb information, great power of concentration, and meticulous habits of scholarship, marred only by the occasional carelessness caused by the speed at which I work. I was academically exceptionally gifted, and being intensely ambitious and competitive by nature, made full use of this gift. Moreover being extremely clumsy and unathletic, although robust and healthy, I had no other field in which to excel.

I am almost the last person in public life to have pursued to the full the classical course which sustained the Church, the Civil

Service, and generally the governing class in this country between the Reformation and the period between the wars. What I went through from the age of 8 (or rather 7, for that was when I started Latin) until the age of 23 seems now so bizarre that it requires description. From about ten until the age of 23 the Latin and Greek languages and culture formed the staple of my instruction, taking precedence of English, French, History, mathematics, science, and everything, perhaps, except the Scriptures. It would be a mistake to exaggerate the limitations imposed by this. When I took the school certificate I obtained distinctions in all these other subjects including advanced mathematics, and, I think, at least two scientific subjects. Moreover, both Latin and Greek cultures, being at the root of modern European society and literature, have an uncanny way of anticipating, and illustrating, modern political and social questions. Still, it remains a paradox that so much effort and so much money were pumped into teaching me the language, the history, the philosophy, and to a lesser extent the art and sociology of a bygone age, the last flicker of whose active life went out in Western Europe when St Augustine, Bishop of Hippo, died besieged by the Vandals in North Africa in the first years of the fifth century. Every week, from the age of 10 until I finished with Honour Moderations in 1928, I would show up a copy of Greek verses, and a copy of Latin verses, a copy of Greek prose and a copy of Latin prose, each designed to reproduce the classical styles of the best period, and each week I would be expected to translate from the originals passages of Greek and Latin tragedians, comedians, historians and philosophers. But it was a pagan culture that was being instilled into me by this means. I knew nothing of the fathers of the Church after the fifth century, nothing of medieval Latin, and had scarcely met a Jew or a Roman Catholic except in the most casual kind of way. From about the age of seventeen onwards my own agnosticism was something of a secret sickness, to be kept very much to myself and not to be paraded in public for the scandal it could cause to those I loved. It was also a sickness to which I was completely indifferent. Life was too interesting and too full of promise to make me unhappy about anything of this sort.

It would be a mistake to regard this education as devoid of moral content. To begin with, the classical authors are full of material extolling civic virtue and patriotism, courage in war, and public service in time of peace. For this reason I have never been particularly patient with those who do not admire these virtues as much as I. I was as fully identified with the heroes of Marathon and Salamis as with those of Agincourt, Trafalgar, or Waterloo, and, as almost all my early education between 8 and 12 took place in the highly charged atmosphere of the First World War, there was nothing to counteract these influences in a gentler sense. I am not, on the whole, sorry for this. The ancient world has much to teach us about the dangers of social disintegration and permissiveness, of treachery and cowardice. The Greek and Latin cultures, with their literature, live on as expositions of natural virtue, and I feel at the end of the day that a very great deal of what I possess of value derives from this non-Christian but extremely relevant source.

I see that in describing the moral content of the classical authors I have used the term 'natural virtue'. At the time I am speaking of I would not have used the description although I believed in the thing. At that time words like 'nature' or 'natural' had much the same effect upon me as Hermann Goering once said was produced on him by the use of the word 'culture'. At the use of 'nature' or 'natural' I would reach for my dialectical six-shooter and spray the offender and his language with verbal bullets.

This was because the words 'nature' and 'natural' are used in so many inconsistent senses. 'Doing what comes naturally' can cover almost any kind of moral obliquity and permissiveness. Indeed, since we are all inhabitants of the natural world, there is practically no sort of action, good or bad, which cannot, in some sense, be described as natural. In another context, 'nature' and 'natural' have come to be contrasted with 'contrived' or 'artificial'. Thus, in relation to law, it could be said that slavery was against the 'natural' law although it was permitted and enforced by the positive law of individual nations, and even by the embryonic international law insisted on by the community of all nations.

These considerations have given 'nature' and 'natural' a bad name amongst philosophers and lawyers. Nevertheless I have come in time to believe that 'natural' in another, if closely related, sense is an indispensable term for those who wish to understand the human condition when applied to nouns like 'law', 'justice', or 'morality.'

I therefore feel entitled to use the words 'nature' and 'natural' to describe the value judgements to which one can come by the unaided use of reason, unassisted by divine revelation or by the authoritative pronouncements of any particular group. Of course, if it so be that value judgements are only emotive noises which people utter to describe their subjective likes and dislikes, I have nothing more to say. Natural justice, and natural morality, must be discarded along with all judgements about beauty and ugliness, about good and bad, right and wrong. But I do not believe that value judgements are of this kind. Of course I accept that opinions on these questions differ, and that there is no objective test by which the philistine's opinion can be shown to be demonstrably less reliable than that of the artist, or that of the saint about morality, or the professional judge in matters of justice more reliable than that of those to whom the subject is a matter of little or no interest. This does not worry me at all. Once you have accepted that observation, measurement and verification are not the only marks of significant truth it need not worry one that parts of experience involve assessments of value which do not involve measurement, and that a consensus, where it exists between those who have studied and experienced a subject in detail, should be accepted in preference to a casual or ignorant assessment of the same matter by others who are either insensitive or indifferent to the subject. In the republic of learning and taste, there may indeed be no room for privilege of wealth or birth, but there need be no nonsense about equality, for this republic at least is not a democracy.

Given the meaning I have sought to give to them, natural justice, natural morality and natural law seem to me to be indispensable, and related, conceptions in any civilized society. I am aware that two of these phrases, natural justice and natural law, are commonly used in the courts and by writers on jurisprudence with different and more specialized connotations. In the courts, natural justice means primarily acting fairly but without regard to the technical rules of evidence and procedure imposed by any state or other system of positive law. In practice this very largely boils down to two main rules, namely the obligation on any quasi-judicial body to hear both sides of a case before delivering judgement upon it, or even privately forming a concluded opinion, and the obligation of any judge not to have any interest in or bias about the subject matter of a dispute, and more especially any interest not known to and accepted by both parties. I am not using the expression 'natural justice' in this specialized meaning. The expression 'natural law' is also commonly used by writers on jurisprudence to describe rules of law which exist in some imaginary ideal world by reference to which the rules of actual law in any given society fall to be judged. I believe this to be a mistaken, even a misguided, way of seeking to express a truth which I am trying to describe in terms of another theory about value judgements.

This theory which is really fundamental to the view I am trying to expound is that value judgements in general, and value judgements about morality and legal obligation in particular, do have an objective value, analogous to, and not different in kind from, the sort of judgement we make about works of art or scenes of natural beauty. It is true that, in these matters, there remains an element of subjectivity, in that, as we say, not all tastes are identical, and even amongst experts insights also differ. But this is not to say that there is no difference in quality between the judgement of an expert in his own field and the untutored judgement of someone who views a subject for the first time, and perhaps with indifference. The mere fact that there is no common standard, other than experience and love for the subject, by which these judgements are to be assessed, does not seem to me to be a reason for disputing their objective validity.

I find evidence in support of this opinion in the extraordinary extent to which sages and religious philosophers throughout all history tend to converge about judgements of this kind. It is, of course, not at all true that the ethics of a high-minded Greek philosopher, let us say, Aristotle, are identical with those of a Christian saint, let us say, Saint Francis of Asssi, or the author of the *Imitation of Christ*. I will come back to this basic difference when I approach more closely the central subject of this book, which is Christianity itself. It is equally not true to say that the ethics of, say, Buddhism, Judaism, Christianity, Islam, Confucianism are identical. They are not. But it is surprising how much they tend to converge.

When my grandfather and namesake, the founder of the Polytechnic, died in 1903, there was found an unfinished letter on his desk which was evidently being written to one of his boys who had confessed to have religious doubts and difficulties. I do not now recall the exact terms in which it was couched, but they made a profound impact on me when I first read them, and they exactly illustrate what I am trying to say. The letter read something like this:

'For ever truth is better than falsehood, beauty than ugliness, justice than injustice, kindness than cruelty. These few truths, believe me, are worth more than half the creeds.' In other words, there is a morality inherent in the human condition which seeks to articulate itself into general guide lines, like 'Honour thy father and thy mother', 'tell the truth', 'love your country', 'do not commit adultery', 'do not commit murder, steal or lie'. They are, of course, no more than guide lines, true, as Aristotle says, only generally, and therefore with exceptions which are always difficult to express or limit. But we disregard general rules of this kind at our peril, and if we accept them and live by them we find that we are living in accordance with the judgement and the precept of the noblest amongst mankind.

I call all this 'natural morality' because it can be arrived at by the exercise of the natural faculties and does not require any direct revelation from on high to validate it, nor any human authority to give it force. In this it differs from the supernatural morality taught by the Sermon on the Mount, the supreme self-sacrifice demanded at times of the Christian, but not because the latter contradicts natural morality. Christ came to fulfil 'the law' (that is, the natural morality prescribed by the Decalogue and protected by the ritual observances of the Jews) and not to destroy it. If one is tempted to doubt the existence of this kind of morality one only need reverse the precepts of the Decalogue, or the generalizations of my grandfather's letter, and then see what kind of a nonsense one gets into. It is impossible seriously, even for a Hitler, to say 'Forever falsehood is better than truth, cruelty than kindness, ugliness than beauty, injustice than justice'. That is why the Devil (whoever or whatever he may be) always tries to deceive his victims by sophistries, pretending that the particular wickedness is not what it seems to be, or is a means to a higher end, or is some special or exceptional case.

When one comes to consider the basic nature of legal or political obligation, it seems to me that the conception of natural morality is absolutely indispensable. It is obvious to us (at least I hope it is) that the purely formal definition of law stated by the nineteenth-century writers on jurisprudence, 'Law is the command of the ruler', leads straight to the concentration camp and to the gas chamber. It is, in fact, indistinguishable from Hitler's definition: 'Das ist Recht was dem Führer gefällt.' One is only entitled to interfere with the freedom of another in cases where it is arguable that that other is already under some obligation to do or to refrain from doing the sort of thing that a proposed law imposes as a duty under penalty or prohibits.

This, of course, is not to say that all moral duties ought to be enforced by law. In many cases no obvious social consequences flow from the non-performance of moral duties. In many other cases enforcement can only be achieved by methods more repulsive than the original wrong. It only means that there must be a relationship of some kind between law and morality, however much the relationship is tempered by the need for freedom (itself a moral concept) or by practical considerations of common sense.

I do not wish to elaborate this in the present discussion. I only wish to conclude this chapter with the philosophical point to which it has been leading up. As I have said, I do not think there was ever a point in time, even at my most irreligious or immoral, when I questioned the existence and objective validity of value judgements in general or moral judgements in particular. I regarded the latter as a kind of categorical imperative, not directly related to any external criterion, such as utility, nor on any particular view of the world, still less to religion. I derived them, or rather my continued belief in them, after I had cast off the religion of my childhood, more from my classical education, and the ancient authors than anything else, in private morals more perhaps from Aristotle and Plato, and the derivative philosophical works of Cicero or Seneca, than the Bible, and, in public morals, more perhaps from the terrible analysis of the consequences of class warfare outlined in Thucydides and from the obvious facts of contemporary society in the world between the wars, the unemployment, the bitterness and the strife, than from any specifically Christian source.

Nevertheless there came times, more particularly after my answer to the question in the logic paper, when I came to ask myself as the philosopher Kant had previously done in his *Critiques of Pure and*

Practical Reason, what kind of a universe it could be in which for ever:

    'Truth is forever better than falsehood, justice than injustice, beauty than ugliness, kindness than unkindness.'

I found myself saying that such a universe could not be only a fortuitous combination of indestructible atoms, or a ghostly ballet of unearthly categories. I found myself believing more and more insistently that somewhere enthroned in the very nature of being, behind the physical world which is itself not self-explanatory, behind the moral world which appears so divorced from physical science, there was Intelligence and Goodness, and Love, which we can dimly apprehend only on the analogy of our own feeble intelligences, and loves, and our own, often imperfect, striving after goodness. For now we see through a glass, darkly, and not face to face. In other words, I was becoming a Theist, and I was being forced into a Theistic position by intellectual rather than purely emotional considerations.

As I am not a person with a really sophisticated appreciation of art or music I have not based my argument so much upon the appreciation of beauty as upon ethical considerations. But there is one field in which I find that my appreciation of aesthetic beauty is not far behind that of the experts, and that is scenic and natural beauty. There have been times when I have almost cried for joy at the sight of a landscape, particularly in the mountains, Chillon Castle from the lake of Geneva with the Dents du Midi in the background, the Blumlisalphorn from the Oeschinensee, the Aiguilles Rouges and Mont Blanc from the Buet. I could go on enumerating these scenes almost indefinitely for page after page by examples both from the British Isles and elsewhere. But the point I want to make is simply that these insights into the sheer beauty of the world can, I think, have nothing whatever to do with man's evolution from the animal kingdom. They have, to use the technical language of Darwinian theory, no survival value whatever that I can see. In the field of morals it is, I think, arguable that the insights that we, on this view, mistake for evidence of the Divine, are really only inherited instincts acquired by the human race during its evolutionary development, things which, although they do not benefit the individual as such, assist the survival of the species, by enabling groups to form and last in associations, children to be protected during their vulnerable years, and so on. I do not think this is right, but it is an argument which is at least plausible to some extent. I do not think this is true of beauty whether man-made or natural. I cannot think what survival value has to do with my enjoyment of the view in the Coolins or from the Domhütte, or viewing a wood full of bluebells or a field full of daffodils, or the colour of the feathers on a cock pheasant, or enjoying the merry tunes of Arthur Sullivan, or Shakespeare's poetry. But, of course, if man is not only an animal, what is he? And what is the Factor in the Universe which explains his value judgements? Am I wholly foolish in thinking of It as He, and having thought of It as He, am I altogether fatuous in bowing to the ground and saying: 'Thou'? This, at any rate, is the point from which I started, and, however much during subsequent years I have doubted or fallen off, it is to this to which I return in the end. To me it is the vital clue.

5

My Religious Upbringing

In the state of mind which I have been trying to describe there was, and is, no religious content whatever. I had had no experience which could be described as spiritual by any stretch of the imagination. I did not immediately resume any religious practices. I did not immediately seek to amend any irregularities in my life. I simply found it impossible to accept the intellectual basis of materialism, and because I had never been brought into contact with any other religious or metaphysical beliefs than the Anglicanism in which I had been educated, at that stage it did not occur to me that there were options other than a fairly colourless Christianity and the agnosticism into which I had drifted as the result of the loss of my religious faith.

This now seems to me so surprising that I think it requires explanation. This involves some description of the religious background with which I was left when my formal education was complete. I never knew either of my grandfathers. Quintin Hogg, the founder of the Polytechnic, died in 1903, before I was born, a victim of one of the early gas geysers, which poisoned him with carbon monoxide whilst he was having a bath. My other grandfather, my mother's father, died in his native Tennessee when my mother was a little girl of 4, four years after the war between the states, in which his health had been undermined. Both my parents were conventionally devout, but not, I think, profoundly religious. My grandmother, Alice Hogg, was a Scots Presbyterian and a saint. She knew the Bible better than anyone I have ever met and she knew it from cover to cover. She was by far the greatest and most loving woman I can remember ever having known. Unfortunately she died of a painful cancer when I was 10. My brother Neil and I were, I think, her favourite grandchildren, but her early death meant that she left little beyond her memory behind her, though I still have a little book she gave me called *Daily Light on the Daily Path*, containing some mixed texts for every day in the month. This particular form of piety did not, and does not, appeal to me. My Nanny was a High Church Anglican, of melancholy disposition. She taught me the Church Catechism, the Lord's Prayer, and the Apostles' Creed, and to say grace at meals and prayers nightly. My schoolmasters taught me the Bible regularly, in the Authorized Version, which gave me a profound love for its magical English, and a considerable knowledge of its contents. This knowledge I improved and turned to good use at Eton when I competed for, and won, the Wilder Divinity Prize. At Eton we also read the Acts of the Apostles in Greek, and two of the Gospels (Mark and Matthew) in the same language, again for the Wilder prize. I read the history of the first four centuries of the Church, and English Church History from the conversion of our Saxon ancestors to a little after the Norman Conquest. Apart from Latin hymns, prayers and graces which we recited at College Prayers and dinner every Sunday, we made no acquaintance with the Medieval Church unless, which I was not, we were history specialists. Preparation for confirmation, although undertaken conscientiously, left little mark on my mind, and from my confirmation onwards I had little spiritual guidance or instruction, except what I acquired at compulsory chapel. Owing to my loss of religious faith I acquired little new at Oxford, except what I required to know about Christian origins for the purpose of my special period of Roman history, and this, so far as I remember, finished with the accession of the Emperor Hadrian. Thus the house was swept and garnished and devoid of a tenant.

Consider me then reflecting about the universe in a purely philosophical mood after I had reached that stage of scepticism which disbelieved even its own unbelief. By this time materialism was rejected as a philosophy, and objective idealism had never seemed to be a starter. Nevertheless I had come to believe that the very essence of the universe must contain that which explained and gave sense both to the fact of consciousness and the objective validity of value judgements, both moral and aesthetic. Because consciousness itself is intrinsically subjective, at least in so far as it presupposes the existence of subjects, that is, personalities, I had come to regard my Unknown God as both Immanent and Transcendent. I thought of him as immanent in the sense that it was necessary for him to underlie the existence of every fibre even of inanimate material, and transcendent because only a transcendent being can be possessed of personality in the same sense as, but on an infinitely higher level than, the human beings with whom I was familiar. In so far as I believed my Unknown God to be transcendent, I was, I suppose, almost consciously making God in the image of man, but without his defects. But I was not guilty of anthropomorphism, because I regarded him as immanent, something of which human nature is wholly incapable. It was, however, wholly foreign to my thinking to regard my Unknown God as somebody or something to be feared or loved, still less as someone with whom to carry on some sort of a dialogue, and it did not occur to me that this divine explanation, be it adequate or inadequate as an explanation, was ever trying to get in touch with me, or that I should consciously endeavour to get in touch with him. He was a postulate, and nothing more, a conception which I found intellectually necessary to make sense of the universe of which I was a part.

This position is so intellectually arid, and so unstable that it could not last, and it did not last for more than a comparatively brief period. It is, however, strange that I cannot at all remember either when, or by what steps, it began to give way to something more positive. I suppose this was because it never was quite so precise and definite as it sounds now that I have written it down, and that the steps by which I arrived at something different and more permanent represent a continuous process of experience rather than a series of dramatic moments.

In a sense, this process has never really become completed, nor I suppose will it ever be finished and completed this side of the grave. But at any rate, by the time I was elected a fellow of All Souls College in 1932 I was beginning again to go to church, or rather to churches, for I discovered a considerable variety to choose from even within the Anglican communion, and to say prayers at night, and occasionally during the day when something especially distressed or perplexed me, and these habits have continued more or less regularly ever since.

Whilst I am quite unable to describe the logical steps which led me on, I am certain that two factors influenced me more clearly than any other. The first was my encounter with the Christ of the Gospels. The second was my gradual appreciation of the living Church, both in history and in the liturgy and language of the Book of Common Prayer, and in the persons of various friends and relatives of different Christian denominations. Before I describe these, however, I think I should make one further purely logical point. It is that it is surely incredible, if there happens to exist anywhere in the universe an Entity of the type I have been trying to describe, that He, She, or It (for it must in one sense be indifferent what gender is used) should not have some communication with the rational human beings whose existence and value judgements provide the main reason for supposing it to have a real being. Such a relationship of communication would either have to be direct, as it would be in experiences definitely mystical, or mediated, as would be the case where the communication became known through the experiences of others, or by the experience of events in the world or in one's own inner field of consciousness. My own experiences obviously belong to the latter class unless, of course, the sheer joy of living and loving, and knowing the external world, the kind of ecstasy I have tried to describe in my appreciation of mountain scenery, or what is experienced in moments of profound emotion, whether of distress or joy, can be said to have an element of the mystical in them. I sometimes think they have, but this can never be known except to those who have had unequivocally mystical experiences. It seems therefore safe to group all normal states of mind whether deriving from books or communication with others, or whether the products of our own inner life, as being natural, and, if divine in origin, then mediated through the natural order.

6

The Christ of History

The Communist world teaches an extremely simple view of Jesus of Nazareth. According to the Communists he simply did not exist. It is not that they disbelieve in the Virgin Birth, the Resurrection, or the feeding of the five thousand or other miracles. It is not, as the Talmud says, that he was the illegitimate son of a Roman soldier called Pandera or Panthera. Communists teach that there was no such person as Jesus at all. He was a Sun myth, like Mithras, or perhaps a rain god like Quezalcoatl. He is the unperson to end all unpeople. It might be possible to ignore this view as too absurd to be taken seriously were it not for the fact that so many people must be growing up to believe just this. There is a second reason why I feel I must now examine this view with some care. It is that the Regius Professor of Modern History - no less - Professor Hugh Trevor-Roper, has expressed in print a modified version of this opinion, which is that though the existence of such a person as Jesus is certain and that it may be reasonably accepted that he suffered under Pontius Pilate, we know practically nothing else about him. Therefore, before I set out to meet the Christ of the Gospels, I must first logically, though this is chronologically out of place in the chronicle of my thoughts on the subject, set down my reasons for rejecting both versions of this modern heresy.

It is a mistake to believe that the Roman Empire was not very fully documented with civil service files. It is a pure fluke that we possess the correspondence between Pliny the Younger and the Emperor Trajan when Pliny the Younger was Governor of Bithynia, and not loads of other contemporary correspondence from the files of the Colonial Office in Rome. I very much doubt whether Pontius Pilate would not have sent some account of the transactions culminating in the Crucifixion to Tiberius, especially after the Jewish notables had hinted at a charge of high treason against him. Be that as it may, it is clear enough from the pagan historians that the Emperor Nero attempted to blame the fire at Rome on a Christian conspiracy, and one of these historians, Cornelius Tacitus, states expressly that the Christians accused in this way were the followers of one Christus who was 'put to death in the reign of Tiberius' (*imperitante Tiberio supplicio afflictus est*). It would be absurd to credit Tacitus with accepting uncritically any Christian account of the matter when, as a leading figure in Roman public life, he had the imperial archives to draw on, and regarded the Christian religion as a 'disastrous superstition' (*exitiabilis superstitio*). The fire of Rome is, of course, a well-known historical event which took place only thirty or forty years after the Crucifixion. Tacitus was writing in the reign of Trajan within a hundred years of the Crucifixion, and in his youth must have spoken to many leading Romans who remembered the fire. I say nothing of the persistent and probable legend that the Flavius Clemens, a member of the Imperial House quite certainly known to Tacitus who was put to death for adhering to a 'foreign superstition' in the reign of Domitian during Tacitus's manhood, was a Christian, and perhaps connected with the author of the epistle of Clement, which is still extant. Nero's Palace, the remains of which are uncovered, contains a strange scribble on the walls of the servants' quarters. This consists of the picture of a figure with a donkey's head hanging on a cross with the words underneath, in Greek, 'Alexander (no doubt a fellow-slave's name) worships his God'. The Christians were perfectly well known in the reign of Trajan and at least as early as the reign of Nero. Pliny writes about them from Bithynia. Marcus Aurelius, a little later, writes disparagingly of their contempt of death as due to obstinacy and not the true indifference of the philosopher. It is wholly inconceivable that if their founder about sixty or seventy years before Trajan had never existed or had never been crucified, someone, Greek, Roman or Jew, would not have said so. One might as well cast doubt on the existence of General Booth.

Nevertheless, there is no doubt that Jesus was something of an unperson by the time Tacitus, and Pliny and their contemporaries, Josephus and Suetonius, were writing. Josephus, who fought on the

Jewish side in the Jewish wars, afterwards surrendered to Titus and Vespasian, took the imperial name of Flavius and wrote a history of his times. In that history he mentions John the Baptist and James, both of whom were related to Jesus, but in the final edition of his work omits all reference to Jesus himself. This is quite clearly deliberate, since it is quite unthinkable that he was not very well acquainted with the history of Christianity and its relevance to Judaism. Whether the early editions of his work (of which there had probably existed at least one) were equally silent I am not so sure, since a good many people have accepted as authentic several direct references in the old Slavonic translations which may come from this earlier version. But be that as it may, the argument from silence cuts the other way. There was a certain amount of deliberate silence, but it was not complete, and the facts were known. Jesus had suffered under Pontius Pilate in the reign of Tiberius and had given rise to a popular movement which was illegal and was a considerable nuisance to the authorities, and had been used as a scapegoat by Nero at the time of the fire.

There is a fashionable tendency to discount the Christian sources. I cannot do the same. Writing about twenty years after the Crucifixion, St Paul describes in unequivocal language the broad facts of the existence of Jesus, his death by crucifixion and his reputed resurrection. One can of course discount the latter as miraculous and therefore suspect, and one may place on one side Paul's own references to his strange experience on the road to Damascus as of the same kind. After all, you may say, he also claims to have been carried up to the seventh heaven. But you cannot discount, twenty years after the event, his reference to the founder of his movement who, he says, was seen after his death by five hundred people at once, some of whom he claims to have interviewed. You may disregard what they say as incredible. You are unlikely to be right if you deny the existence of the man. If he were writing now, in 1974, St Paul would be referring to the early fifties, just after my father died on 16 August 1950. If I said that I had seen my father after his death (which of course I did not), even if I were deceiving myself, it would be rather odd if someone told me he was a solar myth.

If I were arguing the case of Christian origins in full, which, at this stage of my argument I am not, it would be at this point that I would draw attention to the obvious and close connection between the writings of St Paul and those of the author of the Acts of the Apostles and therefore of St Luke's Gospel, and, because the author of the latter obviously made copious use of the earlier Gospel according to St Mark (whoever wrote that) with that Gospel as well. It really does not do, simply as a matter of historical criticism, to divorce St Paul from the Gospels and assume that nothing which was written in the Gospels which he does not expressly mention was known to him. This is particularly unlikely because the author of the Acts of the Apostles, and therefore the author of St Luke (since they were manifestly the same person) incorporates as part of the text some reminiscences in the first person of his adventures in St Paul's company over a substantial period of time. The most obvious explanation of this is that, at the time of publication, the identity of the author and his personal participation in certain of the events described was notorious and perfectly well known to the readers for whom the book was intended, but even if this explanation be not accepted, the connection between St Paul and the author is so obvious that the conclusion for which I am arguing must follow. This is that, going back to a period about twenty years after the date of the Crucifixion there is a continuous written tradition confirming that of secular writers establishing the historicity of Jesus of Nazareth, and the existence of a cult depending for its inspiration upon belief in his resurrection after crucifixion and held together by the ceremony of Holy Communion which, whatever else it does, was intended from the first to perpetuate the memory of the events described in the consecration prayer, an extract from which appears in one of the earliest of St Paul's writings.

I have set out these facts at length because it is a necessary logical stage in the argument. There was a person called Jesus. He had a group of followers who have a continuous existence from about A.D. 50 or A.D. 55 onwards and have left written records ever since, maintaining a cult whose central ceremony is especially designed to preserve the memory of certain events connected with him and alleged to be historical. The existence of this cult, and the crucifixion of its founder, are adequately attested by secular writers of a period at which the true facts must have been available and known. The way is therefore open to enquire whether we know anything and if so what about the original teachings of the man who gave rise to the movement.

I have not dealt so far with a subsidiary argument used by Professor Trevor-Roper because I do not myself attach any importance to it. This is that the extant manuscripts of the New Testament are comparatively late, the very earliest dating from the fourth century A.D., that is, at a minimum, about three hundred years after the events described. This point is an invalid one for a great variety of reasons. The first is that it altogether overlooks the extreme meticulousness with which, before printing, the copiers of ancient manuscripts preserved the integrity of the text they were copying. This is true both of pagan and religious writers. The Massoretic text of the Hebrew Old Testament, for example, depends upon manuscripts, the earliest of which was, until recently, of the eleventh century A.D. or thereabouts. But its basic integrity has not only never seriously been questioned but has recently been amply vindicated by the discovery among the so-called Dead Sea Scrolls of an almost complete text of Isaiah. The truth is that both Old and New Testament scriptures and for that matter the works of a wide range of secular authors are amply confirmed by quotations from a wide variety of sources outside their respective holograph versions, by translations of whole books, by criticisms and references in other authors and, occasionally, by the accidental preservation and rediscovery of actual fragments, like the Dead Sea Scrolls, or the fragment of papyrus, now in Geneva, containing a few lines from a second-century manuscript of St John's Gospel, presumably written within a century of the original autograph.

The second reason which renders the argument invalid is a fact about fakes of all kinds which I learned myself in the course of a case I did in which there was in question the authenticity of a painting purporting to be by, and to be signed by, Modigliani. This painting, as the result of my Advice on Evidence, was shown to be a fake by X-ray evidence. But in the course of my researches I was supplied by my instructing solicitor with a considerable bibliography concerning the nature of fakes of all kinds and how to detect them. There was one point made by the author of one of these books which is of direct relevance to the point I am discussing. Although fakes can often be made which confuse or actually deceive contemporaries

of the faker, the experts, or even the not so expert, of a later age
can invariably detect them, whether fraudulent or not, because the
faker cannot fail to include stylistic or other material not obvious
to contemporaries because they are contemporaries, but which stand
out a mile to later observers because they reflect the standards, or
the materials, or the styles of a succeeding age to that of the author
whose work is being faked. This is true of pictures and statues and,
though less obviously, of written works.

Now, within very few years of the writing of the Gospels, an
immense Christian literature grew up about the life, the manners,
the family, the childhood, the nature, and the alleged miracles of
Jesus of Nazareth, some orthodox, some manifestly heretical, some
even conceivably containing elements of authenticity. Some of these
have been known for a long time. Some have been disinterred during
my lifetime. Some go back to the second and third centuries A.D.
Some, no doubt, are still waiting in the sands of Egypt for some
future scholar to discover, and some may even now be awaiting
transcription and translation. They are as different from the authentic tradition as chalk is from cheese. The authentic books fit into a
particular time slot in history (say from 50 to 100 A.D.) and into no
other. The fact is that we can be as certain of the historicity of Jesus
as we can about the historicity of the poet Catullus or Marcus
Lepidus, or the Rabbi Hillel. But we can be sure of relatively little
about him. We do not know exactly when he was born and, although
we know the manner of his death, we do not know exactly when he
died. An immense literature has grown up in which the authors
seek to disentangle his teaching from legendary and miraculous
accretions added by the pious imaginations of his followers. But it
is unreasonable to doubt the historicity of the man, or the historical
continuity dating back to his immediate circle of friends in the
movement he founded.

7

The Christ of the Gospels

My next task, after the digression of the last chapter, is to discuss the question how much we know about Jesus, granted, as I have now argued that we must allow, that such a person existed, was put to death under Pontius Pilate, and gave rise to a continuous movement originating in the activities of his circle of friends immediately after his death, and that the claims and activities of this movement includes the assertion that he had risen and had been seen alive after his execution, the enactment of a ceremony designed to perpetuate these propositions, and the wholly unverifiable claim that these events, if they did take place, had a cosmic significance in the history of the human race.

I will begin with an analogy, not, I think, altogether far-fetched. We know, *pace* my friend Leslie Rowse, relatively little about Shakespeare. We have his will. We have references, contemporary or near contemporary, in the literature of the period to his existence. We have various contemporary documents about his parents, his baptism and his marriage. But we have no complete biography.

Above all, we have his works. We know so little about him that there exists at least one society dedicated to the proposition that they were written by somebody else. Like Leslie Rowse, I personally regard this last theory as nonsense. But from one point of view it hardly matters. There is a sense in which all true works of genius are self-authenticating. We can argue about textual obscurities. We can argue about which plays, or even what parts of the plays, are properly canonical and which are apocryphal. We can condemn some passages as carelessly written or even as bad. But at the end of the day nothing will destroy the central fact that, at the end of the sixteenth century and in the first few years of the seventeenth, an author was at work of transcendent poetical and dramatic genius whose work tells us, from one point of view, at least as much about himself as one man can know about another.

One must not, of course, carry analogies too far. The Gospels are small in volume in comparison with the plays of Shakespeare, and much that is in them is repetitious. Even the whole New Testament canon is less in volume than Shakespeare's works, and the greater part of it does not even purport to come from the mouth of Jesus of Nazareth. Not one written word of his has come down to us; indeed, the only reference to his writing at all that I know of is the doodling he did in the dust when they brought to him the woman taken in adultery, though I must say I regard as naïve the suggestion I have read somewhere based on the absence of such writings that he could not write at all. His intimate knowledge of the scriptures alone precludes this possibility.

But the point I am making is that so long as one approaches the matter without examining the authenticity of the miraculous element in the New Testament, much of the language attributed to Jesus in the New Testament is self-authenticating in exactly the same sense that Hamlet is self-authenticating, or Catullus's poems about Lesbia are self-authenticating. Incidentally, these last have come down to us from a single manuscript since lost, accidentally found in the Middle Ages, bunging a wine barrel in a cellar in Verona. There is a sense in which I do not require proof of the authorship of the Sermon on the Mount, or the principal parables, or indeed many of the paradoxical or outrageous stories in the Gospels. They are in themselves proof that at the relevant time in Palestine a religious teacher existed whose words make such an impact on the ears of a hearer that they are best-sellers, box-office winners on stage and film to this day twenty centuries later, and it is the power exerted by these stories and sayings which made such an impact on me when I began to return to the Church of my upbringing and which have held me ever since, however much I might try to escape from them. Incidentally, there is at least no Baconian theory about the Gospels. Who was the author of these remarkable utterances? There is only one candidate in the field. No one suggests that they were the work of Caiaphas, Judas Iscariot, or even Pontius Pilate. Either they were uttered by him to whom they are attributed, namely Jesus of Nazareth who, according to Tacitus, was known as Christ and suffered under Pontius Pilate, or these flowerings of religious and moral genius were the product of some anonymous author who has wholly disappeared from history and left no trace behind, except these words, which have been unaccountably and, on this hypothesis, quite wrongly, attributed to the crucified Jesus by the very men who sought to perpetuate his memory. There may be, and indeed are, many things in Christianity difficult to swallow, but I cannot allow that the belief that the main sayings attributed to Jesus are rightly attributed is among them.

8

The Christ of Theology

Up to this point the argument I have been trying to present yields a somewhat arid form of Unitarianism coupled with a belief in the historicity of the man depicted in the New Testament and a fairly warm appreciation of the sayings attributed to him. I suppose that a good many people have got this far in their meditations and have got no further. The views expressed are logically and historically defensible. But there are two difficulties in your way if, having got thus far, you seek to end your journey at this point. The first encountered, both logically and, so far as my own experience is concerned, also the first chronologically, is that it is impossible to disentangle the Christ of history from the supernatural elements in the stories recorded about him, or wholly to disregard the fact that, whatever his critics, past or present, may have thought, or may still think about him, this was not what he thought, or what he seems to have said, about himself. On the assumption, which I think by now I am entitled to make, that the Gospels are, or at least contain, a story about something which actually happened, Jesus seems to have made claims about himself which no ordinarily good or sane man could possibly make. I will not elaborate this argument, because to do so would involve an essay in New Testament scholarship well outside the boundaries which I am setting myself in writing this book. Suffice it to say that I have made the attempt myself and reached the conclusion I have stated. But what is more important, others better qualified than I have been trying to do this very thing for more than a century and, though individuals have believed that they have had a measure of success, what is certain is that none has succeeded for long in convincing the learned world as a whole of the correctness of their own solution. No doubt there are many elements in the Gospel story which are in themselves unlikely or incredible and may well be pious fictions. But nobody can agree a complete list of which these passages are and, in the last resort, the whole endeavour is bound to fail, since the composition of the Gospels and the transmission of their contents to subsequent generations was due to the unshakeable belief of the followers of the Christian cult in the alleged fact of the empty tomb, and the reality of the physical resurrection, which for them at least had been authenticated by witnesses of the post-resurrection appearances. These, of course, if accepted in any form, are the biggest miracle and the biggest obstacle to faith of all.

There is thus no point in getting rid of a selection of the miracles as unhistoric if, at the end of the day, you are bound to swallow, or reject *in toto*, the assertion that in about A.D. 30, give or take a year or two, a man physically rose from the dead. The historical Christ was a person about whom this claim was asserted and, at least in the form in which they have come down to us, this is how the writings about him, from the earliest of the epistles to the latest of the Gospels, have always presented him. What is more, and even if we disregard what he is alleged to have said about the resurrection appearances, this is how, broadly, he seems to have thought of himself. He did not regard himself simply and solely as a mere man.

But there is another and more directly philosophical reason why I found it impossible, having got so far as I have described, to stop where I was. In the last analysis, the gap between man and God is unbridgeable, except to the extent to which God chooses to make himself known to man, and this can only be done by some sort of communicated experience, mediated through the flesh. We may, in an abstract kind of way, theorize about the nature of the universe as much as we choose and, as a result of this, may come to a more or less coherent view of Deity as the ground of our being, and the philosophical first cause which explains both the physical facts and the value judgements which lie at the root of human experience.

We may regard this Deity, this *être suprême*, as we choose, either as inherent reality contained in and underlying all existence, or as a transcendent entity somewhere outside and beyond the realm of experience. But in neither event do we know anything about him, and the mystics, who claim to have been somehow in direct contact

with the Deity, come back talking only of experiences which have
to be translated into physical metaphors like light or water, or into
contradictory propositions which break down into nonsense the
moment they are taken literally. Paganism, of course, is crammed
with deities who were, or became, men or gods who are, or themselves possess, divine sons and daughters. Athena was born fully-
armed from the head of Zeus, with another of Zeus's innumerable
children, Hephaestus, acting as a midwife armed with a hatchet.
Zeus himself was the son of Cronos whom he slew, and Cronos
was the son of Uranus whom he castrated. Mithras was something
less than God and more than man. Adonis was man become God.
There have been divine saviours in Egyptian mythology, male and
female, in the Greek mysteries, in the religions of American Indians,
and in Hindu mythology alike. Some people seem to find the analogies with the Christian Christ so uncomfortable as to be positively
subversive of any faith in Christ, so like, in a sense, he is or seems
to be to those admittedly imagined beings. I do not myself so find it.
Man does not seem to be able to live without religion and religious
practices and beliefs, and even when he comes to regard God as a
Unity, and all the various pagan or animistic beliefs as imperfect
attempts to find and rationalize the ground of all being underlying
natural forces and phenomena, he must still clothe his religious
experience with language, and such language, because it is meta-
phorical and draws on analogies, seems to deny the very unity which
it only seeks to describe. If God does communicate with man, this
communication needs must, at some stage, take on something of
this character in order to manifest itself at all. I do not therefore
find it disturbing to find Christ exhibiting the requirements of man's
limitations if he be the only begotten son of God (whatever is intended by the expression 'begotten' or 'son' in the same context).
On the contrary, I find these other, and mythological, expressions of
deity in some ways as pointers to the reality of Christ, if Christ is
indeed the manifestation of the Divine that I now take him to be.

But at the heart of all the mysteries of life is the mystery of evil.
By itself, pain is a thing I can accept. It is, in fact, the only way in
which a living physical animal remains alive. It is preserved precisely
because it feels pain whenever it damages itself, or allows itself to be
damaged. At my private school there was a boy who, from some

physical disorder, was unable to feel pain in the sense that the rest of us did. Both we and he had to be warned against subjecting him to the physical experimentation which youthful curiosity on all our parts naturally prompted. I often wonder what became of him in adult life, but I doubt if he can still be alive and well. In itself, pain is a useful biological danger signal inseparable from the physical existence of a conscious being. As such it causes me no worries at all.

But evil, though it is often associated with the existence and causation of pain, is a horse of a very different colour. It shakes my whole being with helpless rejection. I once did a case in which my function was to defend a young mother who had beaten her little daughter, aged two or three, to death. I could not open the papers without shaking with sobs because I knew that inside the papers lay the photographs in colour of the beautiful little body, desecrated in death, with all the marks of the blows upon it. And I read in the evidence, happily among the statements not given in court, how the little being just before she died, said the heart-breaking words: 'I'm sorry, Mummy.' She was, and is, as I believe, a saint, and her forgiveness was divine.

I feel the same way about evil of all sorts, real or fictional. When, in the autumn of October 1969, I saw the ruined homes in Belfast, burned out by my own fellow-citizens and fellow-Protestants out of sheer hatred of the occupants, I was deeply moved with horror and rejection, and all the cruelty and suffering which has gone on there since has only intensified my feelings on the subject. I will not, if I can avoid it, read stories of violence, or attend films or plays, or look at programmes which portray evil. This is not because I believe such portrayals damaging to the soul, although I think they are, but simply because they hurt me too much. How can a good God permit such dreadful things to happen, I ask myself helplessly, and I am not really comforted by the beautiful rhetoric of God's final speech to Job out of the whirlwind, since nothing really reverses or obliterates evil, though it may compensate for it. The one thing which keeps me sane and well-balanced in such moods of black despair is the memory of Christ's passion, his shameful conviction, his cruel mishandling, his slow death, and the ultimate hopelessness of his cry of dereliction from the opening words of the twenty-second psalm, and the belief, which I have as a Christian, that this was not simply the despairing cry of a good man, shamefully abused, but a matter of cosmic significance, a statement that God the invisible, the Creator, the ground of all being, without body parts or passions, enters into human suffering with us, and somehow agonizes in all our private Gethsemanes. I know, of course, that this must necessarily be folly to the Greeks, who can visualize a God in human form well enough, as did Euripides when he visualized Dionysus in the *Bacchae*, but cannot visualize a God in suffering. I know too that to Jews and Moslems this seems not merely folly but blasphemy for they cannot visualize a God who, within a single being, can somehow be more than one person. I am not sure what Buddhists make of it, since their religion, like mine, seems based on a rejection of evil as it emerges in the form of suffering, but their smiling Buddha, though he has emerged from a world of suffering, does not seem to me to be involved in it to quite the intense degree of my crucified and risen Lord.

However, the only point of all this is that I do not find a purely unitarian view of God by itself acceptable in a world in which there is so much suffering and so much injustice. There seems to me to be no other way in which God can make himself known to man in an unjust and suffering world save by showing him to be involved in all our experiences, in grief as well as joy, in the appreciation of beauty, in human relationships of friendship and love and parenthood, in weariness and pain, in despair and hope. It is the paradox of Christianity that we predicate this of an omniscient, benevolent and omnipotent creator. Such a view is to some folly, to others a stumbling-block. To all it must involve both paradox and mystery. To the Christian, however, it is based upon a fact of history, and though it does not explain evil, at least it makes it bearable.

Whilst I am on this subject I might as well add that you do not get out of your philosophical troubles arising out of the fact of evil by rejecting God. For, as I have tried to point out before, the real problem is not the problem of evil, but the problem of good, not the problem of cruelty and selfishness, but the problem of kindness and generosity, not the problem of ugliness, but the problem of beauty. If the world is really the hopeless and meaningless jumble which one has to believe it to be if once we reject our value judgements as nothing more than emotional noises, with nothing more in the way of objective truth than a certain biological survival value for the species rather than the individual, evil then presents no difficulty because it does not exist. We must expect to be knocked about a bit in a world which consists only of atoms, molecules and strange particles. But how, then, does it come about that we go through life on assumptions which are perfectly contrary to these facts, that we love our wives and families, thrill with pleasure at the sight of a little bird discreetly dressed in green and black and white, that we rage at injustice inflicted on innocent victims, honour our martyrs, reward our heroes, and even, occasionally and with difficulty, forgive our enemies, and do good to them that persecute us and despitefully use us? No, it is light which is the problem, not darkness. It is seeing, not blindness. It is knowledge, not ignorance or error. It is love, not callousness. The thing we have to explain in the world is the positive, not the negative. It is this which led me to God in the first place. It is this which leads me to think that I know something about his activity in the world through the Christ of history.

9

The Living Church

I have said that there were two factors which led me on from the kind of philosophical acceptance of the divine into a more positive involvement with Christianity. The first, which I have been trying to describe as dispassionately as I can, was my encounter with Christ, both as a historical fact and as a philosophical conception. But the second was my encounter with the Church. At first sight, the history of the Christian Church is not a matter of edification. At the most favourable level, the divine light of the Gospels and the epistles seems to have given place in a matter of a generation or two on the one hand to endless squabbles about unverifiable points of doctrine which continue to divide Christians to this day, and on the other to a mass of pious fables and superstitions, bogus miracles and fake relics, all or most commercially exploited, which have persisted almost continuously from sub-apostolic times, to the *bondieuserie* of shops and shrines which can still be seen all over the Christian world. But this is the least part of it. The cruelties and persecutions, the civil wars and blind hatreds, the *autos da fé*, the burnings and rackings, the hangings, the drawings and quarterings, the anathemas, the inquisitions, the pogroms, the crusades, the sackings, the holy wars, are not, one would think, good advertisements for the divine society, inspired by the Holy Spirit, against whom we are expressly told the gates of hell shall not prevail, that it is to guard the keys, that its judgements are to be endorsed by the heavenly courts, and which arrogantly seeks to spread and perpetuate its doctrines from Greenland's icy mountains to India's coral strand. Although Gibbon's account of the matter can hardly be said to be either accurate or fair, there is enough genuine material available to provide hostile copy for a hundred Secular Societies and, even if one forgets all this, the amount of sheer and self-contradictory nonsense which emerges from clergy and ecclesiastically-minded laymen on the radio and television when they talk about secular and political subjects is enough to damp the ardour of the most spiritually-minded of devotees. It is not enough to say that the same can be said of the history of most other organized bodies of human beings whether secular or religious, Jews, Moslems, Hindus, Buddhists, Communists, Fascists, and so on. The Church claims to be something special, and it is not enough for it to excuse its appalling record by saying that it shares human faults with other human organizations. It is there to redeem humanity and not to share its failings.

This, however, is not the Church, contact with which has helped to give my life stability and coherence. The great difference, it seems to me, between Judaism and Christianity, which is either an off-shoot or the fulfilment of Judaism, and almost every other religious philosophy except Islam (which is largely derivative from Judaism and Christianity) is that other religions are circular, whereas Judaism and Christianity are rectilinear in their fundamental approach to human destiny. Adonis dies, and revives, Demeter is banished and let out on leave every year with the turn of the seasons. India has adopted the wheel as her symbol, and both Hinduism and Buddhism, which seems to me a rationalization of Hinduism, regard the recurring nature of life as at the centre of things. The Buddha smiles serenely because he has escaped from the squirrel's cage of existence into nirvana but, so long as we are in it, for life after life the cage goes round and round. The same sort of conception is found at the end of Plato's *Republic*; although in its recurrent incarnations the soul may mount higher and higher (or for that matter sink lower and lower) and, in one sense, the wheel turns into a spiral staircase, the ultimate bliss is to be out of it altogether. I do not deny the profundity of the myth, though the whole doctrine of Karma and reincarnation, undoubtedly a serious attempt to introduce an element of justice and order into a seemingly unjust and disorderly universe, seems to me to be incredible and, if not incredible, sadly unattractive and productive of melancholy. The recurring nature of the seasons, and the longer and greater circles of the heavenly bodies envisaged by pre-Copernican astronomy, undoubtedly correspond to a genuine reality. But this account of the universe, and the Divine, which gives the ultimate destiny of the human soul as a resolution into nothingness, not merely involves a basic pessimism but seems to me to postulate a relationship between soul and body, between the spiritual and material which is contrary to experience. I do not believe the soul can be extracted from one physical container and inserted into another. The nature of our human existence is shot through with material factors. We are not body and soul, and we are not brain and mind. Nor are we body only, with a computer in the brain. We are made as individuals but any philosophy which seeks to explain our individual existence must neither seek to deny the reality of the spiritual or the physical, nor so to separate them entirely from one another that one can be taken away from the other and continue to exist as if relatively little had happened. It is for this reason that I find the whole Christian doctrine of immortality difficult to swallow, but the more spiritual forms of oriental religion seem to me to be harder still. I do not believe that I ever was, or can ever become, a chaffinch, or that a chaffinch, in some subsequent existence, can be rewarded for its excellence as a chaffinch by becoming a human being.

The rectilinear view of human destiny postulated by Jews, Christians and, I would think, Islam seems to me to receive some confirmation from the physical world of experience and scientific observation. Although spatial relationships are in principle reversible, the time sequence is not. One of the few quotations surviving from the lost works of the Greek tragic poet Agathon is a phrase which says, in effect,

One thing at least God never knew -
How what is done, once done, to undo.

Although there is a sense in which this can be disputed there is a sense in which this is true, and as true as when it was written. Indeed, according to the second law of thermodynamics, the whole universe appears to be running down something like a clock and will require, at a given point of time, to be rewound somehow, unless, of course, the theory of continuous creation (to which I have already referred in another connection) supplies a sort of self-winding mechanism. The same appears to be true of the principle of evolution. Though our own complex bodies and those of bees and wasps, reptiles, elephants and birds may have evolved out of amoeba, there seems relatively little support for the view that they can evolve back again into unicellular organisms.

The weakness and the strength of the view of history postulated by Judaism, Christianity and Islam is that they were formulated at a time when the time scale of human existence on the planet seemed so abbreviated that it seemed not altogether fatuous to date the creation of the world on an October afternoon in 4004 B.C. Other calculations were possible, but the scale was approximately the same. With archaeology putting early civilizations as old as 6000 B.C. and palaeontology dating the age of the human species in terms of millions rather than thousands of years, it is clear that a different kind of philosophical outlook is essential and, in particular, the idea that the whole human race has to be baptized and converted before it can be saved appears more ridiculous than ever. Nonetheless the theory that life is not a perpetually recurring cycle but a progression of some sort from some sort of beginning to some sort of end seems to me to hold the field against all other attempts to rationalize history and experience.

In this world I find myself a member of a society and it is with the life of that society and my re-involvement with it that I am at present concerned. It bases itself on an historical fact, the life and death of Jesus of Nazareth, and an historical assertion, namely his resurrection and ascension (whatever these phrases may mean). I call the first a fact, because, for reasons I have given, I regard the existence of Jesus and his crucifixion under Pontius Pilate as historically certain in the same sense and almost to the same degree as the Battle of Hastings or the Battle of Cannae. I call the second an assertion, because, although, as I have tried to establish, the tradition is continuous to a period at which contemporary witnesses spoke, there is no escaping the fact that none of the witnesses were independent. The Crucifixion was public; the resurrection appearances were all private, and with the exception of Paul on the road to Damascus, confined to followers and friends of the crucified master. This necessarily gives their testimony a different character, though it may be nonetheless trustworthy for that. The Church is a missionary and worshipping society existing in time, and basing itself on this fact and this assertion. Were either of these two historical events proved not to have happened in any sense, the Church ought to disappear and, I think, would do so, though many of the Christian melodies, pictures, buildings and writings would presumably endure for a time by virtue of their aesthetic or ethical value, which cannot seriously be disputed. Their importance may not be unique, but it is at least as important as Chinese porcelain, Greek art, or Islamic architecture.

But the essence of the Church is its claim to the possession of the Holy Spirit, and its dogmatic assertion that this spirit, whatever may be meant by the phrase, is divine, indeed part (though the word used in orthodox theology is 'person' and 'part' is inappropriate) of the Godhead itself. Obviously the doctrine of the Trinity can be presented as a paradox or, as Moslems and Jews would put it, a blasphemous fable undermining the integrity of monotheism, or as orthodox Christians are bound to put it, as a mystery, that is, I suppose, to describe in language something for which language is inherently inadequate. Nonetheless, on a somewhat less sophisticated level, it need not present the same difficulties. All monotheistic religions must think of God in three ways, as God the Creator, underlying all existence, God the Redeemer, demanding and making possible the return of man to communion with God, and God the Inspirer of words, thoughts and actions in man as the result of that communion. The Christian Church is unique in its formulation of the doctrine, its systematization of it, its arguments about the precise use of technical terms like 'substance', 'essence', 'person' and 'begotten', 'created', 'procession', and so on, and in their alleged relation to historical events. But I do not find it unique or particularly obscure in developing a threefold description of divine activity.

For all the case which can be made out against the Church I do not find it false or even paradoxical to say that it did redeem and transform the ancient world and, when that world was overcome by the barbarian invasions, that it did save and preserve not merely the Christian heritage but the tradition of civilization and law through the Dark Ages, and the Middle Ages, to the Renaissance and the modern world, and, whether its religious or historical basis be true or false, that it has remained constant in its protest against the ugliness, cruelty and oppression of the modern age. Whatever can be said fairly against its alliance with authoritarian regimes, new or old, it remains true, in my experience at least, of the events of my lifetime that the moment a society consciously begins to reject Christianity and its values and, for whatever reason, begins pursuing the opposite, the most startlingly evil practices appear once more to emerge from dark corners and flap their hideous wings abroad.

But it is not, as a matter of fact, in its corporate witness that I find the activity of the spirit most convincing. It is the contact between the spirit and the individual which seems to me to show the most spectacular results. How much of what is now taken for granted in what is good in society owes its original inspiration to a consciously Christian motivation, even where the work has been subsequently overtaken, and taken over, by the apparatus of the modern state. Wilberforce was motivated by Christianity when he set about his campaign to end the slave trade. Florence Nightingale's original motivation was Christian, and the source of her expertise when she first sought to revive the almost forgotten craft of nursing was a teaching order of nuns where the art had been kept alive. Our whole system of education, public and private, our network of hospitals, our social security system itself, have each a clear origin in Christian foundations and, whatever can be said against much of the theoriza-tion, and much of the practice which they embodied, the motivation which underlay them was good and, in origin at least, the practice was disinterested. The Christians have been pioneers of good works throughout their history. They have been the originators, and secu-lar society has largely caught up with their efforts, made good their deficiencies of scale, and corrected their faults. No one who has studied the ancient world can get very far without being horror-struck with the hurricane of libido, lust, cruelty and greed of which Jung spoke, and those of us who have an increasing contact with the post-Christian society in which we live are disturbed to find the very same features reproducing themselves under widely differing politi-cal systems, in almost exact proportions as the spirit ceases to be cultivated, and the life of the spirit lived.

10

The Utility of Christianity

I have said already that I could not accept the utility of a religion that I did not believe to be true. I do not consider that it can really be beneficial to believe nonsense, and, even if I found it consoling to deceive myself, I do not think it would be possible for me either to seek or find consolation where I did not think there was truth. The capacity of the human mind for self-deception is almost infinite, and I fully accept that many people have found great consolation in varieties of belief which I personally find unsatisfactory. Indeed, one of the great obstacles to my own religion has always been that I was uneasily aware that the absence of the possibility of verifying many of my own conclusions left me wide open to self-deception myself.

Once, however, one comes to accept the truth of Christianity for reasons which, while obviously falling short of demonstration, nonetheless can be defended as rational, and once one attempts to practise Christianity at least as a working hypothesis forming a rational basis of a life style, one is entitled to reflect upon its usefulness or otherwise as a guide to practical life. I have already made it plain that I do not think it spells out a totally new morality. I do not think it overthrows natural morality in the sense in which I have tried to define the term. Nonetheless it would be an odd sort of religion which, though true, was of no practical value, and the object of what I have now to say is to reflect upon the uses to which it can legitimately be put. Such a series of reflections can serve two purposes. The first is to show that Christianity, so far from being in opposition to the experience of mankind, confirms it. The second is to show that in fact it provides an intellectual basis without which certain values universally accepted to be worth retaining would be wholly absent from human thinking. I will describe the advantages to be obtained from being a practising Christian under two heads. The first discusses the advantages to be obtained in the conduct of one's life as an individual, the second the intellectual foundation which Christianity can provide for a solid and progressive society.

There is, however, one preliminary remark which requires to be made. All Christians regard their religion as in some sense unique, and as uniquely true. But for the purposes of the present discussion this is not quite so. Christianity must take its place amongst other systems of belief, with all of which it has some points of resemblance and some of difference.

I feel, therefore, that I ought to begin by saying something about my attitude to these other systems since there would be no answer to potential criticism if I did not seek both to explain why I do not hold other beliefs myself, and why the fact that other people do hold them does not frighten me off my own quite as much as it used to.

There are certain beliefs and practices that I actively distrust. Among them is Spiritualism, and such elaborate modern organizations as Scientology. The first I distrust because I think the evidence against it is overwhelming. I quite realize that there are things which happen to which I can offer no rational explanation except perhaps conscious fraud. But the sheer banality of the alleged utterances from beyond the veil leads me to suppose that whatever be the explanation it is not that the dead are seriously trying to communicate with us. There have been times, I confess, when I was young, when I experimented with such things as table-turning. It would be quite wrong to say that I got no results. I could never quite persuade myself that the results I did get were not the product of deception on the part of one or more of my collaborators, or else perhaps some honest but nonetheless natural emanation from my own subconscious mind or theirs. But if there was anything more, and I was not wholly convinced that there was not, it was, characteristically, not very intelligent, not very benevolent, and not very nice. So that I gave the whole thing up as undesirable. Since those days I have once or twice attended a more formal spiritualist service conducted by a professional medium, and I formed very much the same conclusion from what I saw or heard. Neither the information vouchsafed through the medium nor the gradual steps by which the information became available seemed to me to be convincing. If it had a supernatural source, which at the time I rather more than doubted at the services I actually attended, the triviality of the information supplied was such that I could only assume that the loved ones concerned were either unusually stupid in their lives, or had undergone a serious degeneration after they had crossed over. I quite realize that many people have found great consolation in messages which they have received and I would hate to hurt them by anything I say or write. Nevertheless, the only advice I can give to the bereaved who may be tempted to try spiritualism is to keep clear of it.

I also accept that there are certain systems of belief, like scientology, which as those who practise them also testify, bring them great consolation. I am reluctant to criticize them in detail for much the same reason. I simply say that I do not find their philosophical conceptions adequate to support their theories and that the factual bases on which they claim to have produced good results on individuals do not seem to me to be fully substantiated.

It is quite otherwise when I examine the great world religions or the different variations on the Christian theme held by different branches of the Christian faith. It is true, of course, that Buddhism postulates, at best, a kind of Deism, and that the differences between Moslem and Jew, between Jew and Christian, and between the various brands of Christianity, Orthodox, Protestant and Roman Catholic, are obvious for all to see. Oddly enough, however, it is not the differences between them which impress me so much as the points of resemblance. All reject materialism as a satisfactory explanation for the totality of things. In one terminology or another, all assert the supremacy of the moral law in human affairs and its relation both to the religious experience of mankind and the spiritual entity underlying all reality and, even in matters of a detailed moral code, the points of identity in practical precept, between Jew, Moslem, Buddhist, Christian and Confucian seem to be much more striking than the differences. When one reflects that what we are concerned with is a series of value judgements, in principle not verifiable, I find the total testimony of civilized mankind in morals and metaphysics at least as impressive as the kind of unanimity which also exists about such matters as natural beauty or artistic excellence.

When I go into a synagogue, I do not find myself shocked by the implicit denial of the Incarnation. On the contrary, I find myself immensely edified and uplifted by the majesty and beauty of the Hebrew prayers and acts of worship in their English translation, quite apart from the Old Testament scriptures and other beliefs which Jews and Christians have in common. Of course my feeling of unity with the various Christian denominations is all the greater. I am not particularly tempted to become, say, a Roman Catholic or a Presbyterian, but I can join in the services of both without becoming conscious of any loss of loyalty to my own communion. It is not that I find the differences unimportant. It is that I am actually strengthened in my own beliefs and practices by finding that they are not at all unique, but form one of a group of related and not dissimilar opinions.

Having said all this, and having said that I do not find it possible in general to spell out of my Christianity any general rules of conduct other than those of natural morality, I feel I must say something a good deal more positive about what my religion has meant to me in the actual conduct of my life.

The first thing I must mention is the feeling of confidence I receive that when I am obeying, or seeking imperfectly first to identify and then to obey, the dictates of conscience, I am not doing something which is plain silly. I am not just deceiving myself. I am, on the contrary, acting in co-operation with something or rather someone at the heart of the universe itself, some Entity which enjoys the beauty of the sunlight, and the stars of heaven, and the sheen on the feathers of a bird, or the qualities I admire and love in my family and my children, even as I enjoy them myself. This means a great deal more than an impersonal Deism. It implies a Creator. I am, of course, aware that the whole appreciation of natural beauty and love is something which I possess in virtue of my body, and that God, of course, is something outside and beyond the physical, and that therefore the relationship between God and his physical creation is altogether outside my comprehension. But the belief that he is there sustains me on my journey as nothing else can. I do not believe that, in the ordinary course, he tells me what to do in particular situations, or that he will help me as a politician or an advocate to map out right courses in my political or professional life. On the contrary, I believe that he has set me in this world to develop my own judgement of good and evil in the light of his universal presence, and that he will not supernaturally intervene in the ordinary course of events, except in the sense that everything that takes place for good comes in one way or another from God. But when I see beauty or seek justice, or try to do right things or avoid evil things I am consciously assisted by the belief that the things of good repute are not just vain imaginings of my own, but correspond to something deep in the heart of the universe itself.

When Pompey invaded the Jewish temple, it is related that he was astonished to find there no image like those of Zeus or Apollo or Athena in the Greek or Roman temples with which he was familiar. The concept of idolatry is of course rather an unreal one to one who has always worshipped in the Protestant tradition, although I am not in the least shocked by the presence of religious pictures, or icons, or statues in churches, and I find the Stations of the Cross an aid rather than otherwise to devotion. But the real idolatry that one has to avoid nowadays has nothing whatever to do with statues or pictures. It is what one worships in one's heart that counts. In the innermost shrine of the soul there must be nothing to compete with God, neither family, nor friends, nor country, nor party, nor wealth, nor profession, nor reputation. The essence of Monotheism is the preservation, empty and inviolate, of the innermost sanctuary of the soul, so that God and God only is there, and God, and God only is worshipped. It is true that a present companion to a Christian is always Our Lord himself, present in the body as a human being and endowed with every human faculty, present in the sanctuary in virtue of his divine nature. But he is not worshipped as an idol, because there is nothing in this temporal world which can take the place of God in the empty shrine.

Some years ago, when the *Daily Sketch* was still a newspaper, I was asked to contribute to a series of articles entitled 'If Christ came back now', and I ultimately agreed to do so. In the main, the outcome of the series was predictable. The Left-Wing parson was saying how the good Lord would go out amongst the poor and the afflicted doing good, and how he would be rejected by the Establishment, and how various useful suggestions would be made by him, and vested interests would in the end get the better of them all, and so on.

The Jesuit predictably, and from his point of view reasonably, made the point that Christ had never left the world. He was present in the Church, and in the Sacrament, and the question what he would do if he came back should be rephrased to ask what was he in fact doing here and now.

I found myself agreeing with a great deal of all this, but thinking on somewhat different lines. Like the Jesuit, I thought the question itself an unreal one. Christians believe that the human life of Jesus of Nazareth took place at the moment of history precisely and uniquely fitted for the work which he had to do. To talk, therefore, of his being born into the twentieth century is basically as artificial and unreal as to talk of his having been born into the Stone Age. Jesus was as much a man of his time and place as any other, and the moment at which he was to be born was unique precisely because it was God's will that he should be born then and there and never anywhere else.

But this led me to face a far more difficult question which, in the end, was the question I sought to answer in my article. It was not the question asked, but it was, I ventured to think, the real riddle underlying the question asked. It was this. The picture we all have of Jesus is coloured through and through with the knowledge of what happened to him at the end of his life and after. It is seen through the dark glass of his remembered passion. He is the man of sorrow, acquainted with grief, by whose stripes we are healed. Alternatively he is the risen Lord, gracious, triumphant, appearing to his astonished friends as the victorious conqueror of death. But this is precisely the knowledge that his contemporaries did not have during his ministry. Indeed, it is related that when he sought to disclose to his friends what was likely to happen they simply did not believe him.

This led me to ask myself, as if I had never asked the question before, a somewhat different question. What exactly was Jesus like to meet? If one had been a fellow-guest when he asked himself to dinner with Zacchaeus, or when he was eating with the Pharisee, what sort of a man would one in fact have seen and spoken to? What was his conversation like? Having asked this question, I looked at the Gospel again, and quite suddenly a new portrait seemed to stare at me out of the pages. I had never previously thought of a laughing, joking Jesus, physically strong and active, fond of good company and a glass of wine, telling funny stories, using, as every good teacher does, paradox and exaggeration as among the most effective aids to instruction, applying nicknames to his friends, and holding his companions spellbound with his talk. And yet, it is a very odd thing that one does not think of him in these terms. Granted that we are told to think of him as having every perfection of human nature, do we not ordinarily regard a sense of humour and high spirits as among the most desirable attributes a man can have? How then can we suppose that he did not have them? As I reflected upon this, I came to the conclusion that the first thing we must learn about him is that we should have been absolutely entranced by his company. Jesus was irresistibly attractive as a man. The man whom they crucified was intensely fond of life, and intensely vital and vivacious. He did not wish to die. He was the last person to be associated with suffering. They called him a winebibber. They abused him for the company he kept. What was it, do you suppose, that kept Mary at his feet when Martha was scurrying about getting the dinner? Was it a portentous commentary on Holy Scripture? I feel sure that it was simply that she found his company actually enthralling. When one begins to think of it, can one see anything but fun in calling the two enthusiastic brothers 'Sons of Thunder', or impetuous, chivalrous, heroic, but often blundering Simon, the Rock? Is there no hint of humour in the foolish virgins, or the unjust steward, or the camel who finds it impossible to get through the eye of a needle, or the comparison of the speck of dust and the great beam in the eye, or the picture of wicked old Tiberius getting back the penny with his ugly old face on it, or the mustard plant likened to a tree, or the trade unionists who complain at the end of the day that someone else has got by with only an hour's work for the whole day's wage? Once one reflects about this, the picture of Jesus suddenly comes to life. The tragedy of the Cross was not that they crucified a melancholy figure, full of moral precepts, ascetic and gloomy. He was not John the Baptist, and the Baptist acknowledged this. What they crucified was a young man, vital, full of life and the joy of it, the Lord of life itself, and even more the Lord of laughter, someone so utterly attractive that people followed him for the sheer fun of it, someone much more like the picture of

Dionysus in a Greek mosaic than the agonized and broken figure in a medieval cathedral, or the Christos Pantokrator of an orthodox monastery. The man of sorrows acquainted with grief was in himself and before his passion utterly and divinely joyous. The twentieth century needs to recapture the vision of this glorious and happy man whose mere presence filled his companions with delight. No pale Galilean he, but a veritable Pied Piper of Hamelin who would have the children laughing all round him and squealing with pleasure and joy as he picked them up.

When I am asked about the utility of Christianity I must point to the consolations of living your life in the companionship of this person who commands your love and adoration precisely because having been through it all and sympathizing with it all he cheers you up and will not have you sad. Your shame at your own misdoings, and shortcomings, your sense of awe and fear of the divine majesty, your broken heart in the presence of sickness and bereavement melts in the presence of this person into the sheer wonder and delight which the happiness of his presence excites. The empty shrine shows the negative virtue of monotheism. Its counterpart is the magical personality of the most lovable young man that was ever born of woman and walked the earth.

There is a third consolation of Christianity about which I am reluctant to write because it is both intimate, and therefore embarrassing, and difficult to explain, and therefore unconvincing. I will call it the consolation of the indwelling spirit. My ancestors who, until one was excommunicated for marrying a Church of Ireland parson's daughter, were Quakers, would have called it, I think, the inner light.

There are two sides to this, the life of prayer and the life of conscience. I will describe the latter first. I know I must have shocked, perhaps even scandalized, many people by writing first that Christianity did not in fact create a new morality or seek to override the morality of the Decalogue or the Old Testament prophets, or indeed morality generally as thought out and practised by the common conscience of mankind, and, secondly, that God does not in the ordinary course tell you what to do in a given situation, but that on the contrary he actually wishes you to work out your own salvation according to the talents and the intelligence he has given you. This doctrine would indeed be shocking were it not for three interrelated qualifications to which I will now give some attention.

The first is that, though the Sermon on the Mount does not in fact create a new morality overriding the old, it does create a new dimension to the existing morality by pointing out the importance which the motivation by love, or its opposite, hatred, has on the determination of human conduct, both by influencing what men actually do and in determining the moral value of what they do even when they appear to do the same thing. The corrosive importance of hatred and bitterness in human affairs, the sublime effect of generosity and self-sacrifice, the dangerous nature of the predatory instinct, are not directly related to moral or immoral conduct in the sense that everybody who hates his neighbour kills him, or that everybody who lusts after his neighbour's wife goes to bed with her, or even that everyone who does a generous act or patiently puts up with injustice acts wisely or rightly. But the influence of these motives on human conduct and human worth is the point which is being made.

The second thing is that anyone who has decided to take the Christian life seriously will begin by questioning himself seriously about his own life and conduct, and will begin to think furiously about the value judgements of right and wrong, virtue and vice which he has been making. He will become a man who suddenly and persistently develops a sort of craze for virtue, as a child will develop a passion for collecting stamps, or a young man or woman develop a feeling for music or pictures. He will want to know much more about the nature of virtuous living than the ordinary people he sees around him. He will begin to study the Bible, Old Testament and New, with a fresh interest. He will go to church and hear sermons and take part in the acts of worship which, almost all of them, contain new and absorbing insights into the whole content of a serious and Christian life. Thus, although Christianity only develops thoughts and insights which are asserted elsewhere, though perhaps with less inspiration than in the Christian literature, he will, as he goes on, acquire an understanding of virtue and morality which is infinitely more cultivated, coherent and sensitive than that of the average man, and will penetrate much more deeply into the subject.

Christianity will make him a new man. Though it will not teach him a morality which differs from the value judgements of others, it will develop the natural moral sense with which all men are endowed exactly as the study of music will develop the natural appreciation of musical sounds with which all or most men are endowed.

At this stage I must say something about the life of prayer which, to my mind, is crucial to the whole matter. I do so with great hesitation because I am extremely conscious of the fact that I am a very bad prayer (I mean a man who prays) indeed. I am not even in the gifted-amateur class. I lack both the concentration and the perseverance which a good exponent of the art will need to show. My prayers are only too apt to be mere repetitious formulae, or naïve and childish orisons of the God-bless-Mummy-and-Daddy variety. If they were not, I would, no doubt, have become a very much better man than I am. What I say, therefore, is only worth writing down to the extent that it may help people who know even less than I do, how a beginner may think about the subject sensibly.

The first point to make is that once you have come to the conclusion that there does exist a Person or rather an Entity transcending Person at the heart of the universe some sort of prayer life is inevitable, and automatic. It is unthinkable that, having reached this point, one should not at least attempt to communicate. When one does seek to communicate one finds at once that one's first thought is not to ask for something. Endless articles are written about the question whether prayer is answered as if prayer was a sort of spiritual penny-in-the-slot machine which would automatically deliver a bar of chocolate every time one operated the machinery, or a sort of letter to Father Christmas which one posted up the chimney. But, in point of fact, it does not happen like that at all. Indeed, half the time I find my prayers are wholly wordless. It consists in a sort of feeling of spiritual sunbathing, turning oneself towards the spiritual light and allowing it to revive the spirit, like the sunlight on a flower, or a mother's smile on the child. Of course, this does not happen every time. There are terrible periods of emptiness and darkness. But it happens sufficiently often and it is sufficiently real to be infinitely worthwhile. There are moments of simple adoration and thankfulness for all the beauty and glory in the world, the goodness of other people. There are moments of horror at the suffering of men, of agony at one's own suffering, of misery and self-accusation at one's past misdeeds or present inadequacy. Ask for things? Why, yes, of course. Obviously if one's mind is troubled about this or that, when one collects one's thoughts and submits oneself to the presence of the Divine, the desire of one's heart comes bubbling forth. There is no difficulty about that. It may be this or that. It may be comfort for oneself that one wants, or something good for somebody else. It may be a purely material good. It may be relief from pain or sorrow. It may be courage or endurance that is needed. The important thing is to hold it up to the light and submit it to the Divine presence and the Divine power. Words come if words are needed, but a great deal of what one does when one is praying is wordless. Moreover, if like me you find concentration and long bouts of prayer impossible or difficult, it is much better to make no bones about it. Little and often has much to be said for it. There is no difficulty about praying in a motor car or in a railway carriage or, for that matter, in the dentist's chair. There is no particular posture in which prayer is impossible, although a regular spell of kneeling twice a day in a closed room with no one else about is obviously desirable. The important thing is not to agonize about it, but to do whatever comes naturally, and I find it does come naturally if one does not try to force it. If by any chance one finds that there are too many distractions, or if, for any reason, one discovers as frequently one does that one is not aware of any subjective feeling of the Divine presence, it is better not to worry, but not to desist. Regular habits in prayer are essential only because there are these long periods in which the Divine presence seems to be withheld, and in which nonetheless some act of submission to the Divine will seems necessary and called for. Otherwise as and when the thought comes to one is often the best time and occasion. Each man must be his own teacher in such matters. I know of no other way, and no guarantee of success. All I can say to those who have given up the habit of prayer is that they should try to resume it and go on trying.

Before I move to the social utility of Christianity there is one other point I feel bound to make concerning its utility to the individual. More than once in my life I have had cause to reflect on the wisdom of the Greeks embodied in one of the two inscriptions inscribed in Apollo's shrine at Delphi. Meden Agan - nothing too much; everything in moderation. There is some reason to think that the Greeks had more need of this advice than most people. Their ebullient spirit was forever boiling over into different varieties of excess. To some extent, I believe, a Christian is more easily able to be proof against excess than the ebullient Greek of pagan times. He is bound to regard, to adopt Kipling's phrase, those two impostors, triumph and disaster, with some degree of caution. I do not use the phrase Stoicism, because I do not think the truly Christian attitude to either is properly one of the indifference prescribed by the Stoic philosophy, and because it seems to me that all the pagans missed the significance and failed to appreciate or perhaps even identify the Christian virtue of humility. Nonetheless I believe that the Christian religion does to some extent proof the believer both against excessive elation at success and undue depression at what is called failure. It is in fact a specific both against arrogance and against bitterness and despair. No Christian dare think of himself as a success if he contemplates seriously any of his shortcomings. Equally no Christian will think of himself as a failure if he reflects upon the love of Christ for himself.

I am moved at this stage to add a footnote about suicide. I had thought of remaining reticent on the subject, but I am impelled to write about it in the hope that at some time someone will read, and heed, my words. My dear brother Edward committed suicide, and there is a sense in which I have never recovered from the blow. He was in every way a delightful person, brave and talented beyond the lot of man. He rowed for Leander, was President of the Oxford Union, earned and received a Double First, was M.P. for Eastbourne, the author of at least one best-selling book, and a rising member of the Bar. He could not have failed, had he lived, to play an important, perhaps even a decisive, part in the history of the country. He killed himself one spring day in our home in Sussex with my 20-bore shotgun which, when I had been a little younger, had been my most prized possession. I will not waste time discussing what led him to do it, except to say that the last phase was insomnia, or to say why I have never failed to blame myself without mercy for my failure to prevent him doing it. I only write this in order to express my profound and passionate conviction that suicide is always wrong if only for the misery it inflicts on others. Bereavement is one thing.

The pain at bereavement is the price we pay for love, and high as that price is, it is not one which one grudges paying when bereavement is suffered. But bereavement by suicide is something altogether different and leaves an incurable wound. If only Edward had known the pain he was inflicting on us all who were left behind, and the ceaseless and incurable self-condemnation we all felt so that even now forty years later I cannot bear the burden of it, he would never have done what he did and, if by reading this some other unhappy family may be saved from woe so intolerable, this book will not have been in vain. As it is, Edward is in the hands of God, and no doubt he is wholly forgiven, since if our poor natures can wholly forgive him as we do, how much more will the infinite compassion of the Saviour take him to his arms. But suicide is wrong, wrong, wrong, and Christians were amongst the first to recognize the fact. Their spiritual insight is to be recognized as among the proofs, as well as the consolations, of Christianity.

11

The Social Utility of Christianity

Having now discussed the subjective value to myself of Christian belief and practice, I would like to point out its relevance to the establishment of a civilized and ordered society. In doing so, I am putting Christianity and the system of belief it offers as one amongst a class of world religions. Many of the advantages I claim will be common to one or more of these other religions. Some perhaps are offered by Christianity alone or by Christianity to a greater degree than others. For the purposes of the present discussion, I do not mind which is which. I am engaged on an exposition of my own beliefs. For reasons I have already given, I am strengthened and not weakened in my own beliefs if and in so far as I find that they are not in fact unique but are shared by other representatives of civilized mankind.

The origin of civil obligation has long puzzled political philosophers. We did not choose to be born. Yet each child born into the world finds himself growing up in a system of authority among people who claim to exercise authority over him. At first these are parents, or those who happen to be in the position of parents. From time to time other authorities obtrude themselves on his notice, more especially the political authorities of the society he lives in, whether they are known by a specific name such as King, or by some generic title such as the State. The common characteristic of them all is that they demand allegiance and respect even though the man or woman has not chosen them himself and does not agree with what they propose to do with him. This, stated otherwise, was what Rousseau had in mind when he propounded the paradox that though born free (I do not know what he meant by this, since it is evidently false) man was nevertheless everywhere in chains (a proposition which, even when he wrote, was at the best a gross exaggeration). His own, and subsequent, attempts to justify or rationalize a political philosophy manifestly failed. There never was a social contract of the kind he envisaged, and, if there had been, it would never have been binding on any save its original authors. The real problem is to justify the use of compulsion by one human being or one human group on another. The utilitarian principle - the greatest happiness or good of the greatest number - clearly provides no answer, since it makes no allowance for the rights of the individual. Participation in the machinery of government by the individual provides no answer since his own will can always be overridden by more powerful or more numerous neighbours. Majority rule provides no answer since majorities can be and often are wrong and as tyrannical as minorities or individuals. What is needed is an explanation of rights which are universally acknowledged to exist both in the individual and the State, and some guidance of what these rights are and what is to happen when there is a conflict of interest. Originally, and until it was seen to be nonsense, the divine origin of society, and of its titular head, was taken for granted, except by a rebellious minority. It never had any intellectual justification, but at least it asserted what everyone knew to be true, namely the individual had rights and the State, in whatever form it had developed, also had rights over him.

It is worthwhile saying at the outset that the problem only arises to those who recognize both propositions. To those who maintain that the King, the majority, the class, the party, the Union is answerable to nobody, or 'only to God', which for this purpose means the same thing, or to those who maintain, at least in theory, the desirability of a purely anarchical society there can be no problem. This is why, on the whole, the nature of civil obligation has been more debated in the West, where there is a long tradition of freedom and a respectable jurisprudence even under authoritative governments, than in the East, where the will of the ruler has been more constantly asserted and the right of the conqueror more frequently accepted.

In the end, however, if we are to seek for a rational explanation of things this is a problem which demands a rational exposition.

My thesis is that Christianity offers such an explanation and the philosophy of the universe which it implies is in fact part of the explanation which it offers.

The answer lies in two propositions about the nature of man. The first is that he is the possessor of free will, that is, he really can, within limits, originate new action, and is thus a first cause. The second is that the value judgements which he makes, and in particular the value judgements about morality and justice, are not mere emotional noises but have an objective validity about which reasoned argument can turn and which respond to something real rooted in the nature of humanity and in the universe itself. There could be no place for law, nor for the sanctions of law, nor political authority if training a man were not different in principle from training a dog or donkey. No doubt there could be sticks and carrots, and in that sense rewards and punishments. But there could be no appeal to reason, and none to justice. There would be no such thing as justice. It is only in a world in which there is morality, and that morality is binding on rulers and ruled alike that there is any room for a jurisprudence in the true sense of the word. This is the world which is asserted by religious belief, and in particular by the world religions. It is, I believe, for this reason that any attempt by the politician to drive religion out from his philosophy has always led to one thing, which is man's almost total inhumanity to man. In the end the utilitarian and individualistic philosophies of the nineteenth century led to the 'wail of intolerable serfdom' spoken of in Disraeli's novels. I need not say to what the collectivist philosophies of the twentieth century have led. The fires of Belsen still stink in our nostrils, and the oppressions of Communism, or the criminal lunacies of the lesser dictatorships, still exist in too poignant a form. It is a belief in man as a creature made in God's image, to use the poetic language of the Old Testament, which forms the protection of man from the extremities of indifference or oppression. It is the objective validity of morality as proclaimed by the sages of all nations which explains and justifies the perpetual tension, the endless dialogue, between individuals and minorities on the one hand and the State on the other, between freedom and authority, between liberty and law. In other words it is the free will and the rationality of the individual, the dignity of the individual, in tension with the

moral responsibility of the individual which explains and justifies
the writings of the political authors, the debates in Parliament, the
regulations made by Ministers, the treaties concluded between
sovereign communities, the demand for freedom, and the necessity
for law which constitute the history of the West, and ultimately of
all mankind. The fact that these things are not measurable, calcu-
lable, or verifiable explains much, perhaps all, of the argument.
But the fact that they remain objective realities proves that the
argument is not about nothing. A law which does not appeal to the
rational in man is no better than a stick or a carrot applied to a
donkey, by whomsoever or whatsoever it is passed. A liberty or a
civil right which does not explicitly or implicitly recognize responsibility to a morality which transcends the right is a mere arrogant
assumption, based on selfishness and nothing else. Law and freedom
are, therefore, not enemies but friends, not opposites but co-ordinates
in a world in which man is a responsible creature with free will and
a reason capable of understanding the difference between good and
bad. Only, I believe, the world religions, of which Christianity is the
one I am discussing, provide a rational working hypothesis of what
this is all about.

I am aware, of course, that this bears only indirectly upon humanism, which was the fashionable doctrine opposed to Christianity,
indeed to any religious view of the world, in the 1960s, though I
fancy that it has fewer adherents in the harsher and more unfor-
giving climate of today. I am myself in one sense a humanist in
political matters. The very word brings back memories of the
Renaissance of classical culture which ushered in the modern world.
I do not regard humanism in itself as hostile to Christianity. Eras-
mus, the first of the Renaissance humanists, was also the author
of devotional literature, and died in the bosom of the unreformed
Catholic Church. In its original meaning, humanism, it seems to me,
brought back an element of much-needed common sense into the
aesthetics, morals and politics of medieval Christianity. Amongst
other things, it taught that, whatever other relationship there may
or may not be between law and morality, a direct correspondence
there cannot be. In its nature, law is concerned with the social
consequences of external behaviour. It is limited by public standards,
by the available methods of enforcement, by the need to reconcile

divergent social goods. With many of these practical limitations morality is not concerned, or not concerned in the same way, whilst, by contrast, morality is concerned a great deal more with motivation than with consequences and more with individual virtue than with its effects. But in so far as humanism purports to pretend that it can do without religion altogether in the social, the moral, the political, or even in the aesthetic field, I think it fails completely to carry conviction. To begin with, it seeks to operate without a metaphysic of any kind and, for reasons I have already discussed, I consider the possession of some metaphysical beliefs unavoidable if we are to hold a rational view of the universe. Moreover, although many of the propositions or values of the humanist are either founded on Christian ethics or indistinguishable from them, the failure to offer any rational philosophy which renders their practice reasonable tends to make humanism an ethic of enlightened selfishness, suitable for the well-to-do, but unsuited to conditions of adversity wherever these are to be found.

When it comes to establishing ethical rules which are consonant with the dignity of man and his spiritual longings, I find humanism sadly lacking. I have never myself underwritten the traditional Roman Catholic teaching on divorce, contraception, or abortion in its entirety. But each in its own way is admirable; if for nothing else, in its unswerving assertion of the dignity of man, and his profound need to behave in a dignified, devoted and un-squalid fashion. Take abortion, for instance. Common lawyers have never taken the view that the child within the mother's womb is to be treated as possessing exactly the same rights as a separate human being with an independent existence. If they did, it would follow that the termination of a pregnancy, even to save a woman's life, is juristically the same thing as the murder of a child. But at the other end of the scale, I find it impossible to deny that the embryo in the mother's womb is a form of human life and, as such, to be reverenced both by the mother herself and by the doctor who treats her. It is quite another thing again to seek to define the circumstances in which the termination of a pregnancy is a crime, when it is a sin, and when it is permissible as the lesser of two evils. I do not seek here to answer these questions. But I cannot answer them without taking into account the holiness and worshipfulness of human life, whether in the mother or the unborn child, and, in so far as humanism leads one to treat human beings as if they were just animals and nothing more or, for that matter, to treat animals as if they were just chattels and nothing more, it seems to me to fall down precisely because it degrades humanity and even animal life in the proper scale of values. Human beings are both other than animals, and despite their animal nature more valuable than animals, just as animals are both other than and more valuable than mere chattels despite their physical and material nature. In so far as humanism asserts the importance of this world in morality and art and ethics and politics, I find myself its ally. One should not be for ever looking over one's shoulder to consider one's prospects in the next world, still less to consider the next-worldly prospects of others. But in so far as humanism seeks to exclude from any practical conclusions in life's conduct a religious outlook, or to limit itself to a view of human beings or animals which does not allow for a religious outlook, I find it wholly wanting, and its failure seems to me to be complete, both in the philosophical field and in its inability to cope with the practical aspirations of the average man and woman. I am fortified in this view by what seems to me the total failure of humanists to agree among themselves about any coherent or constructive view of ethics or social policy to put in the place of the traditional values which they have been so eager to dispute. The sparrow falling to the ground, the rabbit in pain and terror in the field, the child in agony and fear, the old man in loneliness and despair, the maimed body, the tired spirit, need something more than humanism to explain their significance. They need an insight into the divine, and the love of a Divine Creator. Humanism by itself has never redeemed mankind from sin or despair, offers no explanation why, in acting morally, men are also acting rationally, and provides neither explanation nor excuse for the exercise of political authority. In so far as humanism exalts the nature and destiny of man I am with it all the way. But in so far as it debases man to a mere bundle of wants and satisfactions, I find it unworthy of the name of humanism, because it fails to understand the true nature of the humanity it professes to serve.

12

The Bible

At some time or another every Christian, and particularly every Protestant, must ask himself what he thinks about the Bible. Quite obviously the Bible means something very different to me than it did to my Quaker and Church of Ireland ancestors, who lived before the publication of *The Origin of Species*. To them, or at least to many of them, the whole story had to be taken literally, from the talking snake in the book of Genesis to the unedifying passages in, say, the book of Samuel, where Samuel announces the condemnation of Saul because he did not literally obey the command of Jehovah in prescribing genocide for the Amalekites. Quite obviously, I cannot accept the Bible in that sense. There are some stories and passages against which my moral sense rebels. There are statements about history and even accounts of miracles about which, to say the least, I suspend judgement. Moreover, and perhaps most important of all, the historical scale, giving approximately six thousand years of human history between Adam and World War II, is something quite contrary to what I believe about the time scale on which the life of Man has been enacted on earth. I can quite understand how, to an unbeliever, the whole attitude of awe and worship which the Christian adopts towards the biblical canon, whether or not one includes the Apocrypha, must seem wholly perverse and even intellectually dishonest. Nor is this a problem which only afflicts Protestants. Although the right of individual interpretation was, at least until recently, severely frowned on by the Roman Catholic Church, and the authority and tradition of the Church as a living society elevated to a position equal to that of the Scriptures, the Scriptures themselves, interpreted in the light of these doctrines, occupy in orthodox Roman Catholic teaching a position at least as august as that which would have been subscribed to by my own fundamentalist forebears. At least one recent pope has gone on record as saying: '*Scripturae sanctae Deum habent auctorem.*' This, in its most natural interpretation, is almost equivalent to the old simple-minded view that the Holy Spirit simply dictated the book of Leviticus to Moses or the Epistles to the Corinthians to St Paul much as one might dictate a letter to a secretary. Indeed, I suspect that even Ronnie Knox, that wittiest and most urbane of priests, held what one must describe as an ultra-Conservative view when he wrote those splendid skits on biblical and Baconian criticism and thus founded the whole school of Sherlock Holmes Higher Criticism, and proved, as it were, conclusively that Queen Victoria was the true author of (was it?) In Memoriam.

Obviously, therefore, a Christian needs to state his attitude to the Holy Scriptures in the light of what I have written. In what sense, if at all, is it the Word of God? I find myself answering the question positively if not with the same literal interpretation as my ancestors, at least with the same reverence as any of them. I am not put off by the fact that I am compelled to refuse an absolutely literal interpretation. My own reading of the Old Testament books is, to my mind, far less difficult to defend than the extraordinary interpretations placed upon them in the second and third centuries by the Alexandrine Christian scholars, like Origen or even, I believe, the more orthodox St Jerome. I find in them a source of continued inspiration. Apart from the incomparably dramatic stories of the so-called historical books of the Old Testament, I find the moral lessons both in the historical books and in the prophets the best handbook of natural morality and justice in the world. The book of Job is by far the most penetrating analysis of the meaning of suffering I have ever read, maybe the most illuminating ever written, and the poetry and material for prayer in the psalms and the other poetical books is something which has been the inspiration of Christians from the earliest days to the present. As I have written more than once, and will have to say again in the course of this chapter, the Christian religion itself, being concerned with grace and love, is, despite much that is written and asserted at the present time, very largely devoid of political or social doctrine. This is not so of the Old Testament. The moral law here preached is the natural law, and the doctrine reiterated on almost every page is that disregard of the natural law, either by the individual or a nation, leads inevitably to disaster. This is often spoken of as the wrath of God, or divine vengeance, or punishment, and no doubt this is theologically very proper. But the way I see it is that disregard of the natural law, whether we are talking about the precepts of the Decalogue or the more complicated social morality of Amos and the prophets, brings punishment in exactly the same way, and for broadly the same reasons, as driving on the wrong side of the road, or too fast, or cutting in in the face of oncoming traffic brings punishment upon it whether or not the offender is caught up in the meshes of the criminal law or whether he simply smashes his car or kills himself and his wife or someone else. Life is a complex thing, and it need not shock us that if we break the covenants of natural reason upon which we hold its lease, we find ourselves in trouble of one sort or another. What does need to shock us, and what does shock us, is that the innocent suffer so often as the result of the wrongdoing of the guilty. But this is not as paradoxical as it sounds. As the Devil pointed out to the Almighty in the book of Job, if God was always seen to reward the righteous in this world for doing right, it would be seen, and very soon said, that the righteous were only doing right for what they could get out of it. But God does not desire this kind of obedience. He is set on creating beings with a free will, in a world in which they themselves are responsible for the consequences of their own choices and desires the free obedience of intelligent and reasoning creatures. Only when Job begins to suffer unjustly and still will not curse God is it seen that he does not serve God for what he can get out of it. The suffering of Job, like the Crucifixion and Passion of Christ, is seen to be the consequence, not of Job's own guilt, but of the presence of evil in the world, and the need for it to be seen that good must be pursued for its own sake, even, occasionally, at personal sacrifice.

When it comes to the New Testament there are two separate points which need to be made. The first is that the epistles and Gospels provide the necessary authentic link with the historical Jesus. The Church exists, no doubt, and its continuous life is both a link and a testimony. But without the New Testament this would be unintelligible, because the unique personality of its Founder, the meaning of its liturgy, and the source of its inspiration, would have been wholly lost. I mention the epistles and the Gospels in that order because in point of authorship the epistles, or many of them, were written first, and through the link provided by the book known as the Acts of the Apostles provide the stongest guarantee of the broad reliability of the Gospel tradition. The second point is that the peculiar characteristics of Christian theology are rooted in the New Testament and could not wholly be inferred from the Old. In the orthodox Christian tradition, which I share, the Old Testament is only fully intelligible if interpreted in the light of the New.

Looking back on my life I find that the Bible in its coherent entirety has been one of the main influences on my character and conduct. I believe this is true of everyone who has come into contact with it and has not deliberately chosen to disregard its message. My own contact with it became peculiarly intimate in the years between 1950 and 1964 when after my father's death I was living at my home in Sussex and having to read both lessons Sunday by Sunday at Herstmonceux where we worshipped. It is impossible to read the Bible out loud week after week without finding the immense power and vitality of almost every part of it. It seems to come to life and movement on your lips like a living thing. It almost wriggles, like a fish on the line, like a snake in the hand: It is not a dead word, but a living word. Of course, I like best the magic language of the Authorized Version. But the experience is the same whatever version is used. I am not a purveyor of texts to support exact doctrines. I believe that the Bible is an inspiration, a light to guide the feet, not a lamp-post to support moral instability, or one of those handrails you sometimes find in the Alps to stop wayfarers from falling from the path in an access of giddiness. The moment one tries to treat it as a substitute for one's own moral judgements or conscience it becomes a source of potential danger, as one can quote the Scriptures to support almost any kind of nonsense. It is when it is treated as a living source of inspiration and enlightenment that it does its work. It can only be used in conjunction with the life of meditation, self-criticism and prayer. But so used there is nothing like it, and there is no substitute for it.

13

Natural and Supernatural Morality

I am often asked and, when asked, invariably find the question irritating, what difference Christianity has made to my life or, in a slightly different form, what is the relevance of Christianity in the modern world. I am slightly irritated by this because, as I shall try to show, the nature of the question is largely due to a misunderstanding or, perhaps rather, a series of misunderstandings. I like to think that, after about forty years of trying to practise the Christian religion more or less unsuccessfully, I am still not quite so absolutely awful as I would have been had I not been trying to practise it. But that does not mean that other people with nice dispositions or a more effective ability to stick to their principles have not, without attempting to practise Christianity, achieved more than I. What is much more important, it does not necessarily mean that the Christian's idea of what is right or wrong, or what makes a person awful or not, is different from anybody else's, and, as I happen to believe that value judgements are part of the common human heritage and that the failure to understand this is productive of a great deal of confusion, I will attempt to emphasize the point.

I hope by now to have established that one of my main objects in writing this book has been to restore confidence in the belief that our value judgements have an objective validity and are not just emotional noises or subjective expressions of like and dislike. In other words, we can arrive at judgements about what is true, what is beautiful, or what is good, or what is just, which we can discuss with other people as rationally as we can discuss any other questions of disputable fact, even though their validity cannot be verified by measurement or observation. But this means precisely that we can form a judgement on these matters by the use of our natural faculties, and that a Christian's judgement of them does not necessarily differ from an honest agnostic's, and must be judged by the same criteria. I accept, of course, that a person who has thought more about these subjects is more likely to possess valid insights and more likely to hold valid opinions than someone to whom they are uninteresting or unimportant, and if a Christian happens to have given more consideration to moral problems than the average man, which does happen in the ordinary course from time to time, his opinion is entitled to more respect for that reason. But this is true in the same sense and to the same extent in every field of this kind, and not simply that of morals. It is true of musical criticism, aesthetic appreciation, law or political thinking, that an informed and thoughtful opinion is worth more than one which is casual or superficial. In the republic of value judgements there is no privilege of rank or wealth, or race or religion, but there is no nonsense about equality either, and no certainty to be derived from majority votes or opinion polls. It is also true, of course, that a Christian has access to a coherent mass of literature both within and outside the covers of the Bible which may help to sharpen his wits and cultivate his judgements in its appreciation of moral questions. But that does not mean that he applies different criteria or is operating a different type of understanding from that of other people. From this point of view Christianity has no additional relevance which is not given by a special sense of the importance of the subject matter and perhaps a stronger motivation to apply the results of reflection about it coherently and conscientiously. All of which can be briefly summed up by saying that Christ came, not to override the law, but to fulfil it.

But it is precisely in this field of the serious importance of right and wrong, and the duty to study it and to apply the results of study conscientiously, that I wish to make a simple but overriding point. Most people place a considerable value on the qualities of sincerity, simplicity and humility, and I think they are right, provided that they understand these words in their true sense and realize how difficult they are to define and how much more difficult they are to achieve. We are apt to say casually of any loud-mouthed demagogue or publicist: 'I do not in the least agree with him, but of course I do respect his sincerity.' I do not care a fig for sincerity of this kind. Indeed, I regard myself as free to treat it as a mark of particular degradation. I have no doubt Hitler was perfectly sincere in his dislike of the Jews and in his contempt for the namby-pamby attitude of those who objected to their extermination. I regard that sort of sincerity as an aggravation of his criminal wickedness.

Let me put the point like this. There is a sense in which simplicity, which I largely equate with sincerity, is undoubtedly a virtue. In this sense my father was simple and sincere, and he has been an inspiration to me all my life because of it. We are told that, unless we become like little children, we can by no means enter into the kingdom of heaven. But simplicity in that sense is something which most of us lose in childhood, or soon thereafter. When we have lost it, the rest of our lives is very largely spent in an endeavour to recapture it. But this is very difficult. Once it has been lost, simplicity of character has to be rebuilt with infinite trouble, stone by stone, and brick by brick. Sincerity of conviction is part of this edifice. It is no good trying to jump to conclusions, and trying to escape condemnation by saying that facile conclusions and specious arguments have been honestly arrived at or are honestly believed. Once one has lost the native simplicity of childhood, honesty can only be attained by patient examination of each step, verification of each reference, hard and careful scrutiny of each link in the logical chain. This is not an obligation which is confined to Christians. But it is a first obligation upon a Christian who decides to rebuild his life according to the will of his Master, and there is a sense in which it is his only absolute obligation in the field of natural morality, apart from the duty of accepting the imperative his conscience then dictates.

There is, of course, another morality which, if not peculiar to Christianity, is at least characteristic of it. This is the morality of love. But this cannot be explored by the natural faculties. This makes it right to call it by another name, supernatural morality. It does not impose an obligation to do that which it is wrong to do, nor to refrain from doing that which it is a duty to do. But it does mean a doing of more, and better, than natural morality would enjoin. It does involve in refraining from doing a good deal which natural morality would permit. In a sense, this is the whole meaning and content of Christian morals which are based upon the motivation which enjoins them. I have used the word 'Love' to describe it, because it is conventional to do so. But 'Love' is a word for which I have no liking. The Greek word for what I mean was 'agapê'. The Latin word is 'caritas', the art of being a dear, and it is caritas or agapê which was translated by the Authorized Version by the fine English equivalent of 'charity' in the Authorized Version of I Corinthians 13. It is also caritas or agapê which was meant when Jesus is represented as saying that a man can have no greater love for his friends than he can show by dying for their sake. Agapê is both more and less than love. Agapê includes respect for their personalities as well as liking for them. It is what we feel for our nearest and dearest even when we are most exasperated by them. It is this, God help us, which Christ enjoins us to feel for our enemies. It is this against which there is no law.

Yet it is precisely because Christianity is about agapê that it has nothing special to say about natural morality or, as I shall be saying later, about politics which are concerned with justice. It endorses natural morality in the individual and enjoins it. It endorses justice in government and enjoins it. But Christianity invented neither morality nor justice, both of which can be discussed with atheists, Buddhists, or Moslems as rationally as between Christians. A great deal of confusion, I believe, is caused by Christians who seek to import the language of agapê into natural morality and politics. But Christianity is about supernatural morality, or love. Politics is about compulsion and, whatever other limitations this may have, compulsion can only be brought to bear with justice where natural morality enjoins a duty or imposes a prohibition.

But there is another, and more fundamental, reason why I become mildly irritated if I am asked to define the difference which Christianity makes to the conduct and personality of the individual who endeavours to practise it, and this particular point is a paradox. We are, of course, all enjoined to attempt to imitate Christ in our lives. Indeed one of the greatest books of medieval piety which, when I was at Eton, was commonly given as a present at confirmation, is called *The Imitation of Christ*. Now when a number of people seek to imitate a third person they normally begin to resemble one another.

When I was at Oxford, the first Lord Birkenhead was widely admired, as well as violently criticized, as a public speaker and private conversationalist, and it was not long before a sizeable number of aspiring undergraduates began to talk with the somewhat stilted utterance and abusive habit of talk of the great man, oblivious of the fact that even if you succeed in imitating a great man you do not thereby achieve a resemblance, unless you also possess his talents. What you succeed in imitating are his mannerisms – not necessarily his best points at the best of times – and, as you cannot avoid having mannerisms of your own of which you are probably unaware, the combined effect of the two sets of mannerisms is often absurd to the point of being disastrous. Quite apart from conscious imitation, however, there is a great deal of unconscious imitation of people you admire. People often remark how couples who have been married a long time come to resemble one another. Sons resemble fathers in more than physical characteristics, as do pupils their masters. The handwriting of members of one family often show a family resemblance not explained by heredity. One could go on giving instances indefinitely.

But the opposite is true, I believe, of a serious and prolonged attempt to imitate Christ. To the extent that you succeed, you do not become more like other people who are engaged on the same pursuit of excellence. On a superficial level this is partly because the Christ who is our model is not a person with mannerisms we can ape. But on a deeper level, the imitation of Christ does not, and cannot, make us more like other people at all. It makes us more like ourselves. The witty man does not become less witty because he is a Christian. Nor does his fundamental style of wittiness necessarily change. The serious-minded and conscientious man does not suddenly become transformed into a brilliant conversationalist. We are enjoined to be perfect, but our potentialities are infinitely various, and the nearer we approach to perfection the more nearly we shall realize this variety. This is why the conventional picture of heaven is boring and unconvincing. It seeks to paint us a crowd of celestial choirboys clad in white surplices and handling harps of the same pattern coming from some heavenly production line and tuned to the same pitch by a beatified technician. But whatever heaven means it simply cannot be like that. We are to be more ourselves and not less ourselves, in proportion as we receive the beatific vision. In our Father's house are many mansions, and since what we are seeking to imitate in Christ is the Divine image and nature not simply the human, and since the Divine is infinitely various, we are to improve our own talents and not someone else's, only without what the French call *les défauts de nos qualités*.

14

Church and State

A thousand books must have been written about the relationship between Christianity and politics, and none of them are satisfactory. That they are not satisfactory is not necessarily a reason for adding to them, and it would be an act of overweening self-importance on my part if I were to do so in the belief that I can solve the problems which have baffled so many excellent people over two thousand years.

But I cannot altogether shirk the question when I am seeking to give some account of my personal beliefs and I have now spent so much of my life in the political field. I feel more and not less under an obligation to do so since I find so many of the opinions on the subject expressed by my fellow-Christians during the past two thousand years wholly unacceptable, and no doubt they will find mine equally so.

One excuse, which I think is valid, is that I find the problem infinitely complex, and one of the reasons why I find many of the solutions proposed unacceptable is that they underestimate this complexity. But, speaking broadly, I must say at once that I do not think that there is any specifically Christian attitude which all Christians are bound to adopt at any given time (still less at all times) either with regard to political obligation or with regard to international affairs. If there were such an attitude I do not think democracy or a free society could live with it. Nor do I see any sign whatever of that degree of unanimity between Christians even of one denomination which would entitle them to say to their fellow-Christians: 'You should adopt this attitude, or that, because you are Christians' or 'You should refrain because you are Christians from adopting that attitude rather than this'. This is what makes most of

the utterances of Church Conferences or Councils unacceptable to me
What makes the New Testament itself also unacceptable as a direct
guide is that the political attitudes discussed are mostly irrelevant
to the present day. In the Gospels they largely derive from the fact
that the scene is laid in Judaea which was a partitioned and occupied
country ruled by authoritarian powers to which the only nationalist
alternative was a theocracy of zealots. Similarly in the epistles and
Revelation the problems discussed are those of the subject populations outside Judaea during the early phases of the Roman empire,
and the political attitudes displayed by way of solution alternate
between a recognition of the need for justice and law and order even
under a regime of doubtful morality and not of your choosing, and
an out-and-out condemnation of that regime on the limited, if
adequate, ground that, whatever its merits or demerits, the regime
was persecuting and murdering Christians.

Of course what I have been saying is very far from the contention
that Christians should not involve themselves in controversial
politics, or discuss political questions among themselves, or even
that the Church should not make statements about them, even if I am
doubtful of the value of such statements and much of such separate
discussion. Obviously to the extent that Christians are concerned
with natural morality and justice they must be concerned with
political questions in so far as these involve questions of natural
morality and justice. Equally, to the extent that politics are concerned
with the material welfare of our fellow human beings, Christians
are properly concerned with these too, although I do not regard
participation in politics at any level as necessarily the duty of any
individual, whether Christian or otherwise.

I have already explained, however, that I regard such discussions
as concerned with natural reasoning, since I regard arguments about
value judgements as matters for the natural reason. Such arguments
of a political nature, whether advanced by Christians or others,
should be arguments appealing to the natural morality of all men
rather than the specific doctrines of Christianity. I would even go
further and say that, since the limitation on the field of law is that it
is pre-eminently concerned with the compulsion of unwilling
subjects, no morality based specifically upon agapê, which, in
essence, involves the voluntary self-sacrifice of willing subjects, can

be the proper subject of law at all, since that which one accepts as a personal burden voluntarily out of love is not something which one is entitled to force upon other people.

But before I begin a closer examination of these matters, there are three observations of a general character which I feel bound to make. The first concerns the nature of civil society itself. Civil society is not a voluntary organization in its nature, and all talk of a social contract or compact which can bind its members is specious and pretentious nonsense. We no more choose our country, or our fellow-countrymen, than we choose our parents or our brothers and sisters. But our country, whether it be governed by a Nero, a praesidium, or a Parliament makes demands on us which it then proceeds to enforce. It does not seem to me to make much difference to the particular point I am making whether the authority is a king or a tribal council, or a Sanhedrin, or a party executive, or a popularly-elected assembly. There may be occasions when any political authority, however unacceptable in principle, may ask for some measure of support, and there may be occasions, however rare, when a political authority, however acceptable, must expect a degree of defiance. From this point of view popular election may afford a more solid basis of authority and is certainly an alternative vastly preferable, where it works, to the naked exercise of any power which, to use an unpleasant modern phrase, grows out of the barrel of a gun. But popular election cannot give a blanket moral sanction to each and every decree or rule of law.

My second general observation is that any attempt to divorce political authority from moral responsibility or legal rules wholly from moral duties or the opposite leads straight to the gas chamber. One of the great contributions of the medieval Church to European political thought, which it probably owes directly to the inspiration of the Old Testament, is its rooted belief that political authority, however constituted, must obey both its own law and natural morality, and on its subjects must impose duties and prohibitions which bear some relationship to natural morality as it is understood generally at the time in the light of prevailing political, social and economic conditions. I say 'understood generally' because, although I do not regard all opinions regarding value judgements as of equal weight or value, when it comes to compelling other people to act in accordance with them, a very different set of considerations must prevail. I also say 'bear some relationship' to natural morality, because there are many obligations even of natural morality, like good manners, or kindness, which are not ordinarily considered enforceable. The test of enforceability must bear some relationship to the social consequences of the standards enjoined, and the practicability of policing them. Nevertheless, our medieval ancestors were surely right in imposing these limitations on Kingship, and these limitations surely persist even though the present arbiters of our destinies may be the committee of an assembly elected on universal suffrage instead of a monarch ruling by descent from a conqueror but claiming the grace of God from the holy oil poured on him during his coronation.

The third thing I wish to say of a general character is that there is not, and cannot be, an ideal form of society. The various utopias which have been described from Plato's Republic, through More and Swift, to Marx and H. G. Wells, may be models more or less useful as a criticism of existing institutions. Plato's Republic was largely a criticism of contemporary Greek institutions, and particularly Athenian democracy, More's Utopia a criticism of late medieval England, Swift of the early eighteenth century, and Marx of early capitalist society. But useful or otherwise as criticisms, negative or constructive, of existing political practice may be, any attempt made to make them models of universal applicability, either in space or time, is an invention of the Devil. Such attempts have done more harm to the natural development of just human relationships than most of the lucubrations of churchmen or politicians. There just is not a perfect arrangement universally applicable to primitive societies, to urban societies and rural societies, to industrialized societies and societies not industrialized, to societies consisting of homogeneous populations, and societies comprising communities of divergent cultures or different standards of value. Any attempt to find such an ideal and to apply it compulsorily is bound to lead to torture and cruelty and in our time has, in fact, done so to an intolerable and almost inconceivable extent.

When something like thirty years ago I first brought out my *Case for Conservatism*, I included a chapter about the religious background for secular society. I still adhere to every word I wrote then. I believed then, and I believe now, that any attempt to regard society as a collection of animals or the human beings that compose society simply as members of a particular species of mammal, and the world they inhabit as purely material is unacceptable in theory, and in practice leads to deplorable results. I still think this. But I must emphasize that what I was seeking to do then in a limited field, and what now I am seeking to do in a more generalized context, is not to prescribe policies but to rationalize and universalize experience. Then and now I was seeking to defend the objective validity of value judgements, of natural morality and justice in relation to human affairs, and I sought, and still seek, to develop a philosophy and metaphysic which enables those judgements to be relied on and applied. I was not seeking to draw, and I do not think it desirable or possible to draw, particular conclusions from general religious or metaphysical premises. This seems to me one of the great errors into which, almost from the first, Christians have been prone to fall. When they do fall into it, persecution of one human being by another seems to me to be the ultimate, but inevitable, consequence, just as a similar consequence flows from a failure, on materialistic grounds, to concede validity to value judgements at all.

15

The Mythmakers

All religion has its myths. Anti-religion has its myths and its myth-makers no less. Two of the great myths of our time owe their origin to Sigmund Freud and Karl Marx. No myth which has widespread influence can be wholly false, and I gratefully acknowledge the many fresh insights given to me by these two mythmakers. To Freud I owe the sensitivity which most men of my generation have to the influence of the subconscious, and sometimes conscious, influence of sexual motives on human thinking and behaviour. To Marx I owe the realization of the extent to which economic motives and class solidarity have influenced history. Since neither point had been made so effectively before, each is entitled to the fame which has crowned their works, unreadable and dated as I find both of them to be in the original texts. They are, of course, inconsistent thinkers, since each has something to say about unconscious motivation, and, in so far as human conduct has been influenced by the unconscious motivation of class interest, it has not been motivated by sex and vice versa. Of course, too, they are not equally important. Freud has influenced his tens of thousands, Marx, through his apostles Lenin and Mao, his hundreds of millons. But though unequal in effect and inconsistent in doctrine, they have, I believe, done more to under-mine Christian philosophy than any two men since the Crucifixion.

The clinical and scientific basis of Freud's conclusions is now widely doubted and, in some important respects, even his good faith has been brought into question. Marx's prophecies have been falsified many times, and his philosophical framework wholly exploded. Nonetheless the myths they created live on and, if anything, their influence grows. When I speak of their influence I mean less the influence of the authentic versions of their writings, which it is outside my purpose to discuss, than the popular versions of what they are supposed to have written and taught.

Both myths in fact presuppose an almost complete degree of determinism. In so far as our thoughts and actions are causally determined, whether by our sexual nature, or our class interest, or by any other external influence or force, we are not free agents. We are not morally responsible, and if and in so far as value judgements profess to propose moral praise or moral blame on our acts or omissions, it is clear that they are based on a total misunderstanding of our human condition. In the case of Freud, I think he accepts this logical conclusion completely. In the case of Marx and the Marxists, as with their fellow-determinists the disciples of Calvin, we are immediately confronted with a paradox. For, while Freud would have pityingly disclaimed any judgements of praise or blame attached to human conduct with all the compassion appropriate to a physician who recognizes in the worst vices nothing but a pathological condition, there is no group of men practising in politics today who have quite such a vocabulary of vituperation applicable to anyone who disagrees with them in even the smallest particular as the adherents of Marxism, and this whole-hearted condemnation applies to heretical sectaries, who differ on some minor points, no less than the whole-hearted opponents of the whole Marxist doctrine. In part, of course, this can be discounted as mere propaganda designed to inflame the masses, who cannot be expected to know the determinist truth, against their various class enemies. Nevertheless, I do not believe all this vituperation and invective to be as insincere as logically it ought to be and, if I am right in this, I am altogether at a loss to explain it at all.

It is easy, of course, to pick holes in each myth. It is wrong to suggest that human conduct is wholly or even mainly explicable in terms of sexuality. The desire to survive, greed, pride, fanaticism, territorial acquisitiveness, even ordinary self-esteem, are motives every bit as important and as frequently operating at the subconscious level as anything directly or indirectly connected with sex. When it comes to class, I believe that Marxists underestimate the force of nationality, race, religion, and even sheer disinterested sincerity in their estimate of human conduct, and are completely wrong in believing that, once class conflict has been eliminated, there will be, or rather, since I consider the realization of their dream to be impossible, would be a significant diminution in the number of contradictions in human society.

But the main point at which I criticize each myth does not consist simply in an attack on the limited view they postulate of human nature. I attack the determinist assumption as such. I believe in the responsibility of the human being for his actions, limited in practice as his ability to exercise or extend his power of choice may be. I have tried to portray the universe as a place in which human beings - it may be all living things - have a dignity which derives from the nature of the universe itself, from the fact that we are, to use the words of Scripture, made in God's image, and I do not believe that this dignity, or this image, could exist at all did we not possess, at least to a limited degree, that faculty of choice which we call free will, and that it is in exercising it and extending bit by bit the fields in which it is applicable in accordance with our judgements of value that we become most truly ourselves. In a sense it is the capacity to act justly and disinterestedly which separates us most truly from the rest of creation, and it is not logical to suppose such a faculty without at the same time postulating the capacity to do otherwise, that is, the capacity to do wrong. In this sense it is the experience of the sheer misery of having sinned against the inner light which convinces me of the reality of the distinction between good and evil, heaven and hell.

I have mentioned two mythmakers in our time, Freud and Marx. But surely there is a third, and his name is Charles Darwin. It is the greatest of pities that Marx's mind was formed before the *Origin of Species* really penetrated it, for had it done so, the theory of evolution would have destroyed the whole 'dialectical' concept based on a reversal of Hegel on which he founded the formal structure of his philosophy. It may seem odd for a Christian apologist to place so much stress on the Copernican effect which I believe that Darwinism should have on our whole philosophy of life. Nonetheless, I am ready to accept whatever degree of criticism of my own philosophical outlook this admission may bring on my head. For whereas both Marx and Freud, by reason of a distorted and limited outlook, were the progenitors, on the whole, of baneful myths, Darwin's theory was a true and liberating myth. Whatever faults or limitations were found in it, from the publication of the *Origin of Species* onwards, it has been impossible to approach politics, religion, or philosophy in the belief that we are dealing with a humanity whose history extends only over about five thousand years of time and not over a period extending indefinitely into the past and, at least possibly, indefinitely into the future. Equally, I believe, though for slightly different reasons, that it is impossible to evolve a theory of knowledge which does not view the corpus of knowledge, whether in the individual or collectively in humanity, as something growing and developing in a manner comparable with the genetic material of the species itself. It is for this reason that I found Teilhard de Chardin's *Phenomenon of Man*, for all its faults, which were brilliantly pointed out by Sir Peter Medawar, one of the most exciting and stimulating philosophical works I have ever read and, ever since it came out in English translation, I have revered its author as one of the great contributors to modern Christian thinking. But I am prepared to admit that all this does make a big, and largely unexplored, chasm in Christian orthodoxy. So much of our theology and the formulation of our creed is expressed in philosophical or technical language which is at worst obsolete (like 'substance', 'transubstantiation') and at best analogical and mysterious ('begotten of His Father' or 'proceeding from the Father and the Son' or even 'things visible and invisible'). All right, I am prepared to accept all this. But I am not prepared to throw away the torches and lamps which have lit my fathers along the dark roads each of his own present time, and with Christ as my light I am prepared without fear to explore the chasm in my philosophical thinking which the new perspectives of science have given me and which previous generations have lacked.

On re-reading this, I cannot help expecting that many people will find it odd that I regard the Darwinian theory at all consistent with a religious outlook on life. The publication of the *Origin of Species* caused my grandfather in his youth the great spiritual crisis of his life, and in Darwin himself the gradual development in his mind of the principle of natural selection was accompanied, step by step, by a loss of religious belief. I do not see why this should have been so. True, as I have said, the whole time-scale presupposed by the theory of evolution blows sky-high the restricted scale of historical events presupposed by the Bible. This must affect our whole approach to the influence of God in history, and with it the unique character both of the Jewish and of the Christian revelation. It is also plain that the theory of evolution of species from common origins, or a common origin, shows the manner of creation, if that is the right word, to be wholly different from that which our ancestors supposed. But it does not solve, or seek to solve, the central conundrums of philosophy, which I take to be the facts of consciousness and its associated experiences of knowledge and volition, the experience of the value judgements, and the relationships between so-called mind and so-called matter.

Moreover, there is another thought to which the theory of evolution gives rise which I have found extremely stimulating and even exciting. I know I found it in the writing of Teilhard de Chardin, and I think I found it even more explicitly stated in something Sir Julian Huxley wrote about Teilhard de Chardin's works. If I had not made up my mind to verify no references in the course of this book, I would cite them here. But as it is, I express the thought simply in my own language.

One, at least, of the facts which we must regard as differentiating human beings from the animal kingdom is the possibility, at least in theory, of the species controlling, assisting, or disrupting its own evolutionary destiny and the destinies of other species. This possibility was opened up so soon as human societies developed a cultural tradition consciously spread geographically and extending in time from generation to generation. Before that, the process of natural selection governed the evolution of animals and plants, directed by the seemingly impersonal forces of the external environment and the limitations of the genetic material available. But human beings are not limited in this way. We do not start from scratch. We have, from the first, attempted to control our environment; we pass on the experience and habits of our fathers by means of oral and written tradition, and we communicate our own experience to others, to be passed on in its turn, by means of the written and spoken word. The possibilities of doing these things effectively, for good or ill, have spectacularly developed during the course of the scientific revolution of the past five hundred years, and are still developing, perhaps at an increasing speed. To human evolution there is thus added a new dimension. We can raise up children to Abraham, or Mohammed, or Karl Marx, or Christ without any genetic connection with their spiritual forefather.

It is in this context that I view the role in history of the Christian Church. If my reading of the New Testament is correct, Jesus designed to set up a continuing society devoted to the conscious promotion of the Kingdom of God on earth. I do not see any evidence that he promulgated any new, or peculiar, social or political doctrine, or advanced any philosophy within the field of natural morality different from, or better than, the best that could have been found at the time. Indeed his two basic precepts, now commonly recited at the beginning of the Anglican communion service, were both taken bodily from the existing Hebrew Scriptures, and the second of the two, the love of one's neighbour as oneself, was at the very time Jesus was speaking being promulgated as the essence of the Jewish law by the great Rabbi Hillel himself. No, the great contribution of Jesus was not the promulgation of a New Covenant differing from the best that had gone before in the sense of superseding or reversing it, but the creation of a new worshipping community dedicated to a revolution in the nature of the individual himself, believing that this, by itself, would operate to redeem mankind from the domination of hatred and self-interest, and guaranteeing that the new society would possess within itself sufficient means of grace to secure its development and survival in the hostile environment of a materialistic world. The adventures, the successes and the failures of this new society have produced the most significant and exciting factor in the history of the past two thousand years, and the scientific revolution, with all its dangers, and with all its potentialities, only emphasizes, and does not supersede, the essential role of the assembly of God in moulding the destiny of the human race.

Obviously this emphasis on the destiny of the individual human soul is repugnant to those who believe in the essentially redemptive power of a purely secular society. Obviously the emphasis on the continuous role of the divine society operating as a worshipping community through the centuries causes offence to those who see in complete permissiveness the sole criterion of civilization. But neither group of critics really has much objective evidence to support their criticism. The secular society, unrestrained by a religious out-look, moves inexorably towards diabolical tyranny. The individual-istic society in which enlightened self-interest takes the place of agapê degenerates rapidly into chaos and gives way to the same tyranny in the end. The Church which seeks to impose objective sanctions to enforce theological truth or to enact rigid objective codes of practical conduct in the end finds itself deserted by its adherents. But a body of these, returning always to the source of their inspiration, and making use of the covenanted means of grace, always survives to renew the life of the new Israel. This life manifests itself in the inner light vouchsafed to the individual. But it protects itself in little circles of human beings attempting, however un-successfully, to develop the Kingdom by practising agapê towards one another and moving outwards into the hostile secular environ-ment in which they are placed to gain new adherents and to do good even to those who persecute it and hate it.

16

Loyalty and the Crisis of Authority

My parents, particularly my mother, taught me to admire loyalty as a virtue to be prized almost before all other. It may well be that they over-emphasized its importance as a guide to life. But however often I may have allowed myself to lapse from its strict precepts, I have found the influence of this early teaching constantly reasserting itself, and at various periods of my life, notably at the collapse of my first marriage, and at the time of the change of leadership in the Conservative Party in 1963, I have found great comfort in it and sought to mould my conduct in dignity upon its requirements.

Loyalty in itself is something of a paradox. To what extent, if at all, can one justify 'My country right or wrong' or 'my party right or wrong', or 'my parents', or 'my class', or 'my race', or 'my co-religionists right or wrong' for that matter? Clearly one cannot do so at all if the question is put in this form. Nevertheless, according to my parents, one must be loyal to parents, wife, friends, party, country, religion as a consistent theme running through one's life. In the same breath, they would point out the duty of respect for authority wherever it lawfully exists. Of course, this also involves the same kind of paradox. How far was Gandhi right in challenging the authority of the British Raj? Who owed what kind of respect to the authorities of the Third Reich, and when, if at all, did this obligation cease? Was Roger Casement a patriot or a traitor? If he was a patriot, why do we not give the same sort of honour to those who died for the Young Pretender, or the Provisional I.R.A.? If he was a traitor, why do we respect the resistance in Germany to

Hitler, or of the Jews who wished to emigrate from Soviet Russia to Israel, or even for that matter the tradition of Hampden or Pym? St Peter's epistle says: 'Fear God and honour the King.' By 'the King' he meant Nero, no less. But writing of Rome in the era of Domitian, the author of the Apocalypse denounced her as the Mother of Harlots, drunk with the blood of the saints. Winston Churchill, as ever a marvellous phrase maker, solved one apparent paradox of loyalty by saying of the late Kingsley Wood:

'He was a good party man. By this I mean that he put his party above himself, and his country above his party.'

But, however good this may be as an intelligible rule of thumb, it answers no philosophical problems. Presumably one would not belong to any party which did not to some degree represent what one honestly believes to be the interest of one's country. How can one tell which is the greater loyalty or where the true interest of one's country in each conflict?

Greatly daring, and because I think that the modern world needs loyalty and respect for authority more than anything else, I will write a word in support of my parents' beliefs. I regard loyalty as a form of love, or agapê, and without it I believe that all human society would disintegrate. If I were asked for the reasons for the success of the British political system above all others, I would give the loyalty owed by one politician to his colleagues of the same party as an important factor, and the loyalty owed by all politicians of whatever party to certain common assumptions and institutions, the monarch, Parliament itself, an independent judiciary, the acceptance of electoral defeat, as another. When my friends do something I disapprove of, I do not automatically desert them or join in the public condemnation. Either I remain silent or I go and comfort them with loving and gracious words, and encourage them to try again, this time by a better route. I admit that the only ultimate loyalty is to God, and that in the end 'God' must, in this context, mean one's conscience as directed by the inner light, humbly and sincerely sought and followed, in the rather special sense in which I have tried to define humility and sincerity. But all the same, almost everything and everybody is entitled to command some sort of loyalty and respect and, I would add, everyone in a position of established authority with public responsibilities to discharge, provided he is trying in good faith to discharge them, is entitled to a measure of respect and obedience, even though one may criticize the way in which he is going about his task, question his title deeds to exercise authority, or seek by legitimate means to remove him from office. After all, there is no authority in the world today which can establish a respectable set of title deeds if one goes back far enough. The Anglo-Saxons invaded and subdued the Welsh, the Scots came in from Ireland and massacred the Picts, the Hanoverians ousted the Stuarts, the Roman Empire - one of the most beneficent institutions in the history of mankind - was founded entirely on right of conquest and, to the end, substituted authority for freedom and practised brutality as a means of securing assent. Turk and Greek, Moslem and Hindu, Jew and Arab, Ulster Protestant and Roman Catholic cannot agree, and probably never will agree, either as to ultimate political aims or as to the title-deeds to political governance. But unless human beings are to be for ever the butchers of their own kind, there must be some respect accorded to established authority as such, if only, like Mount Everest, because it is there. The degree to which such respect is to be accorded may, in the end, be a matter of degree and therefore of practical judgement, but the hardship and suffering caused by violent revolution and civil war to innocent human beings who wish to live their own lives in peace must be a much more serious deterrent to violent action than is generally admitted in current 'liberal' thinking, and the possibility of radical change by evolutionary if gradual means and established constitutional methods must be very carefully weighed before choosing more direct and violent methods, particularly if these are designed to achieve comparatively narrow or peripheral benefits.

It is clear from what I have said that the obligation to respect authority and obey the law as established by an existing constitution is not unqualified. It cannot take the place of the first, and great commandment of loyalty towards God. Nor is it capable of exact and precise definition. Like other human loyalties, it is ultimately a matter for the practical reason, often to be exercised in the light of the pragmatic principle of choosing the lesser of two evils and weighing the consequences of each of two alternative courses of action. But that does not deprive it of its moral imperative. Anyone who decides to defy established authority owes it to himself and other people to ask himself and answer a number of serious practical problems. What is the nature of the prohibition or precept I propose to defy? Is it a thing which, were I to do it irrespective of prohibition, would be morally right, or morally wrong, or morally indifferent? What are the consequences of what I propose to do on the general respect in which moral or legal obligations are held, or the extent to which they are observed? What is the nature of the regime I propose to defy? Does it itself attempt, however misguidedly and imperfectly, to govern in accordance with law? What facilities does the law offer for peaceful change? To what extent have I exhausted them? What is the urgency of the change I propose to effect, compared with the harm I shall probably do by effecting it (if I succeed) by illegal means? Is the law itself being impartially administered by an independent judiciary? If I disagree fundamentally with the society in which I live, how many of my fellow-countrymen think as I do about it? Does the law of the land allow emigration as a means of contracting out of a system I dislike? These are questions, the answers to which, in most cases, will, at least in my judgement, rule out in practice many unconstitutional courses at present favoured by militant minorities.

But even this does not exhaust the, to me overwhelming, arguments for constitutionality. A feature of our modern times is the pressure group, membership of one or more of which is often canonically blessed, not least by high church dignitaries. But are they really so praiseworthy and democratic as is often suggested? Admittedly the objects of many or most are obviously, or at least arguably, praiseworthy, or at worst morally legitimate. No one would argue in the abstract against higher pensions, or more education, or better hospitals, or more money for medical research, or clean air or the preservation of natural environments of special beauty, or even better financial rewards for those engaged in useful occupations. Those who urge these things are surely worthy of commendation. But the special feature of the pressure group is to urge their own peculiar objective impatiently to the exclusion of other things, at least equally commendable. But what would be the effect of yielding to the totality of all of them? Or of yielding to one rather than another? The most difficult thing in government is the attempt to view policy as a considered whole at any one given time, and pressure groups in themselves, taken singly or together, do little to assist the achievement of this, and many pursue their claims to the point of unreason. To take a small and almost ridiculous example, until recently, and so far as I know to this day, the amenity interests in the Lake District insisted that telephone kiosks be painted green with the result that those who wished to telephone for help in case of a mountain accident could not find them. And what is one to say of the present policy of trade unions? No one in the world would seek to deny the value of such associations particularly when they confront individual employers. But is it so praiseworthy for great monopolies to press demands at the expense of the economy of a whole nation, or to seek to obtain them at the cost of threatening the livelihood or even the comfort of millions? Is it desirable to dragoon the eccentric or the loner into membership, or to be the sole judge as to whether that membership should be continued when membership of a particular union is the sole means of obtaining useful work? And what of political strikes designed, not to improve conditions, but to coerce governments to courses they believe unjustified, by inflicting hardship on a whole nation? These are surely questions which, if answered fairly, would yield answers quite different from those commonly given, and if answers are given by constituted authority in a constitutionally governed country, such answers should be accorded a degree of respect far greater than is nowadays fashionable to do so.

I must, of course, now unmask the philosophy underlying the gist of these remarks. I believe that there is a golden thread which alone gives meaning to the political history of the West, from Marathon to Alamein, from Solon to Winston Churchill and after. This I choose to call the doctrine of liberty under law. It is not a static doctrine claiming to be true for all time, like the gospel according to Hegel or Marx, or for that matter like the original language of the Nicene and Athanasian creeds. It offers no utopias and attempts to define no ideal state of society. It is rather an evolving and living tradition to which there is no exact orthodoxy or precise formula. Moreover, the body of doctrine and tradition is not, and never will be, complete. At different times and at different places it has been interpreted differently. But it is at least opposed to Oriental despotism and permissive anarchy. Somewhere in Gandhi's interesting autobiography I read the sentence that all Western government was based on force. I almost rubbed my eyes with amazement. How about Eastern government? All government is based on force. That is what government is about. But Western government from Solon onwards, even at its deplorable worst, has always gravitated to the belief that the use of force requires reasoned justification, while the exercise of individual freedom to the detriment of another equally requires reasoned justification. This reasoned justification, this constant dialogue, is in fact the essence of law. It has its roots in many places. Since the adoption of Christianity, it has its roots in the moral insights of the Old Testament prophets and ethical legislation of the Mosaic code. These can no longer be regarded as the unique revelation that once they were. They have their analogues in the philosophy of the pagan world, in the sacred writings of the Hindus, and in many ancient codes. But the historical link is with the Jews. In addition, there are direct and earlier sources of the living tradition quite outside the Christian and Jewish tradition. Some lie in Athens where the idea of freedom first found articulate expression and exercised her liberating force. Some lie in Rome with her tradition of definite legal principles and impartial judicial administration following in the wake of military conquest. It is strange, is it not, that three cities, none of which, at their zenith, can have numbered as many inhabitants as modern Birmingham, should have had an influence so disproportionately great? But in this pantheon of moral origins shall we not add that of the inhabitants of the little island moored off the coast of Europe which, inspired by the other three, first pioneered representative government, first insisted upon an independent judiciary irremovable at the caprice of a sovereign, first placed judgements of fact in the hands of a modern jury, first erected compromise and moderation into a principle and, besides all else, sought to interpret positive law in the light of the application of accepted moral principles? Is it altogether surprising that, having said that loyalty is only a special application of the specific Christian doctrine of agapê, I give my love, and therefore my loyalty, first to the tradition itself, constantly evolving over the centuries, and never complete, or in principle capable of completion, and second to the nation which is my own to which the tradition owes so much, and is still in a real sense so much its embodiment? When I say 'the nation', I do not forget that within Britain, or at least the British Islands, there is a multiple national identity, and therefore multiple sources of loyalty, for part of the tradition is the chance it offers of developing unity in diversity, and diversity in unity.

17

Law and Legal Obligation

My professional life has been that of an advocate. I had intended to adopt this profession almost before I can remember. Before I ever went to my private school at the age of 8 my father used to come up to me in bed and tell me about his cases in court. I knew the whole complicated law of defamation long before I had learned the easiest lessons of mathematics. I knew the meaning of the various defences of fair comment, justification and privilege, the difference (as it was then thought to be) between criminal and civil libel, the nature of punitive damages, the difference between libel and slander, and the three cases when slander was actionable without proof of special damage. I knew how to defend the ethics of the advocate against the vulgar and ridiculous charge that he tries to deceive a court or a jury, that he is constantly saying what is not true, that he insists on defending his client 'even when he knows him to be guilty'. My father was the best of teachers, and the best of advocates, and the profession of the law seemed to me at the time among the noblest open to man. I have never regretted this early indoctrination, and even now that I am old and ought to be disillusioned about it all, the gilt has never quite come off the gingerbread.

The ordinary man, and maybe the ordinary legal philosopher, tends to be unduly preoccupied with the criminal law. But my father was not a criminal lawyer and, until he became Attorney-General, had hardly done a criminal case. When I first went to the Bar I did a good deal more crime and divorce than he had ever done. But in those days there was not much money to be made in crime, and I certainly set out to develop a practice in civil cases. One of my first activities was to write a book on the law of arbitration. On the whole an understanding of the civil law has given me a more accurate understanding of the sweep and nature of law than the ordinary educated person obtains when in discussing law he becomes unduly preoccupied with crime and criminal sanctions. Law is the whole framework which dictates the relationship between man and man. It is the law of contract. It is the law of negligence. It is the law of husband and wife. It is the law of property and succession to property. It is the law of banking, and bills of exchange and promissory notes. It is the law of tax, and the law of evidence and procedure, and the complex law of trusts and trustees, and limited liability companies. No doubt the idea of enforceability lies somewhere in the background in any genuine legal structure, a fact which led my father to assert, to the fury of the academics, that international law was not true law at all, since its main source of authority was the textbooks, and the judgements of international law courts could not be enforced. The next time I heard this doctrine promulgated was by Mr Gromyko during the Test Ban Treaty negotiations in 1963. He was not in the least disconcerted when I pointed out to him the close relationship between his ideas and those of my conservative father. 'They were not always wrong, those old people', he said.

But I digress. Having nailed my colours to the mast of patriotism and loyalty, and particularly to my near worship of my own country, I now espouse the cause of law and order. But whereas I quite realize that, to a great number of people, this means an unhealthy interest in criminal law and punishment, and police powers, these are among the least of the things that law and order mean to me, though, of course, they are included. To me law is the first of the social services. Indeed, some form of law is essential to any form of civilized society. It owes its origin to immemorial custom as interpreted by scholarly judges rather than positive enactment. It is founded in common decency and natural morality rather than the command of the ruler. Men must be ruled by force, or by discussion, and law as I see it is primarily the product of usage brought about by discussion. It is true that during my lifetime the common law, constantly being re-interpreted, extended or diminished by unconscious judicial appli-cation in individual cases, has largely been taken over by statute, not always to its advantage. But that ought, in principle, only to substitute discussion in Parliament and outside it, for the learning of judges and argument in the courts. The acceptance of authority, of rules of procedure, of principles of behaviour seems to me the foundation of a prosperous and civilized life.

Law is, of course, in a sense, no more than a gigantic confidence trick. If enough people did not obey the law it would be totally unenforceable. The fact that it is accepted in good faith is what makes it enforceable. If laws bore no relationship to the value judgements about ethical behaviour which men and women are prepared to accept as ethically binding and socially desirable, they would be ignored in practice, because nobody would bother to find out what they were or understand their implication even when legal rules were correctly identified. Obviously, positive law and positive morality are not identical with one another. No one seeks to enforce the rules of kindness and courtesy through the courts, and there are many violent departures from ethical conduct to enforce which either by criminal or civil sanctions is either impossible or would entail far greater evils than their attempted suppression. Nevertheless, any attempt to separate law, or the rule of law, from a generally accepted code of moral conduct would lead straight either to anarchy or to the gas chamber and the concentration camp. If the human race is to evolve in freedom rather than be dragooned, it can only be through a voluntary acceptance of a rule of law based on value judgements of what is right and wrong, just or unjust.

I do not believe that law can exist without sanctions. The one doctrine of the Church which seems to me to be empirically demonstrable is original sin. By this I do not mean the fire and brimstone doctrine of popular Calvinist literature, by which man is regarded as wholly depraved and incapable of salvation without the direct interposition of divine grace. I mean, on the contrary, that man is a series of contradictions, of mixed character, good and bad, capable of almost divine and heroic virtue, but at the next moment muddying his own face, breaking his own toys, and defiling his own divine image. Man is flawed, but strangely perfectible, for ever failing and for ever trying again. If any conduct is wholly permitted the permission will always be abused. Even the virtuous man will not obey rules for long if he observes the unvirtuous getting away with their breach. Law steps in where things have gone awry and to prevent things going awry. It is no enemy of freedom. On the contrary, it is freedom's constant and inseparable companion. It is, after all, the art and process by which men and women can be induced to live together without the bloodshed which has marked the passage of the human race through time. The King's peace is logically, as well as historically, the purpose of law. Law is the consequence of original sin. It is not redemptive like love. It is second best, no doubt. But without it, love could not flourish, commerce could not be pursued, stable family relationships could not be established, and unjustified suffering could not be mitigated. The advocate who has seen many cases has had his sense of justice acutely developed. He is slow to condemn the sinner. But he has come to love righteousness and hate iniquity.

One of the main functions of law is to discourage the use of unilateral force in the settlement of disputes. I do not myself draw a distinction except one of degree between the use of force and other types of unilateral action. This was the point I tried to make to Mr Gandhi when I once met him for tea at University College under the auspices of Lord Redcliffe-Maud, and it was this point I was trying to make to the Welsh militants when I made my speech at Llandridnod Wells. Obviously non-violent action is preferable to violence, just as a gentle push is preferable to a sharp blow with a fist, and a sharp blow with the fist is preferable to a sharp burst with a tommy-gun. But my experience has been that all unilateral action tends to escalate into violence, just as all violence tends to escalate into bloodshed. The transition is one of degree, not of kind, since all unilateral action is based on the premise that one is entitled to enforce one's own judgement of what is right and proper not because one is right, but because one is strong.

I have never myself been a pacifist nor, in private affairs, do I ever rule out absolutely the use of force, still less other unilateral action. It seems to me that such an attitude is wholly unrealistic in a world composed largely of violent and unreasonable men and women, themselves prone to found their conduct on an appeal to their own strength. But before resorting to force, it is surely wise to reflect that, in the nature of things, victory achieved as the result of unilateral action is not a victory either for justice or common sense. In the nature of things it is the victory of superior force, even when force is applied in a righteous cause or in self-defence, and, because it is a victory for superior force, it must tend to perpetuate the doctrine that might is right. With this tendency it is certain that at some time some other persons whose cause is less just will draw the obvious moral and apply force in support of objectives which are either morally questionable or plainly wrong. Even law is at its best when it is most widely observed without force or resort to the courts. But if resort to force is necessary, it is clearly preferable that disputes should be settled by resort to the courts, applying ascertainable principles after argument before an impartial judge than that issue should be determined by threat and counter-threat, followed by a trial of relative strength, whatever the nature of the strength may be. I realize, of course, that in saying this I am bound to offend much Liberal opinion, as well as all Communists and Marxists, and the great bulk of the Trade Union movement, as well as the activists on both sides in Irish affairs, without satisfying the pacifists and Quakers who represent the opposite point of view. Nevertheless it appears to me to be true, and even obvious, and at the age of 68 I am not likely to change my mind.

18

International Obligation

I cannot move from the subject of law without reverting to my father's often expressed opinion that international law did not exist because it was incapable of enforcement and was not, in fact, enforced. Perhaps understandably this is not the view to be found in the standard textbooks on the subject. These point to the extent to which the rules of so-called international law are in fact observed, and to which, in recent years, multilateral treaties and conventions have taken the place of statute law and regulate whole areas of international relations. They advert to the brave, but unsuccessful career of the old League of Nations and, perhaps with something less than their former confidence, to the work and principles of the United Nations Organization, and the various bilateral alliances and organizations based on geographic propinquity, or racial and cultural affinity.

I do not deny any of this, and I am far from endorsing my father's opinion, which was in any event based on the status quo of 1919-39. But the classical doctrine of international law had much in it to reinforce his view. There was an international law of peace with more or less ascertained rules of conduct. There was also an international law of war, perhaps rather more bulky, in which there were also more or less established rules governing the conduct both of belligerents and neutrals. But the transition from one to the other was an act of sovereignty, and there was no law to define the circumstances in which or the procedure by which an independent sovereign might declare, or commence, hostilities. There might be a morality about such things, though this was disputed. But there was no law, and surely any law, properly so called, must start by trying to define and limit the field in which the unilateral use of force is permissible.

My friend Lionel Curtis, whose mien and appearance, constantly, and perhaps designedly, reminded one of a minor prophet, used to make what was basically the same point from a totally different point of view. According to him, the cause of war was the fact of independent sovereignty, and unless this were abolished and some form of international sovereignty established, one generation after another of young men would die, as two generations of young men had died in my lifetime, at the hands of one another in the course of international conflicts, each always becoming rather more horrible than the last.

There is a sense in which I wholly agree with this diagnosis, and for many years now I have quietly, but extremely modestly, been a subscriber to the parliamentary section of the movement for world government. My subscription, however, has consistently been about the minimum, not, I think, wholly because of innate meanness on my part, but because this somewhat exiguous level expresses more or less my opinion of the realism of the movement, and its chances, in my lifetime, of achieving success.

But now that I am seeking to sum up my beliefs about the world, I must spend some time discussing this belief of mine and analysing my feelings about the international scene as it has developed since 1945.

I have already committed myself to the view that the Roman Empire, especially as it developed during the age of the Antonines, was among the most beneficent institutions that the world has ever seen. This is something of a paradox, since the Roman Empire was admittedly based on force and inspired by dreams of something like world aggrandisement, limited only by the art of the possible. Anyone who has a nodding acquaintance with Jewish history and tradition will know that what I have said did not appeal to the Jews of the time, who died in Masada rather than submit to Rome. Nor can anyone who is familiar with the Apocalypse and some, though not all, early Christian literature, doubt that the same hostile opinion was very widely held in the Christian Church. Nevertheless, I believe in the great beneficence of Roman rule over anything which had happened in the West before, and I do not believe that anything quite so satisfactory ever happened in the West again until after the battle of Waterloo.

I say 'until after the battle of Waterloo' because I sincerely believe that the period between 18 June 1815 and 4 August 1914 was the happiest or one of the happiest in the whole history of mankind and can only be matched by the age of the Antonines. Of course, I realize that such judgements are hard to make, since, in their nature, they cover the space of the whole globe, and the whole span of human history. Obviously no single human being knows enough of human history to be confident in such matters. I nevertheless put forward the claim, and if there be anything in it, I do not think that there can be much argument that the credit for this period of comparative peace, amelioration of human conduct, and the improvement of material conditions must be accorded to that maligned institution, the British Empire.

The British Empire is dead and I am not suggesting that it is either possible or desirable to resurrect it, any more than I am suggesting that it is possible or desirable to resurrect the age of the Antonines. But I am not going to apologize for it in any way. On the contrary, although I now regard its disappearance after 1945 as inevitable, I much regret the rapidity with which it was dismantled, and I regret still more the absence of any institution to fill the international void which its disappearance has left.

It seems to me that the problems facing the post-war world are basically international and that the world is engaged in seeking to solve them by means of a series of sovereign nation-states none of which possesses an economic or political basis adequate to deal with the situation. We have done what we can by means of international agreements, like the United Nations Charter, or Bretton Woods, or the GATT, and by military alliances, like NATO. But the fact is that none are adequate for the purpose either to ensure peace and order in the world, or to create a stable period of prosperity. Over wide stretches of international affairs, the United Nations Organization has ceased to operate effectively. But broadly speaking the economic situation has clearly got out of control and the international picture is one of continuing local disorders, happily not, so far, developing into world conflict owing mainly to the deterrent effect of the nuclear weapon. I do not wish to decry the Commonwealth. At the lowest, it is an excellent debating club, and such associations are valuable, in a world where people have ceased to talk to one another, or conduct a dialogue of the deaf. At the best, it provides some admirable bilateral associations within its framework. But it has, and has shown that it can possess, no power structure and no common political aim. More recently the Soviet Union and the USA have shown signs of governing the world by joint diplomacy and pressure. But even if the fears expressed about such a joinder of giants prove unjustified, theirs is an association from which the great mass of mankind is automatically excluded and in which their views are virtually unrepresented. Between the end of the Napoleonic Wars and the beginning of the war of 1914-18, the predominance of the British Fleet at least limited the scope for European rivalries to bring about world conflict and, within the stability provided by British and other colonial rule, conditions of life and material prosperity gradually, but surely, improved on an unprecedented scale, and ideas and ideals of liberty and law were allowed to penetrate to nations and continents where hitherto they had been virtually unknown. There is no pretending that empire had its origins in anything more respectable than national policy. But its effects were generally beneficial and, given the economic and political conditions of the time, the alternatives would have been wholly inferior.

However that may be, all that is past and done with, shattered, as it turned out, beyond repair when the Great Powers of Europe failed to arrest the slide towards war in the summer of 1914. This destroyed the whole basis of continental Europe, and a cloud, at that time, little bigger than a man's hand, in the shape of the Easter Rising in Dublin, led to that which ultimately destroyed the British Empire. Happily, the substance of it remained long enough to prevent Hitler's victory in 1940, but after 1945 world forces, and especially American foreign policy, were too much for us, and we lost both the ability and the will to govern, and were compelled to beat so hasty a retreat that our departure created a power vacuum in almost every part of the world where the presence of Whitehall had previously created at least a semblance of order. No one can regret the assumption of power by independent states where the new authorities attempt to rule justly and shoulder international obligations and responsibilities. This they have not always attempted, and even where they have, the international scale of the problems they face has been too much for the national power bases from which they have operated.

For myself, I have never doubted that, given the dissolution of Empire, we must endeavour to create a power base in Europe adequate to solve our international and economic problems on an international scale. From my point of view, the tragedy came when Mr Attlee's government failed to take the opportunity then offered it to become a foundation member of the Coal and Steel Community. In the House of Commons debate which followed, briefed by Churchill, I made one of the leading speeches on behalf of the Conservative Party. I took particular trouble about the speech since I rightly divined that my father would be dead before the autumn and I thought (wrongly as it turned out) that I would never speak again in the House of Commons. I still look back on that speech as one of the most significant I ever delivered, though at the time it fell on deaf ears. The Labour Government had decided against participation, and the Conservative Party was too divided to vote. When the European project was again mooted in 1962, the situation had become far less promising. All three communities of the Common Market were already in being and had developed along lines less favourable to ourselves than would have been the case had we been members from the outset. All the same, the basic situation remained unaltered. Britain is faced with a series of economic, political and military problems too great to be solved by policies developed solely within the United Kingdom. Obviously neither the United States nor the Commonwealth nor, for that matter, that melancholy collection of semi-subject states behind the Iron Curtain, nor the new states of Africa can be ignored. But Britain's problems cannot be solved any longer without participation in a United Europe. If the attempt to solve them within the Market fails, it is no use looking to America, the Commonwealth, the Union of African States, or the Warsaw Pact countries to solve them. It is ourselves alone, or ourselves as part of Europe, and, of the two, I have no doubt that the latter is to be preferred. Indeed, I have no doubt that it offers the only reasonable prospect if we are to offer to our countrymen a life under the rule of law fit for civilized men.

19

Party

I do not regard anyone of any description, even in a democracy, as under any obligation whatever to embroil himself in politics at any level. At the same time, from my boyhood onwards, I have realized that this was exactly what was going to happen to me. I do not know how I reconciled this determination to make my name in politics with my ambition to succeed at the Bar. From 1922 onwards, I suppose I told myself that my father's success in both fields, coupled with the intention of my lamented brother Edward Marjoribanks to do the same, was sufficient guarantee that the thing was possible. But the truth is that I was already certain from a very early age that my career was to be at the Bar and in public life. I also had an uncanny presentiment that at some time in my life I should be called upon to serve in the army.

Two political memories go back to before the first war, and each in its way is redolent of the high political passions of the time. The first I can date quite accurately to the spring of 1914, at the time of the Curragh incident. My uncle, Ian Hogg, was at that time commanding the 4th Hussars at the Curragh, and his part in the affair still appears in the more specialized historical books about it. However, the only relevance of this is that it explains the intense passions generated in my family, an Ulster family, at the time. In those days, families really were families. It was not simply the question of father, mother and two children living together in a small suburban box as middle-class families do now. There was first of all the staff of eight, butler, cook, two housemaids, a kitchen-maid (or perhaps two), a nanny and nursery maid, and Potty the French lady's maid who looked after my mother. But in addition to these, and two grandmothers (one in America), there were uncles, aunts (great and otherwise) and cousins, first and second, once or twice removed. Quite a lot of them; and my father's house at Sunday lunch in Number 46 Queen's Gate Gardens was often something of a rendezvous. At such a time two little boys from the nursery would be scrubbed and polished and placed in their most uncomfortable clothes and let into the dining-room when the family had reached the stage of having coffee. They would be fed, like little birds, on the remains of the candied sugar in the cups, a treat which they much appreciated. On one such occasion the conversation seemed more portentous and tense than usual, and after a minute or two I could contain myself no longer. 'Daddy', piped up a childish treble, 'who is Winston Churchill?'

My father, ordinarily the most cherubic of characters, became obviously aware that the eyes and ears of the assembled family were upon him, and he determined to rise to the occasion. He began by addressing me as he had never done before, and never did again. 'My son', he said gravely, 'you know I have always taught you that it is very wrong to wish that anyone was dead. But if ever I could bring myself to wish that anyone was dead, I would wish it about Mr Winston Churchill.' Many years later, after they had both been members of the same Cabinet for some years, I reminded him of this event. He did not remember it and denied that it could ever have happened. But I knew better.

The other memory dates from about the same period. My nanny (the melancholy Anglican) was a Liberal in politics, and my mother, during her widowhood in Bath under the tutelage of an old dragon of a mother-in-law, Lady Tweedmouth, my own great-aunt, had become a very prominent Liberal in local politics. I suppose I had imbibed a certain number of their sentiments, and so I remarked to my elder brother Edward one day that I did not, after all, see why the Irish should not be allowed to govern themselves, a fact which my brother immediately reported to my father. 'Then he is a very silly little boy', was my father's judgement on this, an argument which seemed to me to be conclusive when it was afterwards retailed to me. I was then aged 7. I have been a Conservative ever since.

I tell this story because I think it shows how very fortuitous and illogical one's beliefs can be in their origin, however logical and systematic they may become in later life. I make no doubt at all that if I had been born into another family I would very likely have had different opinions, and very likely would have been sucked into the general left-wing trend to which most intelligent young people of my generation subsequently succumbed. But I think one should, in fact, be frank about these things. I see nothing more illogical in beginning, out of loyalty, to side with one's father in matters of politics and religion, than in revolting as have many of my contemporaries against one's father's views. I had an additional reason for loyalty myself. From 1922 onwards my father was very prominent in Conservative politics, and I realized that any open defection on my part would cause him harm and embarrassment quite out of proportion to the value of my own opinions, immature and fluid, as in my conscience I knew them to be. Also my father was a very reasonable man, and a very persuasive advocate. Whenever I criticized his viewpoint, from the time my mother died onwards, he would always answer me reasonably and convincingly which made it difficult for me to differ from him honestly. All the same, on the whole, my criticisms of him were more often from the left than the right, and almost up to the time when I became chairman of the party I was regarded by my fellow-Conservatives as a somewhat dangerously soft and left-wing character. I do not know if they were right. What I do not wholly understand is why since then I should have acquired an opposite reputation, although it is true that, during the two years of my chairmanship, I endeavoured to aim at a more central position in the party than I had done before. After all, when one becomes pope, however fortuitously, one owes one's flock a special duty to avoid unorthodoxy.

Of course, it is difficult for an honourable man to reconcile intellectual integrity and collective responsibilities and loyalties. It seems to me, however, that it is vital for one's self-respect to arrive at some reconciliation of these two requirements if one is to aim at a public career at any time. No two persons' opinions exactly coincide and, even when they do, no two persons' formulation of even identical opinions is likely to be quite the same, and the more intellectual you are, and the more creative and original your views, the more this problem is likely to present itself to you at various times of your life. All the same, if you desire to take part in public life in any parliamentary country, it is no good trying to form a party of one. Collective action is the only way of achieving results, unless one is content to remain a critic on the sidelines of politics, which has never appealed to me, or unless consciously or unconsciously one aims at a dictatorship, a course which appeals to me even less. In some cases, of course, people join parties for perfectly honourable reasons and then find, to their infinite distress, that they have chosen wrongly. More than one person that I know chose the Labour Party in early youth out of genuine sympathy with the unemployed and the poor, only to find in later life they were tied to an uncongenial and rigid society of doctrinaire Socialists, or popular radicals, with whose general cast of mind they had no genuine agreement. I have always thought that this is what happened to Lord Shawcross. Others I know have joined small parties, like the Liberal Party, and have then found that, because they represent a small minority, they are effectively debarred from playing a constructive and creative part in current events, which their natural abilities would entitle them to do. This too leads to unhappiness. I rather suspect that this is what happened to Dingle Foot, who remained a Liberal until, comparatively late in life, he joined the Labour Party and became a law officer, only to find, I suspect, that he was not really spiritually at home among his new colleagues.

My father, and the love and loyalty I owed and felt for him, saved me from all this. He was a truer blue Conservative than I was, or am. But all the same I believe he persuaded me rightly to join that party and not another, and he taught me a great deal about sinking my own personal prejudices and convictions in collective decisions and wisdom without, I hope and pray, a genuine loss of integrity and honour in my public conduct.

When I began in politics, however, the opinions and doctrines of my party mattered to me less than the expression of my own opinions. I suppose this is true of all undergraduates, and the feeling that I have described of having outwardly to conform to my father's opinions increased this tendency rather than otherwise. The highly personalized encounters of the Oxford Union Society also tended to make my opinions personal. I was at Oxford, I think, a little remote from my Conservative contemporaries, partly for these reasons and partly because my classical studies removed me from the general

run of the economic and historical schools in which most undergraduate politicians received their academic training.

As I think I have said, my first years at the Bar were given over
almost exclusively to my professional practice. My father discouraged
political activities until I had found my feet, and it was not until he
had his first stroke in 1936 that I asked him to back me for a constituency, on the ground that I wished to serve an apprenticeship in
the Commons before succeeding to the Hailsham title. In those days
it was virtually impossible for a young man without a good deal of
financial backing to stand as a Conservative candidate, since in the
good Conservative seats it was the custom of the local Conservative
associations to demand of their Candidate or Member an annual
subscription of not less than £400. In one case I knew of, an East
Anglian constituency received more than £3000 a year in this way.
All this was swept away by the Maxwell-Fyfe reforms after the war.
But in 1936 I would not have stood a chance of adoption without my
father behind me. As it was, I had to hawk myself around the constituencies for over two years before I could get anyone to look at
me. It is not always an advantage for a young man to be the son of a
prominent person. The forces of inverted snobbery are extremely
powerful.

In the end, an unexpected opening presented itself by the premature
death of Bobby Bourne, the Member for Oxford City, who was, at
that time, Deputy Speaker of the House of Commons. I learned of
his death quite by accident over the radio when I was staying at a
shooting-lodge in the hills above Pitlochry, and was so disillusioned
by that time by my constant failures that, but for some importunate
pressure from my host, I would never have put my name forward.
However I did, and in no time found myself thrust into the mael-
strom of the Oxford by-election, one of the most spectacular and
controversial by-elections between the wars. After my election, I
scarcely had time to find my feet in the House before the beginning
of the war, when having been a party on that Sunday morning to
voting for it, I felt it my duty to join up in an infantry battalion,
which was not an altogether easy thing to do in those early days. I
mention all this, not because I am thinking better of my resolution
not to write an autobiography in any ordinary sense, but because I
think it necessary to explain that for a young man of 30, who had

got a double first class and had been President of the Oxford Union, and at the Common Law Bar for seven years and a member of a very political family, my political ideas in 1938 were still comparatively immature and unformed. It is also worth pointing out that, although I had planned a political career from the first, had it not been for the purely fortuitous death of Bobby Bourne, and the importunity of my host, I would probably never have been a member of the House of Commons at all. Although I might well have got a constituency in the General Election of 1945, in that Conservative debacle I would almost certainly not have been elected and, since my father died in 1950, I would have succeeded to his Viscountcy without ever having a further chance. All this it is necessary to relate because it would otherwise never be believed that, though my religious philosophy dates from undergraduate days, or shortly thereafter, the moulding of my political ideas dates very largely from periods of reflection during and immediately after my military service. I must now discuss these, and their origin, in more detail.

20

From the Oxford By-Election to the Norway Debate

I am now, in my mind's eye, newly elected to Parliament. It is 1938. I am about to embark on my political career, just as my father has been compelled on account of physical infirmity to leave it. I have been elected in a sensational by-election against a most powerful opponent to support Mr Chamberlain's government. In another chapter I shall give my reasons for thinking that, in the matter of home policy, my opinions were still inadequately formulated and immature. But in 1938, at the age of 31, this was not my own estimate of myself. I had been practising at the Bar for more than six years, and had succeeded as well as, or better than, any of my contemporaries at the Common Law Bar. I had learned the trade and had founded my professional competence so solidly that I was twice able to return to the Bar after long absences and establish my position. I do not believe that this had been achieved before.

But there are two topics which I must now discuss. I had reached manhood after the First and before the Second World War. My contemporaries were mostly left wing and, of those who were right-wing, a few were so far to the right that they were dabbling with Fascism. I was resolutely a man of the centre, somewhere on the left of the Conservative Party, miles to the right of the moderate Labour man, mostly represented by the Morrisons and the Attlees, and of the so-called popular front activists headed by Lloyd George, who had been the most formidable group supporting Dr Lindsay at the by-election.

But in one respect I was typical of my generation. The misery of unemployment and depression had made as deep an impression on

me as on any of them, left or right. It had never led me to be false to
parliamentary government. I had never dallied with Socialism,
which I regarded as authoritarian, or Fascism in any of its forms. I
had not even responded to Lord Beaverbrook's overtures to identify
myself with his Crusade for Empire Free Trade. But the one characteristic of my thinking about home policy was my hatred of unemployment and poverty. I might not accept the Socialist remedies.
But I accepted many of the premises of my Labour contemporaries.

By 1938, however, foreign affairs held the centre of the stage, and
soon after my adoption meeting in Oxford, it was apparent that
foreign affairs were to provide the dominant issue at the by-election.
The Berchtesgaden, Godesberg and Munich meetings followed one
another in a dramatic succession. Fear of an immediate world war
was succeeded by almost universal relief, and almost hysterical
acclamation for Mr Chamberlain. This, in its turn, was followed by
a deepening disenchantment with the Munich settlement, which
showed its full force in the two other by-elections succeeding mine.
In the meantime, I was the candidate in the most controversial by-
election for years, and I had no previous political experience to rely
on.

I remained totally loyal to the Government throughout, and I
have never changed my opinion. My father had warned me of the
danger from Germany ever since 1932, from which date he regarded
war, sooner or later, as inevitable. He had told me of his opinion
consistently since, just before the Hitler regime came into power,
Germany had walked out of the Disarmament Conference. He
regarded this as a watershed, but I disagreed with him, since I was
more impressed than he was by the injustices of the Versailles
Treaties, and more impressed than many of my contemporaries
with the hardships of the German-speaking minorities in Czechoslo-
vakia, Poland and Italy. I was also rather more believing than I am
now of the right of national minorities to join in one national group
and to have political frontiers drawn accordingly. But I was never a
pacifist. On the contrary, I remember, when my father was, I think,
Secretary of State for War during the Abyssinian crisis, urging on
him the necessity of opposing Italy by force of arms and pouring
scorn on the effectiveness of sanctions. During the whole of a dinner-

party with him and my stepmother at the Ivy Restaurant, I kept the argument up, and I was infuriated with his counter-arguments, based largely on our unpreparedness and vulnerability in Egypt. It will be seen, therefore, that I was neither a pacifist nor an appeaser. Neither was my father. But we were on different sides in the Abyssinian crisis because, apart from the arguments he deployed at the Ivy, he regarded Germany as the main enemy and Italy as a potential ally against her.

One result, however, of my arguments with my father was that he disclosed, perhaps more than he ought to have done, what had being going on in the Cabinet since he had rejoined it, after being excluded from the first National Government. According to him, the real protagonists in the government for rearmament were himself, Londonderry, Cunliffe-Lister and Neville Chamberlain and, of course, of the four, Neville Chamberlain and my father were the most important. The remainder were deterred from rearming by the immense power of pacifist opinion, led by the Labour Party, and typified by the Fulham by-election, and given a sort of bogus respectability by the catch-phrase of collective security. Neither my father nor I disbelieved in collective security, but neither of us believed that it could be made effective unless Britain first rearmed on a massive scale. For this doctrine my father argued in the government, and during these arguments he always told me that his most reliable ally was Neville Chamberlain. I have always regarded the way history has dealt with Neville Chamberlain as basically unjust, and this must be right if what my father told me was correct.

When Munich came, I have never had any doubts, nor had my father, that it was in truth a great deliverance. I did not then, at any time in the Oxford by-election, place my justification of it on an acceptance of Chamberlain's optimism, to which, I still believe, he gave vent only in a revulsion of feeling engendered partly by relief at escaping war and partly by popular acclamation. I made two points, and both of them, I still believe, were valid. The first was that the country was deeply divided and could only hope to win a war if it went into it united in the knowledge that everything had been done to preserve the peace. This it could not do if it fought over the Sudeten Germans. This was generously acknowledged to be a cogent point by Churchill in the little gem of a speech he delivered in

Parliament on 3 September 1939 in that short Sunday morning sitting at which the declaration of war was announced.

But my second point was to me even more important. It was that we had fallen behind so far that we needed the time to prepare against the possibility of war, and I believe today that this was even more important than the first. It was the delay of almost a year, nearly a year and a half if you discount the months of so-called 'phoney war', which enabled the eight-gun fighters, Hurricanes and Spitfires, to go into service in the RAF. If they had not done so, we well might have lost.

The arguments which had to be confronted in the by-election of 1938 were, I am satisfied, all forms of self-deception. I have already dealt with the argument about collective security. The most frequently repeated argument against me was that the dictators were bluffing. It is difficult today to realize that this was the argument most strongly pressed by my opponents. Those who put their faith in Russia were, as subsequent events showed, completely deluded. Russia was suffering from the astonishing purges of 1937 which could be seen, even at the time, to render reliance on her completely futile. Churchill, unlike my father and Chamberlain, wholly miscalculated the military power of France under the Third Republic. I still believe that, without the respite given by Munich, which enabled public opinion to consolidate behind a war policy following the entry into Prague, and the RAF to acquire the eight-gun fighters, Hitler would have been triumphant in Europe, and over Britain, if she had tried to oppose him.

My own private declaration of war against Hitler took place in March 1939 when Hitler, in breach of the Munich agreement, went into Prague. At the railwaymen's dinner in Oxford, with all the absurdity of the butterfly who stamped its feet in the Hans Andersen tale, I predicted that the dogs would lick the blood of Hitler as they had licked the blood of Ahab in the valley of Jezreel. This pompous utterance at the time only lost me the support of a valued ally, Jock Lynam, the headmaster of the Dragon, who came up to me afterwards and said that he could no longer support a Member who used such intemperate language of a friendly head of state. 'Wait six months before you say that', was my reply.

I joined the army by the back door in September 1939, just after war was declared. I do not wish here to say anything of my military career, which was sufficiently undistinguished. But I do make the point in my own favour that, having voted for the war in Parliament, I showed my willingness from the first to expose myself in it in an infantry battalion, and not in an administrative job, and, in the event, I did, in fact, have the honour to lead an infantry platoon in a minor battle and numerous night patrols in the desert in the summer of 1941.

The only other thing which is relevant to the general thought lying behind this book is the Norway Debate, which brought the Chamberlain government down at the beginning of 1940 and within a matter of hours before Hitler's attack on Holland and Belgium brought to an end the so-called 'phoney war'.

This was by far the most difficult political choice I have ever had to make. At that time my battalion was stationed in Lincolnshire and I was deeply disturbed at its lack of training and equipment. I knew that it was in no condition to fight a battle and I thought that after more than six months of its embodiment as a territorial battalion this was little less than a scandal.

But this was not the main source of my discontent. After months of war all the old party rancours seemed to be unhealed. It did not seem to me that we could win a war without a change of government and a new administration containing all parties, with Churchill, and not Chamberlain, at the head. My own admiration for Chamberlain remained undiminished.

On paper, the Norway Debate offered an opportunity to declare my misgivings. But in fact the Speaker, then Fitzroy, did not call me, and in retrospect I would be grateful to him, since I am quite certain now that I would have made an ass of myself. But this only made my vote all the more difficult since, when it was delivered, it would be wholly unexplained.

The difficulty was that Norway was very largely a naval operation and was, almost certainly correctly, considered to be the brain child of Winston Churchill. It seemed, therefore, logically absurd to bring down the government in order to put in charge of the war the very man most responsible for the policy under criticism. The choice was rendered even more difficult by the impeccable behaviour of Churchill when he came to reply to the debate. Chamberlain himself had made a speech which provoked a good deal of hostility because, under provocation, he made, for the second time in a few months, a reference to his parliamentary majority, to which he referred in correct parliamentary usage as 'his friends'. But Churchill excelled himself. Never for a moment did he betray that he must have known that, in the corridors, people were saying that the only salvation was a national government under his leadership. Earlier he had formally rejected a fly cast over him at the end of his speech by Lloyd George. I can see him now, crouched over the dispatch box and scowling defiance at the critics of the government. The debate ended in uproar. Emanuel Shinwell, standing somewhere in the gangway two or three benches behind the opposition front bench, and a little behind the Speaker's chair, shouted an interruption. Churchill engaged him at once. 'There is the Right Honourable Gentleman skulking in a corner.' The rest of the sentence was lost in shouts of protest and counter-protest. But Churchill rose, like the prow of a ship temporarily battered by a gigantic wave, and proceeded to his peroration. 'Let all the strong horses pull at the collar. Let party rancour be forgotten.' The noise was terrific, but he dominated them all. The Speaker put the question. On which side was I to vote? How could I vote at all? Until the question was put a second time I was wholly undecided. I had come in late to hear the final speech and had found a place on one of the Cross-benches. I hesitated until I saw the Speaker rise to order the doors to be locked, when a sudden impulse drove me into the 'no' lobby, brushing the attendant aside as he moved to obey the Speaker's order. When the result was announced, the Government had won by eighty, an attenuated but still viable majority. I thought I had achieved the worst of all possible results. I had weakened the Government without removing it, just at the very moment when, as we all knew, the 'phoney war' was about to end. And when Chamberlain left the House to the jeers of his enemies and the silence of his friends, I felt more alone than I had ever felt before. I could neither triumph with the one nor identify with the other. Nevertheless, events justified my decision. It was undoubtedly the votes of a few of us who had hitherto been his supporters which brought about his resignation. Important choices are often better made instinctively with one's whole being and not simply as the result of a logical train of thought. But I had still to drink a fairly bitter draught. I went back to Lincolnshire on a slow train in a carriage with old Walter Liddall, the Conservative Member for Lincoln, who had voted with the majority. 'Mark my words', he would say every fifteen miles or so, 'you'll regret what you did last night all the rest of your life.' Again I replied, but this time without much spirit, 'Say that again to me in six months' time.' And when the post came from Oxford, my first wife told me that she had never seen so many letters of criticism and abuse. So ended the first phase of my political career. After a spell in the War Office, which kept me in London throughout the blitz, I followed my battalion out to the Middle East, and was there posted to a regular unit, the second battalion of the Rifle Brigade, which by that time was basking in the glory of our first great victory of the war, Wavell's advance to Benghazi.

21

Political Re-Awakening

As I have said, although my family was intensely political, and my training at the Oxford Union had made me a formidable debater and speaker, my political philosophy really began to develop much later in my life, that is, from my period in the army which arrested my legal career and gave me much more time for reflection and meditation than I had had since I read Greats as an undergraduate. During my first seven years at the Bar I had acquired a good deal of social experience, both by my practice, which was very mixed, and by my serving in alternate weeks at a Poor Man's Lawyer centre in Deptford. This and the traumatic effect of living through the period of the General Strike, and mass unemployment, and the rise of Fascism in Italy and Germany, which was common to all my generation, was really the sum total of my involvement in social affairs. The Oxford by-election was almost entirely involved with foreign policy, and my army service took me away from the service of the House except for spasmodic periods of leave, one of which coincided with the Norway Debate, and two years of it was spent in the Middle East, part of it in the desert. I did not return until the last days of 1942 when, owing to an attack of infective jaundice, I found myself, at the age of 35, degraded medically so that I could never again form part of an active service unit. I decided from that moment that my duty lay in the House of Commons, and that in particular my role would be to prepare for the post-war world. I did not resume my practice at the Bar until 1945, partly because I thought it my duty to dedicate myself to this role and partly because I did not wish to steal a march on those members of my own profession who were still in arms. I was out of the fighting against my will, and thought my duty to the younger generation the paramount consideration. I believe that, whatever else I may have done wrong in my life, in this at least, and at this time, I was wholly sincere.

Curiously enough it was my period of active service which set me thinking most strongly about politics in the post-war world. Army service has many periods of boredom inseparable from it, and it was natural that, as a young MP in the army, I should spend a number of idle hours reflecting by myself on the nature of the problems which we should be facing when the war was over.

The first of these, curiously enough, was actually in a sense commissioned by the military authorities. For a brief period of time during 1940 I was made part of a supposedly highly secret outfit in the War Office called M.I.R. The commanding officer of this outfit was a highly intelligent colonel in, I think, the Sappers, called Holland, and at about the time of St Valery he set me the curious task of trying to produce a written appreciation of how I thought the war, which was obviously going so badly, could possibly be won, and he sent me away from the office for a week or so to write down my thoughts. The document was eventually sent forward and received commendation from the highest quarters, and amongst other people who received a copy was none other than Hugh Dalton, at that time Minister of Economic Warfare. He was sufficiently interested to ask for the name of the author and, when he learned it, actually offered me a job in his Ministry. I turned this down at once because I had joined the army as a matter of honour at the beginning of the war, and I did not intend to change my mind by joining a civilian Ministry when the fighting had only just begun, even if, as was arguably the case, I would have been more use there. For the same reason I gave up my captaincy in the War Office shortly afterwards in order to join a fighting battalion in the Middle East, and was for a time the junior subaltern in my unit, and the oldest officer, with the solitary exception of the Colonel, the second in command, who had sat next to me in school at Eton, and the Quartermaster who had risen from the ranks in the regular army.

However, one section of what I wrote I did not show my superiors. I was concerned about the morale of the people of Britain. It struck me then, in the atmosphere of the time, which was one of impending crisis, that, in order to sustain the hardships of indefinite duration which seemed to me to be looming ahead, it would be advantageous for the people of Britain to be given a glimpse of a post-war world which was more full of hope than the world of the interwar years which had bred so much bitterness and strife. I believe that, somewhere among the mass of paper I have accumulated in the past fifty years, this document still survives, but since it went far beyond my original instructions, I kept this part of it to myself.

My next period of reflection took place whilst I was serving on the staff in the Lebanon. Service in the desert did not afford much opportunity for writing or thinking, but after I was sent away I found myself employed as a staff-officer again on the staff of General Maitland Wilson at the headquarters of the 9th Army in Broumana above Beirut. It was an intensely lonely period of my life. A decree had gone forth from Caesar Augustus that no one over 25 who had not attained the command of a company could be allowed to stay in the desert, and as the only purpose for which I had gone out all that way was to be allowed to serve actively in that active theatre, I was extremely miserable, in spite of an intensely interesting and active set of duties. I agonized and fussed about my young friends in the desert, especially those who became casualties. I do not think my work suffered, since, without any staff training, I was promoted GSOII. But all the time I was meditating and thinking of matters of general import to Britain and the world. It so happened that almost exactly at the time when I was recovering from my attack of jaundice, and making my decision to return home, the Beveridge Report appeared which, in the rather popularized versions that reached us in the Middle East, made an immense and almost universal impression. Unknown to me, Brendan Bracken and others had actually written to me to return. I never received their letters until after I had done so, but when I did come back and began to formulate my ideas, I found that they had a ready welcome from many others, and there gradually formed a small body of Members of Parliament in which I took an active part. This group came to be called the Tory Reform Committee.

Among the first of my former friends to welcome me was my somewhat older contemporary Hugh Molson, who took me to dine at the Athenaeum, then the most gloomy and desolate place imaginable. I well remember his expounding his own views which I found quite compatible with my own, and he remained a close ally during almost the whole of the active period of our committee. The most vigorous members also included Lord Hinchingbrooke and Peter Thorneycroft.

Briefly speaking, during what was virtually a period of three whole years of seclusion, I had formed a fairly coherent view of the internal policy which I wished this country to pursue. As I have said, I was gratified to find that I was by no means alone, and as the ideas came to be formulated more precisely in the constant meetings we held, they formed the basis of the book *The Case for Conservatism* which I came to write in the period following our defeat in 1945. At the time I am speaking of neither the philosophy nor the policy of the Tory Reform Committee was popular among the more orthodox-minded of the party. But again and again in recent years I have come across people who say they were profoundly influenced by what we wrote and said, or by my book when it came out about 1947.

I can truthfully say that at no time during the period I am describing did it occur to me to join the Labour Party. This was not because I did not recognize that at various times Labour spokesmen had been emphasizing important truths, which had either been ignored or forgotten. In the party system which we have inherited it is both normal and desirable that each party should basically recognize the valuable and indispensable role played by the other, whilst indulging to the full in all the rancour and controversy of party politics. But the Labour Party never presented to me a package which I would have been capable of accepting for myself. To begin with there was too much theory - at the time I am speaking of, specifically, Marxism - which I was wholly unable to accept, and to go on with, the attack on property and profits, which is still characteristic of it, appeared to me too like an assault for reasons basically sentimental upon the goose which laid the golden egg.

But once forget the theory and there was much in the motivation of Labour politicians which I could whole-heartedly admire. It seemed to me intolerable that we should have to return to massive unemployment and the low wages throughout industry which went with unemployment, and my experiences at Deptford and in the County Court had led me into a profound sympathy with the housing deficiencies and lack of medical facilities from which the urban working class suffered. All my life I have somewhat over-estimated the intelligence of what were known at one time as 'C' and 'D' educational streams, and I was passionately anxious to make available to all educational chances the equivalent of those I had myself enjoyed. In short, what I believed in was publicly-organized social service and privately-owned industry, and it seemed an ill service to the system of free enterprise in which I believed to assume that it was to be for ever associated with the under-employment and inadequate social services with which I was familiar. Like everybody else in the political field, I was, of course, unaware of the ease with which full employment would be achieved after the war, and as the whole of my adult life had been lived in a period of severe deflation and recession, the problems of inflation never really crossed my mind. I was irritated and impatient with those of my party who found Beveridge impracticable and extravagant. I looked forward after victory to a gradual liberalization of the British Empire, but not to its liquidation within a quarter of a century. I wholly underesti-mated the hostility to the West of the Soviet Union under Stalin and his successors. I did not foresee the domination of Eastern and Central Europe and its consolidation into a Communist bloc. I greatly underestimated the speed at which Germany and France would recover from the devastation and demoralization of defeat. I did not foresee the Cold War, or the permanent division of Germany, or the emergence, whether on the scale, at the tempo, or in the direc-tion it has taken, of the Third World. In this, I think, I was fairly representative of the younger Conservatives of my time. I greatly overestimated the extent to which Britain would retain her prestige and influence in the world, and developments like the Common Market were almost wholly concealed from me until after the Cold War had permanently split Europe into two separate camps. On the contrary, I looked forward to a gradual liberalization and humani-zation of the Communist philosophy, and, under the influences of a continued comradeship in the period of reconstruction between the wartime allies, a gradual loosening of ideological differences. Whilst I had not expected a Conservative victory in 1945, I was wholly taken aback by the extent of the Labour victory, and completely antago-nized by the arrogance and want of generosity of the triumphant Labour majority. However I set myself quietly to rebuild my practice at the Bar and to play my part on the opposition back benches in the House of Commons. As a former Under-Secretary in the coalition and caretaker governments I was entitled to a place on the Front Bench, but I gradually came to realize that under the dominant influence of Churchill and his closer friends the best contribution I could make could be made in relative independence. Moreover, my father, who had had a stroke in 1936, could obviously not live long and I determined that, unless I were allowed to resign the hereditary peerage to which I would succeed when he died, I would devote myself to the law for the rest of my life. When, shortly after I became a peer in 1950, the 1951 General Election took place, I let my friend Randolph Churchill know that I would not welcome a place in his father's government. This message, as I had intended, he passed on, and I was not offered a place. Shortly after the Churchill government took office I became embroiled with my party over the introduction of commercial television. As I said to a journalist in 1950, when my father died, I intended to devote myself to my profession; I added, rather oddly in view of my subsequent fate: 'Perhaps about 1970, if there is a Conservative Government, some ass may make me Lord Chancellor.' So far as I was concerned, and apart from this apparently remote possibility, my somewhat undistinguished political career was at an end. My highest ambition was to become a judge.

22

The Admiralty

I seem to have become far more autobiographical than I had intended when I set out upon this journey, without, however, I hope, becoming false to my resolution not to write memoirs. In any case, having pursued the matter so far I had better proceed. I find that although I can express my philosophical and religious beliefs in a more or less abstract kind of way, the development of my political ideas requires something of an autobiographical background to render them intelligible.

I have reached the point at which my father had died and I had determined to abandon politics and aim at a judicial appointment after a successful career at the Bar. When my father died I was still a junior barrister. My legal career had been seriously damaged by my political activities. Solicitors and clients do not like to brief barristers who are known to have outside interests. However, I had at last made a considerable breakthrough with a junior practice both in commercial cases and in personal injury cases and, three years after my father's death, I decided to apply for silk. I was successful on the first application. I wish my father had lived to see this. Very shortly before he died he had lamented the fact that he had not lived to see me in the front row.

The year in which I became a Queen's Counsel coincided with my one serious breach with my party - over commercial television. I had always taken an interest in broadcasting. It seemed, and seems, to me an essential adjunct to public life, and I have no doubt that, like advocacy, it can only be learned the hard way. Too many public men begin broadcasting at an age when they are not prepared to endure the necessary apprenticeships and humiliations. Broadcasting is quite different from public speaking, and though the techniques of communication and persuasion are to some extent subject to the same general laws, much of what one learns in platform speaking or court advocacy is a positive disadvantage in radio and television. Political leaders usually attach so much importance to their prestige at any given moment that they fail to realize that in broadcasting, as in fighting, you cannot acquire the necessary skills without getting hurt from time to time.

My experience in broadcasting in 1953 was already quite considerable and I was frankly shocked when a lobby in my party succeeded in persuading Mr Churchill's Government to overthrow the then accepted doctrine of public service broadcasting, which had been established between the wars by a succession of Conservative Governments, and to go in for the American system of broadcasting financed by advertising. In the end, the Government avoided some of the worst features of the American system of directly sponsored programmes, and in many ways the opposition for which I was partly responsible affected the ultimate structure for the better.

I still think, however, that there was considerable force in the criticisms I made. The great case for the Government was based on freedom of choice. But looking at a programme when there are only two, or at most three, channels available, is not like buying a book at a bookshop when you can choose anything you can afford between Liddell and Scott's Greek Lexicon and the most vulgar American paperback. Moreover, once you establish two competing systems, so far from increasing the freedom of choice you would get if you had one system, producing at any given time two different types of programme, you tend to get the two systems competing for the same audience in producing similar programmes at the same time. Quite apart from this, I am not at all sure that the introduction into the home of the most powerful advertising stimulant ever devised, giving rise to constantly increasing desires for new domestic expenditure, has not been an important contributory cause of the wage demands and inflation which have so characterized the past twenty years of economic life. What I did not realize was the high level to which the licence fee would have to be raised to cope with the popular demand for television, and the phenomenal success from the financial point of view which the commercial network would enjoy. I doubt whether anyone did realize this and, if they did, I do not think they stressed

these points. However this may have been, the disenchantment I felt
with my party at this time (which I was only too well aware was
heartily reciprocated) only strengthened me in my resolution to give
up politics and stick to the law for the rest of my life. Matters turned
out somewhat differently from what I had expected. At about the
end of 1955 my friend Kenneth Diplock, then the head of my
Chambers, became a judge, and I succeeded to his place. I naturally
looked forward to the most lucrative and most satisfying period of
my professional life. At this time Lord Salisbury, the Leader of the
House of Lords, sent for me to his room, and I came up from the
Temple wondering what on earth he could want with me. He told
me that he was authorized by the Prime Minister, then Anthony
Eden, to offer me the position of Paymaster-General, then, as now,
an unimportant sinecure carrying no departmental responsibilities.
My reply was practical. What, I asked, somewhat crudely, is the
screw? I was informed that it was £2000 per annum and, as at that
time I had a wife to maintain and four young children to educate,
I was able to give an immediate answer. The project was impossible,
even absurd. I returned to my Chambers rejoicing that my task had
been so easy, and glad to think that, after all that had occurred, I
should not be troubled again. I was wrong.

Somewhere about six weeks after my summons from Lord
Salisbury I received another, this time from the Prime Minister
himself. He told me that Jim Cilcennin, then First Lord of the Admiralty, was retiring in the spring and asked me to succeed him.
The salary was only £5000, a mere fragment of what I could hope
to earn professionally and, quite frankly, the invitation, although
flattering, was unwelcome. Quite apart from the financial sacrifice,
there were my duties as head of a Chambers only recently bereft of
their former head. I consulted my wife, my clerk, my colleagues,
and I accepted. My reasoning was as follows. It was then late 1955
or early 1956 and I calculated, correctly, that the next election would
not be later than 1959. It seemed to me unlikely that we should win
that election and I could then, I thought, go back to my practice at
the Bar without irreparably spoiling my chances. To be the political
head of a fighting service and that the Royal Navy was a noble
chance. I thought of the great First Lords of the past, and the great
opportunity for service that this opportunity offered. I felt I would

be mean-spirited to turn it down. I prayed earnestly for guidance and, as usual, felt quite convinced that God does not help you to make up your mind in cases of this kind. I think I was correctly motivated at the time. But if I had known what the future held in store, I think it likely I would have refused, as the direct and indirect consequences of my decision upset all my plans. At this stage I simply make the point that, apart from my marriage, the two crucial decisions of my life, to enter Parliament at the end of 1938 and to become First Lord of the Admiralty in 1956, were purely the result of chance, the first the death of Bobby Bourne, without which I would never have been in the House of Commons at all, the second, the weakness of the Government Front Bench in the House of Lords, which led to the persistence of Lord Salisbury in pressing the Prime Minister to offer me a place. I shall have to return to this theme as I proceed with my story, as it will become apparent that none of the things which have happened to me have been the result of conscious planning on my part at all.

A period of months intervened between my conversation with the Prime Minister and my actual appointment in September 1956. Some delay had always been intended, but a singular mischance led to an embarrassing postponement. The Khrushchev-Bulganin visit took place in the early summer, and at the height of it occurred Commander Crabb's fatal exploit in exploring the bottom of the Russian cruiser in which, it was alleged, the Admiralty was involved. The result of this was that Cilcennin refused to resign on the ground that, if he did, it would be construed as disgrace. Although I perfectly understood all this, the result was highly embarrassing to me, partly because I had laid all my plans on the assumption of a May appointment, which had been promised, and partly because the proposed appointment had somehow leaked out into the press to the great detriment of my legal practice. In the end, I wrote to the Prime Minister telling him of my difficulties and hinting that, if matters were not brought to a head, I would have to reconsider my assent to the arrangement. The ultimate conclusion was that the appointment was announced at the beginning of September. My wife refused to live in Admiralty House, which was constructed for I do not know how many servants, partly on the ground that it was unmanageable and partly because the flat at the top in which we would have had to live was highly dangerous for young children, who would certainly have fallen down several flights of stairs. As Lord Mountbatten, then First Sea Lord and, technically, a subordinate, was living at his own house in Wilton Crescent, we were installed in the flat above Admiralty Arch, the official residence of the First Sea Lord. It was inconvenient and noisy, and our sleep was much interrupted by the noise of lorries accelerating under the arch, and pigeons making love at unseasonable hours on our window-sill.

I had used the months in which my appointment was pending to reflect about our defence policy and, in the course of these reflections, thought it right to call on the greatest ex-First Lord, then living at his house in Hyde Park Gardens, in the hope that some kind of mantle might descend upon my shoulders.

The old man received me with elaborate courtesy. He had already heard of my appointment. 'I congratulate you', he said, and then, after a pause, 'You must get yourself a sloop.' He was referring to the absence of the *Enchantress* which had been raised from the bottom of the sea and then sold off to a millionaire. Talking with Winston at this period of his life was a curious experience. His mind was not so much failing as withdrawn into himself, and from the dark caverns where it reposed it would suddenly return with devastating clarity and perception, only to disappear again as suddenly. We began to talk about the nuclear deterrent, whose military characteristics he understood perfectly, though he was presumably completely ignorant of its technical details. His conversation was punctuated by long pauses. At the end of one of these he suddenly looked at me with startling intensity and said in a voice of immense virility and strength: 'Indestructible retaliation. That is the secret. Never forget this. Indestructible retaliation.' In the context in which we were speaking, I understood him perfectly. He was speaking of the necessity for a second strike weapon, located under the sea, which, if a first strike were launched against us, would deal retribution after we were dead. The possession of a first strike weapon would only encourage a preventive strike. A weapon obviously intended to be used only as a second strike weapon would deter one. At this time Polaris did not exist, or at least was not in our possession. I thought then, and I think now, that with his immense understanding of the big issues in war, Winston, then in the retirement of advanced old age, had nevertheless penetrated to the heart of defence policy.

My recollection of this conversation with Winston prompts me to make one reflection about his career which I first made in a letter to Brendan Bracken written when I was serving in the Lebanon in the summer of 1942. The context was the attack contained in a motion criticizing the 'Central direction of the war', made in the House of Commons. I felt deeply concerned and thought that, as a Member of Parliament, I ought to make my views known at home. I cannot now remember why I wrote to Brendan in particular, but I think he had written to me. It has always seemed to me that Winston's extraordinary life is the nearest thing to an actual miracle that I have seen or can think of. Cardinal Newman wrote, as a believer, that he had always been puzzled by the absence of any sign, in history, of divine intervention. It was, he said, as if he looked in a mirror, expecting to see the reflection of his own face and, instead, saw nothing there. This is very much my own position. But if I were to make an exception, I think I would make an exception about Winston. Winston was not, in the ordinary sense, a religious man. But from the first he had a conviction that an extraordinary destiny awaited him, and when he fell from power in 1915 after a meteoric rise and a dramatic series of adventures, he felt as much puzzled as frustrated. Apart from his own works, I have in my library a set of books about Winston dating from different periods of his career and written in each case by candid third parties. The first dates from about 1908 when he was Under-Secretary for the Colonies, and the second from about 1921 by, I think, Bechofer Roberts writing under the name of Ephesian. The estimates of these various writers of Winston's virtues and shortcomings are various, and in the light of what was subsequently to happen, full of unconscious irony, but the constant factor in all of them, as in Lady Violet Bonham Carter's account of early conversations with him dating from an earlier period still, is his own premonition of destiny.

Winston is one of the few men of genius that I have ever known and studied at close quarters in my life, and it is idle to deny that men of genius possess, in general, shortcomings commensurate with their qualities. Winston is an example of this. His attitude to India in the 1930s although strategically correct, was politically insensitive, and his attitude at the abdication was basically as wrong-headed as it was obviously chivalrous. His realization of the German menace between the wars has rightly been given the credit that is due, but I can testify myself that he was, as the targets of his criticism were not, wholly unaware of the potential weakness of France under the Third Republic. The fact is that from 1915 onwards it was as if Winston was being deliberately reserved by Providence for the part he was ultimately to play. I think he would desperately have liked to be in office in the thirties. But it was precisely his alienation from the party leadership at that time which in 1940 enabled him to take over the Prime Ministership after the Norway Debate without any of the embarrassment of responsibility for the failures of the pre-war policy and to unite the nation at a moment of peril after the fall of France, an eventuality which, as I have said, he had not foreseen. He has not yet been given enough credit for his resistance to the 'Second Front Now' campaign of 1942. Almost everyone was against him, the Americans, the Russians, the Left Wing here, and many right-wing elements, including his close friend Lord Beaver-brook. But Winston, with his personal acquaintance with trench warfare in 1915, was on the other side and, apart from all the other claims upon our gratitude, men of my generation and after should never forget that it was he who saved us from all the horrors of a renewed Vimy and Passchendaele in 1942. If we had opened a second front then, I cannot say what the end of the war would have been. What I can say with certainty is that, if we had won in the end, it would only have been after another generation of young men had been senselessly slaughtered.

However, at the time when Winston was instructing me never to forget his formula of 'Indestructible Retaliation' I was more con-cerned with conventional than unconventional warfare. I believe that the only way to foretell the immediate future is by looking at the immediate past, and though I thought then, and think now, that nuclear warfare presents an almost incredible horror in the inter-mediate or perhaps even more distant future, warfare with con-ventional weapons on a limited scale was what was most likely to happen in my time. This, apart from the 'indestructible retaliation', ought to be prepared for or guarded against during my coming term as First Lord of the Admiralty. The role of the navy was being seriously underestimated by the Press, by the public and by the chiefs-of-staff. I did not believe in an invasion by Soviet troops across the border of the Iron Curtain dividing Western from Eastern Europe. Looking at the immediate past, I saw a series of what the Americans called brush-fire operations taking place at short notice in quite different parts of the world. For these I did not expect that the West could safely count on guaranteed over-flying rights or air bases. If we were to have any influence in the maintenance of world peace, it followed that we must have means of transport and an air strike potentiality independent of such rights and bases, and this meant then, and to some extent means now, seaborne aircraft and some form of surface fleet, mobile and ready at reasonably short notice. I was fortified in this appreciation by the knowledge of the immense development since the war of the Soviet navy, and particularly of their submarines. It did not look from that as if their general appreciation differed very much from my own. It also seemed to me perfectly absurd, despite my already developed commitment to Europe, that large numbers of British land forces should be stationed in Germany when Germany, France, the Benelux countries, Italy and America had immense resources in manpower and economic strength which were only partly being used for the purpose. Thus, at the time when I was appointed First Lord, I had reached a position in which, at least to a greater extent than was the general opinion, I favoured a blue water attitude to defence.

However, again, it was the unexpected and unplanned which took control of my life. Between the time when I consented to become First Lord and the time when I was appointed, Nasser had nationalized the Suez Canal. I still think that this was a wholly lawless act, but it did not occur to me then that it ought to be visited by other than economic measures concerted between a number of user nations. What was apparent to me, and to everyone else, was that a number of contingent preparations of a military kind were taking place and that naval and military operations were at least a possibility. I did not foresee what was actually going to happen, and for a considerable time after my appointment even the contingent plans were withheld from me, and when, on my insistence, they were ultimately disclosed, they were disclosed in a rather misleading form. When some short time before the Suez operation some actual ship movements began to take place, I was not in fact told the truth about their actual purpose until later.

It so happened, however, that I had formed conclusions of my own about the probable course of events, and although they did not actually tally with what took place, they were not so far out as all that. My service in the Middle East in the war had led me to take a more than usual interest in Middle Eastern affairs. At first my emotional sympathies had been largely with the Arabs. I had acquired a smattering of Arabic between 1941 and 1943 and had made a number of Arab friends, and, after the war, the murder of a British sergeant and the blowing up of the King David Hotel, in which a personal friend, Peter Smith-Dorrien, had perished, had alienated my sympathies from the Jews. All the same, in 1948, when Israel was admitted to the United Nations, the civilized world had admitted unequivocally her right to exist as an independent nation, and therefore, under Article 51 of the Charter, had accepted her right to self-defence. I do not understand this right in a pedantic or legalistic sense. Quite the contrary, if a conspiracy of states agrees to destroy a small nation, I believe that the right of self-defence may justify that small nation in using a pre-emptive strike. It has always seemed to me that a long war must destroy Israel, if she is confronted by a union of the Arab states. In theory at least these states must mobilize at some millions of men, and Israel can muster, I suppose, about quarter of a million, and then only at the price of virtually stopping her whole economy. It seemed, and seems, to me quite intolerable that a number of Arab nations claiming to be members of the United Nations, and claiming all the privileges of membership of that body, should nonetheless assert for quarter of a century the continuance of a state of war between themselves and another member-state based on the mere fact of its existence. This was the basic factor in the situation in the autumn of 1956, and again in 1967. This did not mean that I was in any way Zionist in my convictions, or that my thinking was based on a desire for Israel's interest as such. It seemed to me that the Arabs, however powerful their initial case had been, had stated themselves out of court by adopting a position inconsistent with their continued membership of the United Nations. The few contacts with Arabs that I had had since the war led me to believe that nothing short of the destruction of Israel as an independent state would satisfy them, and, if this were once permitted to happen, the entire framework of international peace aimed at by the Charter would fall apart. Moreover, I had the distinct conviction that the calling together of the chiefs-of-staff of the several border states by Nasser distinctly presaged that in their view the time to strike had come. When they closed the narrow entrance to the eastern arm of the Red Sea and so interdicted the approach to the port of Eilath to Israeli merchant vessels, it was certain that, if they wished to save their national existence, the Israelis would have to fight, and because they could not afford a long war, they would have to take the initiative. What I did not anticipate, and what I believe at that time few people did anticipate, was the extent of the superiority of Israeli over Egyptian and Arab troops. I believed that the Western powers would have to come to the aid of Israel to prevent an initial tactical victory of the Israeli armed forces developing into stalemate and defeat. I am not even now sure that this was wrong. I had thus reached an appreciation of the facts which led me to expect something not wholly dissimilar from what occurred.

On re-reading this, I am not sure that this fully represents my attitude at the time, because I remember that I had the gravest reservations, amounting to agony of mind, about the nature and the timing of the Anglo-French intervention when this was ultimately made known to me. I suffered very great qualms of conscience in the initial stages, and I think that only the fact that I was the titular head of a fighting service in which men were risking, and losing, their lives really reconciled me to supporting it whole-heartedly until I found Britain herself assailed from within and without and I felt it my duty to defend her with all my might. However, when the time came at the end of a week's actual fighting that the Government agreed to a standstill, I was even more against this than I had been critical of the original intervention. I thought we should have occupied the entire length of the Canal, cleared it, and then departed. I still think that if we had been permitted to do so the tragedy of the 1967 and Yom Kippur wars might have been averted, and the fatal rift between Britain and France which led to our exclusion from the Common Market in 1962 and again under the Labour Government, would not have taken place. It is, of course, impossible to re-write history, but if the kind of negotiation which has since taken place under Henry Kissinger had taken place in 1957, the world would be a happier and safer place today, and Britain would be enjoying a more secure role in it. However, I had no doubt of my immediate duty, which was to pick up the pieces as best I could and not allow Britain to remain a scapegoat or to be traduced. Since I was not a member of the Cabinet, I could only do this by staying at my post and defending the position against all-comers. Again fate had given my life a new twist. I had expected to spend the next three years in satisfying and constructive work and then to return to my profession. Instead I had been flung into the middle of a national and international crisis which was not of my making, the indirect consequences of which was to keep me away from the Bar for the next eight years and, as I then believed, destroy for ever my chances of becoming a judge.

23

Education

With the actual Suez crisis behind me it was urgently necessary that I should continue with the visits which a new First Lord used usually to undertake, and in particular that I should visit the Fleet at sea. The Fleet was in the Mediterranean, and much of it was actually in Port Said awaiting the agreement that it should withdraw. Moreover, we had assembled a formidable group of salvage craft, British and foreign, to take part in the clearance of the Suez Canal, including one unarmed naval vessel, the *Discovery*. I was determined that, whatever happened, these should be used, and used they were. I was quite aware that, before they gained admission, it would be necessary to put them under international command, probably of the United Nations who, despite a certain number of over-confident statements by Dag Hammarskjöld, would, I felt sure, need them. The arrangement was that I should confine myself to visiting Malta and the Fleet at sea. But I felt in my heart quite certain that, if I got so far as this, the Navy woul dinsist that I visited the Fleet at Port Said, and, by one means or another, ensure that I did so. This, in fact, happened, and one day, when I awoke in the captain's cabin in a cruiser, I saw the unmistakable figure of de Lesseps' statue sliding past the window. Even then I had hoped to keep the visit fairly quiet. But when I got out of the cruiser into a launch which was to take me round the harbour, it was obvious to me that the entire Press of the world was watching me from the deck of the submarine depot ship *Maidstone*. It was obvious that I would have to give a press conference and I did so. By the time I got back to England instead of a second line Minister I had become a national and international figure of some consequence. I expected to have to resign as the result of what I had said and done. In fact, the reputation that I gained launched me on a new career.

Soon after my return we were giving a children's party in the bottom two floors of Admiralty House when a summons came that I was to see the Prime Minister. Thinking over my various offences, I assembled a collection of controversial files and walked across the Horse Guards Parade to Downing Street. I was soon joined by the Secretaries of State for War and Air. Each had been afflicted by guilty conscience in a similar way and was clutching a similar bundle of documents. Instead of receiving a rebuke, when we got into the Cabinet room, to which we were summoned together, we were told by Anthony Eden that his doctors had ordered him to resign.

I was appalled. It needed only this, I thought, to make confusion worse confounded, and the next few days were spent in the profoundest gloom. To my astonishment, I next found myself summoned by the new Prime Minister and asked to join the new Cabinet as Minister of Education. After four months of office this was promotion with a vengeance. But strangely enough I was not at all pleased. I had given my heart to the Navy, and I believed I was popular. Such rapid changes are not good for morale, and I was afraid that there were people who would accuse me of careerism, as of course they did. But in this they were wrong. What I had done, I had done solely for my country and the service, and I neither expected nor desired reward.

I took stock of my situation. I had been a Governor of the Regent Street Polytechnic since the early thirties and of the Quintin Grammar School for some years before my promotion to the Cabinet. But the structure and administration of the Education Ministry and of the Local Education authorities were strange to me. Moreover, I had agreed to join the Government as First Lord, and I was apprehensive that my promotion would make it more difficult for me to return to my profession after the next election, as I had planned to do. However, I gave everything that I knew to my new task, and I believe the Ministry, the local authorities and the teaching profession came to recognize this. I still visualized myself as returning to the Bar in 1959. But I learned the new work thoroughly. I had to fight a losing battle with my colleagues over the general grant controversy, and a winning battle with the profession after the first battle was lost. I lengthened the teacher training course to three years, laid the foundations of the development of the Polytechnics, to the needs of which my attention was attracted by my association with the Polytechnic in Regent Street, and gave much bigger assistance to the denominational, mainly Roman Catholic, schools than they had received up to that point. But my most important work during the eight months I was there was my attempt, which I believe to have been successful, to restore the morale of the educational world, by compelling it to believe that the Conservative Party was at least as enthusiastic as its Socialist rivals about the role of education in a free society.

Looking back on my eight months in the education world, which I had expected to be but the prelude to two and a half years' constructive work, I am left with one or two compelling thoughts. I believe now, and I believed then, that no modern society, particularly a society which is devoted to liberty under the law, can afford to be without an educational structure commensurate with its needs, and that the apparatus which I inherited was quite inadequate to serve the needs of Britain at any one point at which one chose to examine it. But I was convinced then, and am convinced now, that any attempt by the State to control the intellectual content of education was incompatible with the preconceptions of a free society. I therefore found myself profoundly antagonistic to the enthusiasts of the left who try to make the educational machine a vehicle for social engineering. It is not possible or, I think, desirable to avoid moral teaching at a school, and Christian and Jewish parents and, so far as I am concerned, the parents of any sizeable minority, have every right to expect facilities to be provided within the educational framework, for their children to be brought up to practise and believe their particular doctrinal tenets. So far as general morality is concerned, it follows from what I have said earlier about the basis of my moral and political beliefs that the morality inculcated must at least be consistent with what I have been bold to call natural morality, things like telling the truth, courage, self-control, and the last six commandments of the Decalogue. It used to be said that every teacher is a teacher of English, and I would count it a bad mark against any teacher in any subject that his or her English was ungrammatical, slovenly, or imprecise. But every teacher is also a teacher of morality, and parents have a right to expect that the people to whom they entrust their children during the greater part of the daylight hours should, at least by the standards of the time and the society in which they live, observe and assume the precepts of natural morality so that, at least when the child leaves school, the simpler moral judgements and moral choices will, if possible, come naturally to him.

My experience both at the Ministry in Curzon Street and in life generally has led me to have no specific dogmatic views about the structure of education. I have no particular preference as between single sex or co-educational schools; secondary boarding-schools are, of course, more easily organized on single sex lines, but this system has its perils. Unlike most people, I prefer boarding-schools to day schools, and this has been borne out by my experience in my own family where we have used both. A boarding-school wastes no time in daily travel, gives more leisure to the pupil, absorbs less time on household chores, and gives better lessons in living in a community. But it must necessarily be a minority taste and even a minority possibility, if only because it is prohibitively expensive.

I am completely contemptuous of those who decide to force comprehensive schools as a single pattern for all secondary education. If parents prefer comprehension they can have it. Some areas are too sparsely populated to support any other type of school. But as a general rule comprehensive schools are too large, and have to be too large, for young people. They have to be too large because, if they are to supply a viable sixth form it must be at least sixty strong; if they are not to do so, they are not comprehensive, and on the basis of a five-year course and an entry of all streams of ability this puts the minimum number at well over a thousand pupils. The Sixth Form College solution is far more elitist than any grammar school, deprives its pupils of the last year of responsible authority, and the schools from which the pupils are taken of their natural leaders. Observation leads me to believe that, while bullying is an evil in all schools, bullying and contempt for authority is most rife in comprehensives, since all the problems of discipline are made more difficult in schools so amorphous in quality and so large in numbers. I do not believe, and in this I am reinforced by teachers of experience, that teaching of most subjects in all ability classes is a viable proposition. I am not prepared to admit that children of exceptional ability are in general given a fair deal in the comprehensive system especially if they do not excel in games and suffer from emotional tension, and an educational system which gives less than a fair deal to children of exceptional ability is every bit as unjust as a system which gives less than a fair deal to children of ordinary or sub-normal ability.

There are a number of points as to which I have changed my opinion since 1957, or as to which my views have crystallized on subjects which I had not then identified as problems or as to which I had no positive views of any kind. At that time, like most educational enthusiasts, I was a dogmatic supporter of the policy of raising the compulsory school leaving age to 16. I am now, at best, an agnostic, at worst an unbeliever. At that time I was mesmerized by the success of the earlier operation of raising the age from 14 to 15, by the higher leaving age in most other developed countries, and by the history of the period between the wars, which first fixed the age at 18 and then failed to make any advance on 14. I was determined that the policy of the 1944 Act should not suffer the fate of the 1918 Act, and both whilst I was at the Ministry and up to and including my membership of Mr Heath's government I was almost fanatical in my support of raising the age to 16. I was strengthened in my belief because it was shared by most of my friends and colleagues whom I regarded as progressive and enlightened.

I am sure now that I underestimated the case on the other side. In the first place, the ratio of pupils voluntarily staying on was going up all the time and without compulsion. The quality of the education the willing pupils receive in their last years can only be impaired by the addition of a number of indifferent or actively resentful recruits, who are usually constantly strengthened in their attitude by the indifference or resentment of their parents. In the second place, and viewing the matter simply as a matter of social priority, I now think that an improvement in the pupil/teacher ratio throughout the system ought arguably to have taken precedence over the compulsory education of the unwilling pupils at the top end of the age scale. In the third place, I underestimated the attrac-tion of early leaving in a high wage economy, and perhaps I attached too little importance to the more rapid emotional and physical development amongst boys and girls of 15 and 16, and the consequent degree of resentment felt by many of them of a continued schoolboy status after the age of 15. I found even amongst my own children, two of whom successfully entered the University, an increasing restlessness after the age of 15 was reached. If education is ever to become universally compulsory to the age of 18, I feel confident that a period of student status education at local colleges, with a strong practical or vocational slant for those who want it, will be the only way of attaining it. I wish I had come to this view earlier, but I doubt whether, if I had, I would have turned the course of history even by a hair's breadth.

Whilst I was at the Ministry, strictly industrial training was solely in the hands of what was then called the Ministry of Labour. At the time I did not question this orthodoxy and, owing to the hostility of most trade unions to any change, I doubt whether any Secretary of State for Education would get away with empire-building today. I now find myself questioning an arrangement which, so far as I know, is to some extent peculiar to Britain, now gradually becoming an industrially backward country. The craft unions, based on a long history of carefully protected journeyman status, are, except in the party political sense, among the most conservative bodies in the country, in the most perverse and unintelligent sense of the word conservative. When it came to training Spitfire and bomber pilots in the war we managed to produce some of the best airmen in the world in a period of about eighteen months. But the period of apprenticeship during most of my lifetime has been in the neighbourhood of five to seven years. The academic content of the apprentice course has been inadequate. There has been little flexibility in the acceptance of mature students or late entrants. Until recently the facilities for the retraining of redundant workers has been derisory. Although much progress has been made since I was at the Ministry in 1957, it has been on a scale which is quite incommensurate with our needs. On the whole, I put a good deal of this down to the debit account of the unions. But I am not at all sure that they would have had the same debilitating influence on government policy had the Education Ministry played a bigger role in prescribing the whole structure, and the Ministries of Industry and Employment less.

When I was first at the Ministry of Education - and that is the stage which I have now reached - the universities were wholly outside my responsibilities. The Robbins Report and student unrest were things of the future. It was, as a matter of fact, during my second period of office at the Education Ministry, this time as Secretary of State, that responsibility for the universities and schools were finally brought under the same office. Mr Michael Stewart, in the first Wilson administration, completed the present structure by leaving the polytechnics and the technical colleges with the local authorities instead of taking them over and placing them under the University Grants Committee. I thought myself at the time that the transfer of the university element to the Ministry of Education was mistaken and, when I went there as Secretary of State, I tried to mitigate the evil by leaving Edward Boyle in charge of it in a different building and with separate Cabinet membership. The unification of responsibility for the universities with the rest of education was always part of the orthodoxy at the Ministry and was strongly supported by Iain Macleod during his brief editorship of *The Spectator*. Logically it was irresistible, but practically I believe it to have been an error. It is more than a coincidence that student unrest and domination of university politics by party politics and philosophies largely date from the change. The retention by the local authorities of the polytechnics was, I now think, another step in the wrong direction. I accepted it as inevitable in my second period of office, and believe that I will be found to have said as much publicly when I spoke from the opposition benches. But the argument for the acquisition by the Ministry of its new empire and the retention by the local authorities of their old responsibilities in the field of higher education was the same, and basically sentimental. Sentimentality is the bane of democratic politics. The argument was that if these decisions were not made there would be two forms of education, higher and lower, and that this would involve a form of elitism, as it was already beginning to be called, which would operate to the detriment of school education. This is basically a nonsense argument, since the differences between school, further, and degree standard education will continue to exist whoever is responsible for their organization. If the words 'higher' and 'lower' offended the nostrils of our inverted snobberies, by all means let them be changed, although, on the whole, I resist changes of nomenclature to suit sentimental prejudices. After all, no one complains that some floors of a building are called higher and lower, and the words, as applied to education, do not involve a value judgement of any kind, but are applied analogically, because to achieve the higher one has, on the whole, to climb the lower flights of intellectual stairs.

The effect of both decisions in real life has been to render both polytechnic and university education more political and less independent. To pretend that they were the only causes of student unrest would be greatly to overstate the case. But that they were a minor, but still significant, contributory cause I do believe. What is much more serious is that, despite the buffer of the University Grants Committee, the intellectual integrity of the academic world has been significantly invaded, the more so since the effect cannot be precisely demonstrated or measured. In its higher ranges, university teaching is closely related to research; indeed, I would go so far as to say that neither can properly be carried without the other. The researcher needs to be constantly brought to earth by constant association both with the teacher and the learner. The teacher becomes stale without at least some recourse to research, or at least some intercourse with the researcher. The student, as he approaches the frontier of knowledge, must acquire at least some glimpse of what is going on at the frontier itself, if only to understand the significance of what he is learning as a student. Moreover, if the frontier is to advance, the body of researchers needs to be recruited constantly from the army of students who have just acquired their first degree.

Of course, at the time of which I am now writing, that is in 1957, the Robbins Report was in the future. Nevertheless, since I was, at a later stage of my ministerial career under Mr Harold Macmillan, largely responsible for its immediate acceptance within forty-eight hours, perhaps I ought at this point to set down some of my thoughts about it.

It was at the time greatly criticized by a strong body of conservative university opinion, on the basis that it was too ambitious. It is difficult to say that they were either unintelligent or wrong. There is no doubt that many of the troubles which have beset universities, new and old, since Robbins was adopted, have stemmed from our whole-hearted acceptance of its recommendations. There is a sense in which 'more' does, at least for a time, become 'worse'. The quality of the teaching force is diluted. Admission standards are relaxed. Student conditions (by which I do not only mean grants) become strained, and in particular accommodation and other facilities tend to become squalid and overcrowded.

All this leads to discontent. Perhaps worst of all, the sudden availability of large sums of public money coupled with the need for rapid expansion encourage cranky educational projects, like a new 'university without rules', and ludicrous architectural experiments, like large high buildings of gaunt and repulsive appearance, unsuitable for housing human beings of any kind, whether students or families. Such buildings can only be described in terms of Professor Tolkien's Mordor. When they exist by themselves without adequate recreational facilities you get the Alton Estate at Roehampton, the design of which was in part responsible for one of the nastiest murders of our time, the 'queer bashing' murder at the entrance to Wimbledon Common for which, alas, the butcher's boy who delivered meat to our house is even now serving a life sentence. When you get these architectural monstrosities allied to zany educational fallacies, you get Essex University at Colchester, about which no more need be said at present. Talking of educational architecture, however, I must now claim credit for what I believe may have been the largest personal achievement of my eight months at the Ministry in 1957, if one disregards my missionary efforts amongst my colleagues and the public at large in the cause of education generally, and my morale-boosting crusade amongst the local education authorities and the teaching profession.

When I came to the Ministry in January 1957 I came at a time when the design of schools had probably been passing through the greatest period of improvement that it had ever enjoyed, and I was led to believe that English schools were in advance of the rest of the world in this respect.

That this was so was a direct result of the vast expansion in the building of secondary schools after the 1944 Act and the raising of the school leaving age from 14 to 15. Moreover, the improvement of design was accompanied by very great economies, the credit for which largely belongs to a fruitful partnership between a young Jewish Civil Servant now, alas, deceased, on the financial side of the Ministry, and a brilliant team of architects.

The result was that when I came to the Ministry, and surveyed the scene, I was politely informed that there was not much more to be done in this field. Nevertheless, like all Ministers in charge of spending departments, I was chronically short of money. I am not amongst those who regard the Treasury as the root of all evils, although, like most other human institutions, they are productive of many. It is their business, amongst other things, to save candle ends, and it is by no means universally true that candle ends are good things to save. Nevertheless, amongst users of candles, the discipline of cash shortage can only be beneficial. 'No money', the great Rutherford is credited with saying. 'No money. Then we must use our brains.'

There was not only a chronic shortage of cash but a really pressing shortage of schools. This was not only due to the policy of the 1944 Act but to the very considerable movements of population which had occurred since the beginning of the war when most of the existing schools had been built. Moreover, the shortage of cash was intensified by the fact that the actual expenditure on school building had to be incurred by the local authorities who were small, numerous (146 in my time, I think), sometimes absurdly self-centred, often extravagant, and competitive with one another.

I found that they were actually driving the cost of school building up in a variety of different ways. They tended to employ their own architects, with the result that their designs were markedly more costly than we knew to be necessary, and had none of the advantages of large-scale production, which even in a labour-intensive industry like building, can greatly reduce costs. They also placed their orders with the main firms in such a way that the starts would take place in competition with one another and not on a co-ordinated plan.

The problem was to make them work together, without impairing their independence. As so often happens when a problem has been correctly identified, the providential ram caught in a thicket is to be discovered near at hand. In this case the animal took the form of a special type of building design invented to deal with mining subsidence. It was pointed out to me that local educational authorities which had a subsidence problem had a common interest in building schools to this design and, of course, what they could not be made to do by compulsion, a group of local authorities did willingly enough when they could be persuaded that it was their own idea to co-operate, and could be given the credit for their supposed farsighted-ness. The system was, I believe, called CLASP, the letters of which, I suppose, represent the initials of some words of significance, but I have forgotten what. On this idea was founded the first consortium of school building and authorities and, modestly, I claim the credit for it now. The secret, I may say, was that at the time I claimed none. But many new schools were built much more quickly at lower cost.

To return to the Robbins Report, however, I remain wholly im-penitent about having embraced it with open arms. Higher education has always been the Cinderella in England. Scotland has had at least three universities since the Middle Ages. For centuries England had but two, Oxford and Cambridge. For centuries after the Reformation these were largely somnolent, largely clerical, entirely Anglican, and the courses available at them absurdly restricted.

Of course this was no longer true either of Oxford and Cambridge, or of English universities generally, in the 1950s, of which I am writing now. But the consequences of our English neglect of uni-versities were still plain to be seen. The whole apparatus was in-adequate to take the strain of a modern society. Universities must represent the central point of a nation's intellectual activity. They must also provide vocational training for a number of the pro-fessions, and for the administrative cadre on which the actual process of government depends. Many of the political figures in any rational society ought ideally to emerge from the university machine, and in this, at least, Oxford and Cambridge, socially restricted as uni-versity education was until recently, had not failed. All this aside, the universities should produce the new knowledge and ideas, alike in the sciences and the humanities, without which society becomes static and torpid. Research is essential to learning, and learning is one of the features of civilization.

The weakness of English university education was, however, in some ways productive of blessings in disguise. So restricted was the public system that private benefactors, like my own grandfather, Quintin Hogg, had supplied the want, and, being unrestricted by conventional ideas or the social morality of the establishment, in many ways supplied it more intelligently. The polytechnics were always democratic institutions, in the sense that they supplied felt needs and not preconceived educational ideas, and I had been brought into contact with the Regent Street Polytechnic since I was about eighteen months old, when I was first brought, almost as an exhibit, to its annual fête.

Allied with local authority money, the polytechnics had set out to give just what the university system did not. Moreover, the professions, initially the Inns of Court, then the fighting services and finally the engineering institutions, had been in the business from the start. There always ought to be more than one route to the top, and ladders should be available to mature students as well as to adolescents and to part-time students as well. This is not realized by the Communist countries, or those parts of the United Kingdom where Socialism is endemic. It was not consciously and sufficiently realized by the professional classes here until recently. But the result has been a more variegated educational pattern more precisely tailored to felt requirements than if it had emerged as the result of a preconceived plan.

Nevertheless, what was vital in the early sixties when the Robbins Committee reported was that the scale on which degree level courses should be available should be vastly increased. No one can regret more than I do now some of the absurdities and extravagances which have followed. Moreover, the time has come for consolidation before further advance. But I do not regret or disparage the general thesis of the Robbins Report or apologize for my own precipitancy in embracing it. I have already described the eagerness with which I embraced the Beveridge Report in 1942, despite its manifest weaknesses and occasional errors. I was much criticized for doing this at the time, just as I am now much criticized for wishing to repair some of its mistakes. But I do not regret my enthusiasm for Beveridge or Robbins. Big decisions like this need to be taken with the heart rather than the head.

24

Party Chairman

My life had taken an extraordinary turn as the result of my giving a
positive answer to Anthony Eden's invitation at the beginning of
1956. What was now to happen was even more unexpected and
wholly undesired. I had joined the Government in order to hold an
historic office for a short sharp period before I returned to the Bar.
I had thought that in 1959 there would be an election in which, in
the ordinary course of events, a Labour Government would be returned to power. I would then be free to resume my career at the
Bar and become in due course, as I had hoped, a judge. When Anthony
Eden retired after the Suez operation, I was invited to join the
Cabinet as Minister of Education under Harold Macmillan. I was
almost heart-broken at leaving the Admiralty after only four months
but threw myself into my new work with all the enthusiasm of
which I was capable. Nevertheless, my ultimate objective remained
the same. I remember that one of the first things I said in Cabinet
was that it was our duty to clear up the mess we had made as the
result of Suez, and that we should be extremely lucky if, in the
confused state of public opinion at the time, we were not skittled
out by July before we had had an opportunity of doing so. That this
did not happen is to my mind one of the most remarkable political
non-events of my life, and the credit for it must undoubtedly go
to the virtuosity of Harold Macmillan as Prime Minister. What
followed was in some ways even more remarkable. It was that after
two successive General Elections in which the Conservatives had been
successful, and having about hit the bottom in public estimation in
1957 and 1958, we came out with a third successive win in 1959 and
with a majority of about a hundred. I do not wish in any way to
reduce the credit of Harold Macmillan in achieving this. But I do

not think he would have done it without me. After all, this does not reduce his credit. He had appointed me and backed me when people said I was no good. I do not know how he thought of the appointment, but Oliver Poole, the existing Party Chairman, may have suggested it. If he did, I do not know why. But I think I know the factors which helped me to succeed. There were three basic reasons. The first was that I was before all else a tough professional advocate and applied the principles of what I had learned to the political situation in the run-up to the General Election of 1959, and subsequently in the conduct of the election campaign. The second was that one of the first decisions I made was to cling on to Oliver Poole as my deputy Chairman at all costs. He is a man in many ways the opposite of myself. But of all the partnerships I have ever had with anybody, my two years' partnership with him was the most nearly without flaw. It would be much too much to say that he did the administration and I the talking. I am myself a reasonably good administrator, and he is a fluent, cogent and effective speaker. Each knew the other's job, and each did the other's job for extended periods of time. For instance, when he went to America on business I did the entire administration, and he did almost as much speaking as I did when I was away or too preoccupied with other things.

The third reason why I succeeded was that I was an hereditary peer confined to the House of Lords and therefore no rival for Harold Macmillan, since there seemed at that time no conceivable possibility of my succeeding to the leadership of the party. Of course, this sounds silly now, because of the Life Peerages Act, 1963, and the fact that Harold Macmillan ultimately selected me as his successor and very nearly succeeded in placing me in that position. Nonetheless it was not only true but extremely important to my success. It is absolutely vital to the work of a Conservative Party Chairman when his party is in office that he should go round the country doing what, in the nature of the business, the Prime Minister cannot do, that is, stirring up the faithful and explaining the policy of the Government in the constituencies. In other words, he must actually act to some extent as if he were the leader of the party and exercise many of the functions of leadership while leaving the real decisions to the real leader, and all this without exciting the real leader's jealousy. This can only be done if you have no ambition whatever to become leader yourself, and if the thought never crosses the actual leader's mind that you might succeed him. During my two years as chairman of the party it never once occurred to me to think that I could ever be Prime Minister. Nevertheless, I deliberately studied Harold Macmillan's character and set myself to do for him exactly the things which he was occupationally or temperamentally incapable of doing for himself. I acted as his professional advocate, making myself as much a contrast to him as I possibly could. Where he would understate, I would be strident, where he would be serious, I would be humorous, and vice versa. Where he would play the Duke's son-in-law, or even the Duke, I would be eloquent and ostentatious to the point of vulgarity. On the other hand, where he was devious, I would be plainspoken. Only a professional advocate could have done this. It was not natural to me. It was even more unnatural because the whole training of a barrister leads him not only to avoid but to hate personal publicity, and the whole essence of being Conservative Party Chairman is that, when the party is in office, he must get and seek to get personal publicity of whatever kind is most beneficial to the party and its leader.

I have stressed the words 'Conservative Party Chairman' because the Labour Party is quite differently structured. They have a titular chairman. During part of my time it was Barbara Castle, who was at that time a far less prominent figure in the Labour Party than she is now. Nevertheless, part of the function of the Conservative Party Chairman needs to be done under our system whichever party is in office. Herbert Morrison did it for Attlee during the Attlee administration and, so far as I can judge, he did it extremely well. There must be someone inside the Cabinet listening to their deliberations and wholly committed to their decisions. A mere party functionary outside the Cabinet will not do, whether based on the constituency parties or on the parliamentary party. He must represent the party conscience and party feeling while government policy is being discussed, although he must always subordinate this to the needs of the nation where a conflict arises. On the other hand, he must be seen constantly in the regions and constituencies fighting the party battles, absorbing the party atmosphere and, among the faithful constituency workers, expounding the policy of the Government and relating this policy to the party philosophy and party principle.

This two-way movement of ideas is absolutely vital to the working of our system. Party activists tend always to be more jealous for party faith and party orthodoxy, than those who are responsible for policy in government, and those who are responsible for policy are always apt to be more responsive to pressure from events, from opponents in the House of Commons, from the Civil Service, from financial stringency, from the circumstances of international alliances than are the party faithful. Hence the legend that they are out of touch with the grass roots of the party, which the party faithful always identify with public opinion, that they sacrifice principle to expediency, and that any electoral misfortune which occurs is due to these shortcomings. Hence when the party is unpopular, or beaten, it tends to become more extreme and dogmatic, while the real lesson to be learned is often one needing greater moderation.

I also express the view that the role which I have described is incompatible with being leader of either House of Parliament. Both my immediate successors as Party Chairman tried to combine Chairmanship of the Party with Leadership of the House of Commons. Both failed as Party Chairman in consequence. Since ceasing to be Party Chairman I have led the House of Lords, and I know what I am talking about. The essence of being a good leader of either House is that one should always seek to conciliate one's opponents unless they subject one to an outright challenge. The essence of playing the role which is played in the Conservative Party by the Party Chairman is that one should always dramatize differences, point contrasts, and challenge opposition. Party zeal thrives on controversy. Parliamentary management, especially when one is in power, frequently, perhaps usually, involves reducing party and personal tensions.

When I was first appointed Party Chairman my appointment was challenged by the opposition on the ground that being paid as a Minister, namely as Lord President of the Council, I would be sacrificing public policy to party interest, or alternatively, pursuing party interests at the public expense. One particularly foolish critic even went so far as to say that by accepting the appointment I was involving the monarchy in party politics. It is true, of course, that Lord President of the Council has a fairly regular and formal relationship with the Queen, because about twice a month or more he is received in private audience and attends the formal Privy Council meetings, standing as a sort of left marker (Privy Council business for some reason is always conducted standing) in the line of Privy Councillors, while the Monarch stands at the table, with a chair behind. But the Lord President never, or practically never, tenders substantial advice to the Sovereign, except formally on matters devoid of party political interest. The political advisers of the Sovereign are the Prime Minister and, less importantly, the Home Secretary or the Chancellor of the Exchequer, and, of course, on judicial appointments, the Lord Chancellor, and these are the great figures in a parliamentary party and in the country. The functions I am describing, although in my view indispensable in a parliamentary democracy, and occasionally hitting newspaper headlines, are considerably humbler. As I say, I do not believe they can be dispensed with, and where attempts have been made to do so, the substituted arrangements have been considerably more open to criticism precisely because they have been less openly avowed. My Party Chairmanship was essentially part-time. I always gave Cabinet and Parliamentary business and Lord Presidential functions absolute priority, and though I drew, by the standards of those days, a generous expense allowance which I fully spent, I accepted and asked for no salary as Party Chairman. In retrospect I have no qualms of conscience about any of this.

What I have not yet said, but what is equally true, is that I accepted the Party Chairmanship with extreme misgiving, and very reluctantly. I had not joined the government for this kind of enterprise. If, as I have said, I was almost heart-broken at leaving the Admiralty after only four months, I was equally broken-hearted at leaving the Ministry of Education after only eight. I was fully aware that people would say, as they did, that I had made both posts only a stepping-stone in my political career. I was wholly innocent of this. I had thrown myself whole-heartedly into each, and wanted nothing better than to continue. On the very day that my appointment as Party Chairman was announced, it was my fate to be asked to speak and then to dine at the Roman Catholic Teachers' Training College at Strawberry Hill. When dinner was over they drank my health and asked me to reply seated. I found that before I had ended I broke down and cried, a silly habit which I have always despised as I believe that a man, however emotional, and however much he may feel it, should always have himself completely in hand. After describing what I had had it in mind to do in the Ministry, and how little after eight months I had actually been able to accomplish, and 'now', I said, 'they have given me the dirtiest job of all.' The contrast was just too much for me. If I had realized, as I did not, that the result of my accepting it would be that I should not go back to the Bar for eight years, I should have been in one way more distressed than I was. I thought I should fail as Party Chairman in achieving the task I had been set, and I knew that if I failed I should be blamed by my friends and despised by my foes. Moreover, I thought that by taking this politically controversial post, I was shutting the door for ever on any judicial appointment. When my father died I had said to a newspaper man who interviewed me that perhaps in 1970, if there was a Conservative Government, 'Some ass might make me Lord Chancellor.' I had visualized this as happening to me because by that time I might have made my name as a High Court Judge, and perhaps even as a Lord Justice of Appeal or a Law Lord. The chance, I believed, had gone for ever, through no fault of my own. I believed that I had sacrificed all the hopes I had ever had, and for what? The chance of being branded as a failure by my friends and incurring the hatred of my enemies for having embodied, albeit unsuccessfully, all that they most disliked. I was well aware that, as Education Minister, I was fairly popular, because I had been whole-hearted in my pursuit of educational excellence. I was now to leave constructive work for what I then regarded as the squalid field of party controversy.

25

The Chairmanship

It is difficult now to recapture the complete spirit of disarray into which the Conservative Party had fallen in September 1957. For a brief moment, during the Suez operation, public opinion had been largely with us, and party opinion, though divided, had been uplifted. I was then the odd man out, having been doubtful, or worse, about going in, and even more doubtful of stopping when we did. I learned afterwards that this was also Churchill's view. I did not know it then. But by the autumn all had gone awry. Worse, our popularity was still deteriorating. The economic situation was unattractive. The by-elections were going wrong, yielding Liberal victories in safe Conservative seats, and Labour victories in the marginal seats. When I held my first press conference, the assembled Press of the world, and there were a lot of them there, openly sneered at my statement that this was a battle which could be won (I always think it bad luck to prophesy victory as assured or likely; there is something about my classical education which warns me against it). The Central Office pundits continued to prophesy electoral defeat for more than a year. Senior members of the Twenty-Two Committee were actively or covertly disloyal both to the leader and myself, and spent the next months writing to the leader asking for my removal and talking to the Lobby saying that the leader was no good. Just as things were beginning to get better, or at least show definite signs of improving, the Thorneycroft resignations deprived even me almost of hope. Then there was the Bank Rate Tribunal, and the trouble at Bournemouth over Nigel Nicolson. There were those who had opposed Suez all along, like Medlicott and Anthony Nutting. Most of these, like Edward Boyle, had returned to the fold. There were others who had opposed our leaving, including my own successor at Oxford, who formed a little cave of Adullam called the Suez Group. On the extreme Right there were the predecessors of the National Front who, not yet having found their national bêtes noires in Commonwealth immigrants, persecuted me, because one of the last things I had done as First Lord of the Admiralty was to secure the triumphal return of the British into Egypt under the auspices of the United Nations. Most of these were merchant vessels, but one, at least, was the *Discovery*, an unarmed research vessel of the Royal Navy. This, to them, was called 'hauling down the White Ensign'. The situation of the party was, in truth, almost desperate. The only solid asset I had was the party in the country, the National Union of Conservative and Unionist Associations, which, under Oliver Poole, remained loyal but was much disheartened by failure at the by-elections and press and parliamentary criticism of the government.

What, then, were my assets? The first, of course, was a total belief in the national, and even international, importance of what I was trying to do. I shall have to come back to this later as it is absolutely fundamental to what I am trying to say. Whatever may have been my reasons for becoming a Conservative at the outset, I had come to believe that the continued health and vigour of the British Conservative Party was absolutely vital for the continuance of parliamentary democracy in this country and, indeed, for the defence of the values of Western civilization. Paradoxical as it may sound today, I sincerely believed not simply in the validity of the cause for which I was fighting, but my own disinterestedness in fighting it. As I have said, whatever other people thought, I myself believed that I was making the supreme sacrifice of my whole planned career in accepting the office of Chairman. As he left my first press conference, I was later told that, among the world Press who had sneered, one American journalist was heard to say: 'The strange thing is that the guy actually believes what he is saying.' I did believe, and today that seems to me the first reason why I won through.

My second asset was that I approached the actual conduct of the matter with the professionalism of a member of the Bar, and with whatever gifts of leadership I had acquired in my short and unsuccessful career in the lower ranks of the army. I had always believed that it was absolutely vital if you wanted to win a case to analyse it thoroughly, and when you had analysed it to concentrate on a single point. When I came to fight the election I fought on the single point of the financial unsoundness of Labour's policy. I had great difficulty in making my colleagues see it that way, and I never convinced the Treasury, the then Lord Chancellor, or even, I believed, Harold Macmillan. But, if he needed convincing, I convinced Oliver Poole. Or rather, he did not need convincing, for after the election had been running a week on the rather wishy-washy lines on which we had been condemned to fight, I was rung up somewhere in the provinces by Oliver who began rather abruptly by saying: 'You know, we are losing this election.' 'I know we are,' I said. We then planned our own private enterprise campaign which immediately began to yield results. In fact, it yielded a result wildly beyond my dreams, because someone in the Labour hierarchy apparently got rattled. I never knew how or why it happened, and I have never been able to find out. Quite suddenly, someone persuaded or, I rather suspect, bullied, Hugh Gaitskell, who had throughout showed himself sensitive to the campaign I was fighting on the financial viability of Labour promises, to make a speech claiming that, so far from the promises being impracticable, he would, if elected, actually reduce the income tax. When this was reported to me I was speaking at Doncaster on behalf of the up-and-coming Conservative candidate Anthony Barber. The promise seemed to me so extravagant in the light of what I believed about the Labour programme that I vouchsafed the comment: 'The Lord hath delivered them into our hands.' And so it proved. I believe that Oliver's and my unorthodox conduct of the campaign converted what would have been a defeat into a victory, but that the unexpected bonus of Gaitskell's ill-advised speech turned what would have been a victory of fifty into a victory of about a hundred. If it is said that such things cannot be, I disagree. I remember listening to Churchill's first election broadcast in 1945 in the Carlton Club, when he referred to the possibility of a Gestapo in Britain with rather more perspicuity about fundamental political attitudes than practical advocacy or wisdom. The club was entranced. 'You might be interested to know,' I said offensively, 'that that speech will cost us at least 250,000 votes.' I was not popular. 'It must be wonderful to be as certain of yourself as that,' said a critic. But I was certain, and am now, that though it was written in the stars that we should be beaten in 1945, that broadcast turned what was certain defeat into a calamity. Incidentally, it was not an unmixed blessing for the Labour Party. Attlee's Government in 1945 would have been a better Government than it was with a smaller majority and a more effective and stronger Opposition. But in 1959 my tactics were successful. More important, however, than election tactics was the strategy I had been pursuing since 1957.

This brings me to my third asset. I had a plan, and with the aid of Oliver Poole I proceeded to carry it out. To some extent it was the product of necessity. But necessity is the mother of invention, and what I aimed at was, in fact, the consequence of thought. Broadly, all the media were against us, radio, TV and the press. Therefore my main thrust would not be through the media, though I would make use of them, so far as they would let me, and certainly at my first main opportunity, the party conference, the media did me proud, if anything too much so. But my theory has always been that, in the main, the media reflect public opinion as much as they create it. Nothing would achieve my purpose except a change in public opinion on a fairly massive scale, within a fairly limited time. At the most I had till the autumn of 1959 in order to effect it and, as matters turned out, I needed every minute of that. I did not think that if opinion had not changed by the autumn of 1959 I could hope for a significant improvement by the spring of 1960, by which time the Parliament theoretically ran out. Though technically I had until then, I reflected that things seldom go right for a government that has exhausted its mandate and manifestly dare not face the electorate. In order to effect a substantial change in opinion it is useless to rely on the media. They have their own fish to fry, their TAM ratings, their circulations, their Charters, their editorial policies, even their advertisers. Who shall blame them? I have always held the view that so far as it is not created by events, public opinion is largely made by a relatively small minority of people. It is difficult to define who these are. Obviously they include Members of Parliament, contributors to the press, and television and radio producers. But the opinion makers are not confined to these obvious groups; they include all those whose word counts with their fellow men. A hairdresser, a taxi-driver, a doctor, all have a little more influence on public opinion than Mr Average voter, or even Mr Average voter of their own class, education and degree of articulateness. I took particular care by various means to cultivate the articulate rather than talk down to the multitude, or rely on gimmicks or glib phrases. But particularly, I cultivated the party activists, who are certainly among the most important of opinion-makers, and to a party chairman a group of opinion-makers most accessible to his persuasion.

Some of the makers of opinion are beyond reach, because they are on the other side. But before an election even these can be pressed into service. They can be made to take notice, to twitter with rage and scream in derision and, if they can be made to twitter and scream at the right things, or, rather, from their point of view, at the wrong things, powerful allies can be wheeled into support from sources normally neutral or, occasionally, even unfriendly.

But of course the opinion-makers *par excellence* are one's own party activists. These are eager to be convinced, and the whole party organization is designed to organize and move them. Though I had nothing whatever to do with it, my appointment was timed to be announced one month before the party conference. Long before I was informed by Harold Macmillan of what was in store for me, which was conveyed in the course of a *tête-à-tête* lunch at the Turf Club, I had accepted an invitation to address the annual meeting of the Conservative Political Centre at the Brighton Aquarium during the week of the conference. No doubt this invitation was offered by design, presumably Oliver Poole's, but I accepted it in ignorance. After my fate was made known, I realized that this was a heaven-sent opportunity to make the maximum impact on the party. True, not more than a thousand could crowd into the Aquarium, and there were many more than four thousand delegates at the conference. But I could be sure that my audience would include the most powerful opinion-makers in the party. The CPC is the great focal point of intellectual Conservatism. I could not afford to fail and, if I succeeded, the message would be all over the conference by the morning. The speech was ready in print and would be read by the delegates. The television cameras would be there, to capture the atmosphere of the meeting and broadcast selected passages of the speech. At the end of a long, hot hour I knew that I had succeeded in this the first of the many hurdles I would have to surmount. I have had occasion to re-read my speech at the CPC meeting. I still think it was one of the best I have made, intended to appeal to the head, but phrased also so as to move the heart.

The other incidents which made the 1957 conference famous were as spontaneous and unplanned as the CPC speech was carefully prepared. My boyhood was largely spent in Sussex, at my home at Carter's Corner, near Hailsham. It has therefore been my habit from childhood to swim in the English Channel as and when opportunity presented. I knew, what other people have never taken in, that in the English Channel the sea is warmer in November than it is usually in June, and in the middle of October there is usually a finer spell of fine weather than in most of the summer. I came down therefore fully prepared to swim in the sea as I had done countless times before, little knowing that this innocent and beneficial activity of mine would shortly become as highly publicized as Beecham's Pills. I confess at once that my bathing at Blackpool the following year was less innocent. I like bathing at Brighton. But in October the sea at Blackpool is a good deal colder and, at least in my opinion, the sea is unacceptably dirty. In 1958 it was also extremely rough. I bathed at Blackpool in order not to give offence. I had bathed at Brighton for the sheer pleasure of swimming in the sea, which I love above all other forms of swimming. The effect of the photographs, though I heartily disliked them, was altogether beneficial. It gave the impression of physical vigour, a certain amount of hardihood, and a capacity to be unafraid of ridicule, all of which I suppose was quite genuine.

The bell-ringing episode at this conference, which for better or for worse has somehow attached itself to my name and fame, was quite different again. Every year to this day, at the end of the conference, there takes place a ceremony at which the Chairman of the Party presents to the Chairman of the Conference (a quite different person) the Chairman's bell which has been the symbol of authority throughout the conference. It is a pleasant ceremony, if slightly ridiculous, and the bell, duly inscribed with the Conference Chairman's name and date, is kept as a souvenir by the recipient. Those whose duty it was to attend to such things were officious to remind me at intervals of my duty in this respect and, to tell the truth, I was rather irritated at being told more than once.

At the same time my own mind was preoccupied with a different, though related, and more technical, problem. In those days, but not now, it was the business of the Party Chairman to sum up the theme of the conference immediately before the handing over of the bell. There was then no official opening speech by the leader of the party giving a keynote at the beginning, and, though known to be in the neighbourhood, the leader of the party was not present at all during the conference itself. He delivered a great oration after the conference was over at a mass rally in the afternoon. It therefore behoved the Party Chairman to wind up the conference in the morning, the actual debate at which was devoted to some relatively trivial matter, in a mood to receive the words of the leader in a suitable spirit in the afternoon. I was considerably troubled as to how all this was to be done, how to send away the conference in a suitable mood, after a minor debate, with fire in their bellies and a laugh in their hearts and, at the same time, bring the proceedings to an end with the handing over of the Chairman's bell. It was not a really vital matter, but it was a difficult one, and in this sort of matter I seek to solve this kind of thing professionally. For a long time I pondered in vain, but during the wearisome debate which preceded my winding-up speech, everything seemed suddenly to fall into place. I would pronounce some solemn words concluding the conference and then swing into the handing-over ceremony with a heart-lifting but humorous symbolic gesture. My words are no doubt recorded somewhere, but I have not bothered to look them up. At the conclusion of my remarks, I took up the bell, complimented the Chairman on her conduct of the business and told her that the bell was for her - I then tinkled it mildly, in the manner of a Victorian hostess ringing for the fish after the soup, and told her to ring it gently from time to time to remind herself of us. Then, said I, ring it more loudly, and suited the action to the word, symbolizing it with a more warlike challenge. Finally I said ring it more loudly still, and followed with a menacing if not verbally accurate reminiscence of Donne's 'For Whom the Bell Tolls' passage, adapting it to suit the coming demise at the polls of our Socialist opponents. At this point I clanged it as loudly as I could, waving it above my head. The effect of this impromptu pantomime was electric, far more and, I must add, better than I had ever intended, or supposed possible. The conference rose to its feet, cheering and laughing. The television cameras, caught by surprise at the original performance, made me continue waving and clanging until both they and the press photographers were satisfied, and as long as I continued, and for some time after, the delegates went on waving and cheering and laughing. What had been thought of spontaneously as a modest but professional solution to a difficult technical problem had become a symbolic gesture and a legend which has lived with me ever since to my infinite boredom and disgust. The repeat performance at Blackpool the following year when victory, though twelve months off, was well on the way, was, of course, a contrived affair, like the Blackpool bathe. It was, in its way, equally successful. But it was not in the least enjoyable. What one has done once spontaneously it is never pleasant to repeat again to order. However it was a success. The CPC speech, on which so much labour had been spent, was the more important success, because by it the atmosphere was changed. But, alas, what is remembered now is the bathing and the bell-ringing.

There remained, however, as I knew would be the case, a long grind ahead. The delegates had been sent back to their constituencies in good heart, and with a message to deliver to their fellow-workers which, in due course, their fellow-workers would deliver in the streets and on the doorsteps. But as I had predicted all along, you cannot change public opinion in a few days – not in my judgement in less than six or eight months. The by-elections continued to go wrong. I laboured at each by-election, except at North Torrington, which yielded a Liberal victory, and one other, and I made an elaborate progress into each of the thirteen areas in which at that time the party organization was divided. Trouble continued at Bournemouth over Nigel Nicolson (how I solved this problem before the election is not for this narrative). I would have no truck with the Liberals. I deliberately and, as I think, honourably attracted any blame for failure to myself, so that neither the leader of the party nor my colleagues in the Cabinet would be compromised by what I still regarded as my certain failure in the end. This is part of the elementary ethics of the professional advocate. But I continued to carry out my plan and, at this stage at least, I was loyally supported not only by the faithful Oliver Poole but by Harold Macmillan, which was all that mattered. By January 1958, only five months after my appointment, I saw the first faint objective signs that my plan was yielding dividends. Immediately after this, the Thorneycroft resignation took place and everything was back to square one. I was as near despair as my temperament, and my religion, will permit.

As I am not writing memoirs in the strict sense of the word, I will make no comment on the merits, the causes, or the motivation of the Thorneycroft resignations. When a Chancellor of the Exchequer and his two junior colleagues resign in concert on a question of policy, it is no small thing, and a government as tottering and unpopular as ours was must be considered to be near the end. My own duty, I thought, was absolutely plain. As I had not supported the resignations it would be my duty to minimize their effect with all the speed and all the authority of which I was capable. I met Oliver Poole, and together we concerted a plan. That very night telegrams went forth to every Chairman of every area Conservative organization and association giving our account of the matter. Our critics were astonished at the speed and manner with which we acted, and the principal critics, including the resigning Ministers, were very angry. To my mind they had nothing to be angry about, since, although I had been effective and prompt, I had done nothing dishonourable. I believe my actions steadied the party at a very critical time, at least as much as Harold Macmillan's studied insouciance on his departure at the airport on leaving for his Commonwealth tour, which he would not put off. His judgement was correct, although his reference to the 'little local difficulty' which is how he described the loss of his Chancellor of the Exchequer had more panache than accuracy.

In using the network of the Chairmen, I was using a device which I had invented for myself as a means of keeping feeling in the Party and policy in the Government in step with one another. On no other occasion, I believe, did I communicate by telegram, but every month, or so much the oftener as circumstances required, I sent a confidential letter to anyone who could describe himself as a Conservative Chairman, whether of an area, a constituency association, or a trade union or teacher's association, containing my own version, over a

facsimile signature, of the most sensitive topics of the day. No particular security precautions were taken, and I never could understand
why they were not regularly leaked to the press. But this happened
only about once. I believe some chairmen kept them to themselves
and perhaps produced the arguments as their own. Others read them
out at committee executive or branch meetings. This was an important factor in keeping party opinion in step in different parts of
the country.

After the Thorneycroft resignations things, as I have said, became
worse for a time, and all my efforts seemed to be wasted. It is heart-
breaking to face a situation in which one believes that one has put
up a thoroughly competent professional performance, only to meet
with failure, and with the necessity to accept all blame without the
slightest attempt to pass it on elsewhere, and even with the maso-
chistic purpose of attracting to oneself some blame which might
naturally go elsewhere. This is an experience which all professional
advocates must undergo from time to time. But I was an advocate
with only one client at this time, and only one case, and it was a
case in which I thoroughly believed. In the end it did not end in
failure. The first local elections in May 1958 were almost as bad
as they could be. But the borough elections which followed showed
modest but significant improvement, and this time there were no
more resignations to nullify the result. By autumn we were well
ahead, and at the conference in Blackpool I was able to strike a thank-
ful, indeed almost a triumphant, note. By May 1959 there was a
strong movement in the party to hold an immediate election. I
advised Harold Macmillan against it, since, on a cautious calculation, I could not promise a result within the margin of error which
a wise man would allow. I thought we would win by a small majority.
But small majorities can easily evaporate in the three weeks of an
election campaign during which public opinion is at its most vola-
tile. So it had to be October and, when October came, I prophesied a
majority of fifty. We got a hundred. I was worn out, mentally and
physically, for I had fought an exhausting battle in the constituencies
with my stomach in violent revolt. Above all, I was exhausted
spiritually, as I have been only twice since, once after negotiating the
Test Ban Treaty, and once later in 1963 after disclaiming my peerage.

However, I had won when I thought I would fail. As I have said, the real credit must go to Harold Macmillan, whose control of policy and Parliament at this period was at his most impressive. I do not mean to detract from this, however, when I say candidly that I do not think he would have done it had he not been aided by my efforts.

26

The Party

The time has now come to take stock of the position before I go on to a new and less happy chapter. I have said that, during my two years of Chairmanship, my most important asset was that I most sincerely believed in what I was attempting to do. By the time I was appointed Chairman I had acquired quite a different attitude towards the Conservative Party and its principal rivals from that with which I had begun my political life so many years before.

After the defeat of 1945, I had tried to rewrite the basic thinking, or philosophy, of Conservatism in the Penguin which was published in 1947, and republished with a section devoted to an edited version of my Chairman's speeches in 1959, with the help of Peter Goldman. But by 1957 I had come to think of the Conservative Party less as the embodiment of a philosophy than as an institution, in fact, as one of the most important bulwarks of parliamentary democracy in the free world, more important than its continental counterparts in Europe, and far more important than either the Republican or Democratic Party in the USA. At the same time, I had become much more antipathetic to the Labour Party here than I had ever been before. Before the war, although anything but Socialist, I had been much more sympathetic than most Conservatives to some of the social policies of Labour. This had reflected itself during my period of seclusion in the army in all my post-war thinking about politics. It had shown itself in my whole-hearted advocacy of the Beveridge plan, in my active membership of the Tory Reform Committee, and in my somewhat critical attitude towards Churchill and his Shadow Cabinet's policies in the period of opposition between 1945 and 1950, when I was spirited away from the House of Commons through my succession to my father's Viscountcy. My hostile reception of commercial television had done nothing to improve my popularity. At this time I was regarded with some suspicion by the right, and even by the centre of the party, as a young man in a hurry with some dangerously unorthodox and in some ways semi-socialist ideas. As I have said, the formula to which I was working was 'privately-owned industry and publicly-organized social service'.

But by the time I was appointed Party Chairman I had become fully ready for the role I now felt it was my duty to play. Others might play a useful part on the right of the party, or on the left. For, after all, all parties, if they are to be national parties, must, after their fashion, be coalitions. But it is always better for the Pope to be orthodox and, by the same token, I felt it was the duty of a Party Chairman to reflect the exact centre of party orthodoxy, and whatever I had been before this time, from this time onward I have endeavoured to be just that.

I think I can best explain the development of my thought after 1945 by reference to social policy. Historians will no doubt concentrate on the liquidation during this period of the British Empire, and no doubt most politicians have had economic problems more in the forefront of their minds. Both of these attitudes, no doubt, are right. But it was mostly in the field of social policy that I began to observe most clearly the weakness of my own position. I did not repent at all of my previous attitude in embracing what subsequently came to be known as the welfare state. What I did begin to question was whether the welfare services we had achieved were those best fitted for our post-war needs as these had come to be identified, and this led me to try to identify the policies required by the new needs which experience was constantly revealing. I have come to observe that, after each war, we have attempted to win what I can only describe as the last peace. Thus we founded the United Nations on a model which was designed to defeat aggression on the Hitler model. But this aggression has never taken place. The post-war dangers have been of a different order, and these the United Nations have signally failed to meet. Except in Korea, the organization has proved useless against Communism and, in the third world, UNO has done nothing to arrest the anarchical tendencies of the new nationalisms and dictatorships. It has shown itself equally inadequate to stem the rivalry, unchecked except by the fear of nuclear war, between the super powers themselves, that has permitted the new nationalism to flourish. Finally, it has proved impotent in the face of aggression by subversion, terrorism, and the urban guerrilla.

The pre-war world was dominated by the fact of unemployment and the various kinds of evil which were brought about by the under-employment of the working population. These were not limited to the direct effects of actual unemployment. The wages of an under-employed population are insufficient to enable even a fully employed man to make adequate provision against old age or sickness or against the cost of even an average family. The Beveridge Report, on which our present social services are constructed, is basically a pre-war document put together during the war on the basis of pre-war experience, and put into practice immediately after the war before the true pattern of post-war experience had become clearly observable or established. The Beveridge Report was built on the assumption that, even in post-war conditions, unemployment would run at a rate, on the pre-war basis, of calculation of 10 per cent (on the present basis 8 per cent). This was why Lord Beveridge demanded as conditions of the adequacy of his provision against poverty, which turned out to be pitifully low, a family allowance scheme, a health service virtually financed out of taxes, and a social security payment based on a disproportionately large exchequer contribution. I remember that I once said in the House of Commons before the end of the war that after the war we must expect the unskilled wage to be as high as £4 and the skilled wage at least £6. This was considered at the time to be greatly daring. As I write, the average male weekly wage is over £40, and miners earn about £5000 a year. In itself this is, of course, wholly to the good. But it does stultify many or perhaps most of our social calculations of 1943. At the same time I remember incurring the wrath of an ancient dame for saying that, after the war, every house would require a fridge as part of its standard household equipment. The almost universal provision of television sets, increasingly in colour, multiple motor cars, washing and washing-up machines, and other household appliances was almost entirely unforeseen. Indeed, many of these appliances were almost unknown. It is manifest that, in an age of growing affluence, many of the social benefits we have provided are on a scale and financed in a manner adapted to an age of poverty, and are increasingly unnecessary unless they are paid for either as a cost on industry or at the point of consumption by the consumer. It is significant that post-war societies which were rather slower off the mark than we in devising their social security systems have financed them differently, while providing benefits which are actually more generous than our own.

It is also clear that although a great number of people talk very loudly about a fair society, or a just distribution of wealth, they continue to think in pre-war terms as to where the injustice lies and in what it consists. The contrast is less between the wage-earning class and the professional class than between people of any class who have handicaps of one sort and another which prevent them from joining in the general benefits of a fully employed and affluent society and those whose health and industry and bargaining power put them in a situation in which, whilst they may need insurance, they do not need much looking after unless they fall into one of the special situations which need assistance. A great deal of sympathy is wasted on imaginary evils. If any attempt is made to assist classes of particularly vulnerable people instead of increasing benefits across the board, a wail of indignation is raised about a means-tested society.

The method of financing social spending on benefits mainly out of taxpayers' money has meant on the whole that we have spent less on medical treatment than comparable societies abroad, and the health service in particular has gradually fallen behind. The immense expenditure has meant that there was less money available for genuine social investment, and public investment of all kinds.

The Beveridge proposals were avowedly based on the assumption that it was desirable to transfer part of the national income to the wage earner. With average wages at the present level and continued full employment this is simply not required. What has become desirable is a form of wage-related insurance designed to meet the growing gap which is likely to exist between the worker in work and one who from age, handicap, redundancy or the like suffers some sudden diminution in his income. This is only now gradually understood and has rather unfortunately become something of a party political issue.

The real necessities of social policy have been obscured, I fear deliberately, by a set of bogus figures designed to show that an absurdly high proportion of the nation's wealth or income, as is even less plausibly alleged, is owned by an equally absurdly low proportion of the nation's population. I thought that I had exploded the dishonesty of the methods of calculation involved as long ago as 1947 in my *Case for Conservatism*. It has recently been done again, and more scientifically, by a group of researchers who have published calculations based on a fairer and more accurate method. The result is altogether different from that alleged in the propaganda figures. The crucial fact is that it largely depends on what rights are designated as proprietary. In a modern industrial society the average man and woman, apart from the property he owns himself, which includes, often enough, a house and its contents, a motor car, and the various household appliances I have described, enjoys various contingent rights which in any other age would have been described as proprietary but, because they have a statutory origin, are not seen to be charged upon the property of the nation. He can educate his children free, as if he had paid an insurance premium to do so. He has free health insurances in the form of a national health service, and partly free insurance against old age, sickness, or unemployment, – even when the last is caused by industrial action. In addition, he has shares in various provident and pension funds and, of course, he notionally owns his own share in the vast capital value of public property and of nationalized industries. Given the fact that he is, in fact, better off than any previous generation of British subjects, I cannot myself see on what principle of justice or common sense he has a moral or social right to demand a proportionate share in wealth as wealth, or what good it would do him if he got it. I can see, of course, what good it does power-hungry politicians to bribe him to vote for them with the promise of other people's money. I can even see that, in a misguided moment, a sufficient number of electors in a nation with universal adult suffrage might even in theory be taken in by such promises. What I do not see is the justice of it. In the last resort I believe it would be difficult to devise a policy less likely to promote an increase in total wealth or more likely to create a progressive decline into anarchy and class war. Moreover, I cannot see that as a political device it is less morally corrupting than any other form of bribery.

This leads me to my increasing antipathy towards the Labour Party, particularly that part of it which is actually elected to the House of Commons. When I first got into the House of Commons, the typical Labour back-bencher, and many members of the front bench, were old-fashioned cloth-cap socialists, like little George Griffiths, as far as I remember the Member for Hemsworth. They bore the marks of harsh physical work, sometimes in dangerous occupations, upon their bodies, and not infrequently one could see that their youth had been darkened by the fact, or the fear, of actual poverty. They were harsh, even bitter, men, and they often said harsh and bitter things, and I did not agree with them at all either as to remedies or as to the analysis of the evils they sought to remedy. But they were genuine from their notional cloth-caps downwards, and much of their energy was spent in describing actual conditions and needs which demanded attention and had every right to sympathy.

But the Labour Party today presents a wholly different spectacle. Of genuine working men with experience of labour they seem to have relatively few. Their places have been largely taken by university graduates with a grievance against society which seems psychological in origin rather than to arise out of some hardship or injustice actually suffered. While the old Labour Party was typically based on Methodism, its present-day members tend to a harsh and uncompassionate 'humanism'. Apart from this the party itself is, in fact, an almost wholly-owned subsidiary of the trade unions. By this I mean that four-fifths of the money comes from the trade unions, and four-fifths of the votes which control the sovereign body are trade union votes. I regard it as wrong in principle that any national party should be controlled by an interest in this way. But whereas in the past this was a factor on the whole which tended to control the extravagances of constituency parties, it seems now to be a factor producing a distortion of policies in the direction of the interests neither of the worker nor of the nation but of the trade union machine, and to be run more and more through demagogic methods towards an end clearly subversive of the interests of society as a whole and, over a longer period, of the interests of those whom it sets out to represent.

The Labour Party of the present is one of the most doctrinaire and bigoted organizations in the world. In contrast to the social democratic parties of Europe, it is the only Western party which still clings to public ownership as a shibboleth instead of seeking to make industry responsible, public spirited and enlightened, and of seeking to place a framework of legal rules to control anti-social activities. This puts it into a wholly different class from the social democratic parties of Scandinavia, Germany and the Low Countries. It is, I would think, the only socialist party which seeks penal rates of taxation for their own sake rather than for the sake of the social services and benefits which can be financed out of them. It is among very few similar parties which put its head in the sand about the Common Market. It has no conception of the extent to which Britain is falling behind other industrial nations of which it used to be the envy. Wherever, as in the north-east of England, and parts of Scotland and Wales, it has secured something like permanent domination, it appears to have achieved economic stagnation and petty tyranny, tempered only by local corruption. It always claims to be dominated by its moderates. But from the outside it appears to be schizophrenic in its attitude to society. It can never really make up its mind whether, on Marxist premises, it desires to destroy our society by exploiting its contradictions, or whether, on reformist premises, it seeks to save it by curing its deficiencies.

No one with the political or moral philosophy I profess could possibly desire his own party to be the only party in the state, nor for it to have permanent domination. But I regard the fact that the other main party is tied to a theory - socialism, and financed and controlled by an extraparliamentary institution - as a disaster. There was a time under Mr Gaitskell when I hoped that it might be at least beginning to outgrow its bigotry and doctrinaire ideology and develop into a genuine radical party. This, though it would not have attracted a man of my views, would have provided an alternative instrument of government which could have preserved the steady evolutionary development of our society and balanced any weaknesses and shortcomings that we might show. Under its present leadership, and with its present constitution, I now see no hope of this. There was a time when I hoped that a further setback after 1959 would have shattered it in its present form and driven its fragments into some alliance with the Liberals, and perhaps with some left-wing Tories, to form a new party on the lines I have described. In my younger days, and given the kind of hostility to new ideas with which left-wing Conservatives were then sometimes treated by the older members of my party, I might even have joined such an alliance. I see no hope of this now. With the left wing in the Labour Party and in the trade union movement in their present dominant position, and the right wing and moderates in the main captives devoid of initiative, I do not at present see this happening.

Of the Liberal Party I have always entertained very different feelings. The old Liberal Party of my childhood days, before the great schism which destroyed it after the First World War, had a solid social basis in religious dissent and industrial management. I do not think a national party can survive or have a useful purpose unless it has a dominant ethos and represents solid and permanent social forces. This is not to say it must be either a religious party or a class party. If it is either, it can only harm the national interest. But a party cannot take a coherent line, so as to form one of the main contending armies in a parliamentary democracy unless it represents solid social interests spread over the nation, though no doubt in different proportions in different regions, and not simply a bundle of good ideas which can be changed indefinitely with each change of opinion.

The great schism in the Liberal Party destroyed its old social and ethical basis, and to my mind it has never recovered from the blow. By the beginning of the First World War, advanced Liberals were becoming more and more collectivist and, when the great schism came, gravitated more or less naturally into the ranks of Labour. The pity of it is that they there became more or less captives of the dominant socialist ideology. Instead of forming the leaven in the lump, they were gradually incorporated in the lump and became part of it. Other Liberals, interested in the retention of free enterprise and committed to cautious national finance, gravitated by one means or another into the Conservative Party where they did a great deal of good, preventing it from becoming a purely class party, and forming the basis of a good many useful and rejuvenating radical groups.

But the Liberal name lived on. Since the great schism it has always lacked the elements of a really adequate national party. It has sometimes had policies which were extremely well thought out, and might have benefited the country had one of the national parties taken it over. An example was Lloyd George's election programme in 1929. Sometimes it has proved extremely irresponsible. But so, incidentally, have other parties with more claim to support, as, for instance, in the United States the Republican Party when it adopted Goldwater, and the Democratic Party when it adopted McGovern as a presidential candidate. But since the schism the Liberal Party has never seemed to me to make the grade as a national party. Its only consistent advocacy has been of proportional representation in one form or another, in the mistaken belief that this, if adopted, would enable it to survive and prosper, whereas its true effect would be to cause both it and probably the Conservative Party to disintegrate into various warring groups. Its function is to provide the doubtful voter with the illusion of a half-way house between Conservative and Labour, and a number of intelligent young men without mature political convictions with the opportunity of standing for Parliament without a chance of getting in or, if they do, without having to share the responsibilities of power or official opposition. Because of the relative solidity of the hard core of Labour voters to whom the word 'Labour' is almost a substitute for a religion, and the relative volatility of the Conservative vote, its abiding influence has been to weaken the Conservative Party. It claims to be a party of the left. But it never significantly divides the hard core of the Labour vote. Its successes are won at the expense of Conservatism. Its supporters are mainly those who could most appropriately make their influence felt by leavening the Tory lump, where their real allies are to be found among forward-looking Conservatives. In addition to these, it collects a fairly large number of random voters. On occasion, these included even rabid and extreme Conservatives of the right, determined, as they would put it, to teach the Conservatives a lesson and not quite liking to go to the extreme length of voting Labour owing to their hatred of the very word 'Socialist'.

When I was Party Chairman I was under very constant pressure from well-meaning persons of various colours to make some sort of deal with the Liberals of that day. Apart from two or three constituencies where ad hoc arrangements were made on a local basis under pressure from the leader of the party, who in this matter had his own interest to pursue, I did not respond to this pressure. Indeed, I could think of no more certain way for a party in office to ensure its own defeat than to be seen to make an arrangement of this kind before holding an election. But, in truth, such an arrangement was not to be made, and what would have done the damage was not the making of it but the fact that I had attempted it. If I had set about it, it would have been necessary first to make an arrangement with the National leadership of the Liberal Party and to have persuaded my Cabinet colleagues, the 1922 Committee, which was a body designed to have a will of its own and never slow to take umbrage at the action of the leadership, and the National Union. The terms demanded by the Liberal Party would have consisted of two parts, each of which would have presented insuperable difficulties to one or more of these bodies. The first part would have consisted in a demand for some form of proportional representation, probably the single transferable vote. This would have split all these sections of Conservatives, but particularly the Cabinet and the Parliamentary Party, the members of which would have gone scurrying back to their own constituencies to see how far the proposed arrangement would affect their individual chances of survival. The second part of the Liberal demands would have been even more difficult. They would have been driven to suggest that in a given number of seats, say thirty, Conservative candidates would be withdrawn, in return for a promise that in another given number of seats, possibly not the same, Liberal candidates would be withdrawn. This would have been an impossible exercise with virtually no sitting Liberal members, a very large number of sitting Conservative members, and a very limited number of Labour-held seats where either a Liberal or a Conservative candidate had a real chance of getting in. It must be remembered that, on the withdrawal of either a Liberal or Conservative candidate, the votes he would otherwise have got are not automatically transferred. A number of voters would abstain in disgust. A number of Liberals would certainly vote Socialist in the absence of a Liberal candidate, and the corresponding switch would also take place in some areas where there are a number of strong working-class Conservative voters. When it came down to designating the particular constituencies concerned, the task would be impossible unless, between the local Conservative and Liberal associations, there was already a feeling of cordiality sufficient to make the association lined up for sacrifice willing to withdraw its candidate. Such feelings of self-sacrifice cannot normally be imposed from above and, on the level of constituency organizations, nothing can be more disheartening or destructive for years afterwards of morale than such a request coming from national headquarters. Finally, and most ludicrous of all, if all went through up to this point, in a number of cases at least, no sooner would the official candidate be withdrawn than out of the undergrowth an unkempt John the Baptist type figure would emerge calling himself, as the case might be, an Independent Liberal or Conservative, or, in the case of some Welsh and Scottish constituencies, a Nationalist, and carry off all the votes which had been bargained and sold as the result of the arrangement. I think the Conservative Party owes me one or two debts of gratitude. But none is more demonstrably owed than this, that I absolutely refused to countenance any negotiations so obviously based on sloppy thinking.

I said some time back that a national party must not only attempt a policy which aims at the well-being of the whole nation, and all regions and sections within it, but must have some solid foundation in the social forces whose interests are at stake in the give and take of political controversy. The Labour Party is too completely dominated by the organized Trade Union movement to satisfy the first condition fairly, though obviously the same fact entitles it to claim that it has fulfilled the second. I have no doubt the Liberal Party sincerely endeavours to fulfil the first. If it fails, and I think it does fail, it is rather from insufficiency of knowledge and experience than from an insincerity of intention. But I have already said that it shows no sign whatever of being able to fulfil the second of the two conditions.

It remains for me at least shortly to discuss the ability of the Conservative Party to satisfy these conditions. It has obviously endeavoured to achieve the first ever since Disraeli said that the Conservative Party is national or it is nothing, and at the time of which I have been speaking the same was true. I must return at a later stage to current policies and philosophies. What I am more concerned with at the moment is the nature of the social forces which underlie its continued influence and outlook.

In the days when the Liberal Party represented Dissent in religion and the manufacturing interest in industry, I have no doubt that it was fair to accuse the Conservatives of representing the landed interest and, in England, the Church of England. I see nothing to be ashamed of in representing any of these forces, and the national character of the two parties was sustained by the numerous persons who formed exceptions of these over-simplifications. Gladstone, to the end of his days, remained an ardent churchman. Many of the leading Conservatives were manufacturers, especially after the Chamberlains came over at the time of the Home Rule controversy. Some of the grandest of the landed nobles, like Trollope's Dukes of Omnium, were, and had always been, Liberals. But of course all this had ceased to be at all true by the time I came on the political scene. By that time Labour, claiming to represent, and certainly dominated by, the organized Trade Union movement, was the main rival to the Conservatives. So far from the Church of England being the Conservative Party at prayer, if it can be said to have a political flavour at all, the Church of England is predominantly pink in outlook. But, in truth, religious differences as such have little direct party political significance. Certainly, as far as it is represented in politics at all, management in industry is Conservative in sympathy and, so far as I am concerned, I am glad to see it so, since it seems to me essential that management, as management, should have a political voice. But quite obviously management by itself would be quite insufficient to form the basis of a national party. When I was Party Chairman, I was, of course, quite well aware that many of our large subscriptions came from the management side in industry. But we were always careful to insist that, unlike the Labour Party, we should not in any way be controlled by our subscribers. Indeed, on the whole, industry tended to complain that we studied their interests insufficiently. I am glad to think that, so far as is possible in a country with a predominantly urban population, the natural representation of agriculture has remained Conservative, and the hold we have retained over the rural counties shows that, on the whole, we have done our work well, in spite of a strong undercurrent of complaint from the National Farmers' Union. On the whole I am quite sure that we do well to make the interest of the middle class our special concern. Class is no longer, even if it ever was, mainly a matter of income. This is one of the factors which leads so many of the pollsters astray, as I suspect that their samples, as well as being extremely small, are largely based on income groups and are thus biased samples. In particular, I have become more and more convinced that the professional classes and the salaried worker should become more and more the concern of Conservative candidates and members. This element in the nation is greatly in danger of suffering social injustice, far more so than the wage-earning class whose actual remuneration, owing to the increasing ruthlessness and bargaining power of the unions, vastly overtops that of many people who have spent years of their lives obtaining difficult professional qualifications and maintaining high professional standards.

The truth, as I see it, about Britain and, I would add, the British Isles, for the conception of Britain which I hold extends certainly to the Channel Isles and the Isle of Man, and, without impugning in any way their national independence, the Republic of Ireland, is that we form a unique collection of peoples. We possess interests some of which are identical with and some of which are wholly distinct from the continent of Europe, yet common to one another. Our relationships with one another may be, indeed they certainly are, anomalous. But the very anomalies are valuable if they illustrate, and maybe even safeguard, an important truth. This is that our future lies in, and our prosperity depends upon, diversity in unity, and unity in diversity. I cannot think of my own country as any unit less than the whole of the British Isles. It embraces all the parts of Britain, Wales and Scotland, no less than England. It includes both parts of Ireland, the Channel Islands, and the Isle of Man. I want some form of unity and some form of diversity in and between all these geographical and cultural entities. Above all, I wish to see diversity in unity apply to all class interests and other groups within the different portions.

I know there are those who wish either to suppress the wide variety of our cultural and social life in the interests of uniformity or of the so-called classless society, or else to separate, say, Wales, Scotland and Ireland and for aught I know the Isle of Man and the Channel Islands, from their largest partner, England, in the interests of independence. I find myself wholly and passionately against both tendencies. Separatism is the plain road to ruin and could only lead to chaos and economic regression. Classlessness could only be obtained at the price of continuous conflict and enforced only by oppression. The unity I am talking about has nothing to do with uniformity. Uniformity is the badge of tyranny wherever it is enforced. But unity is the price we pay for independence and freedom from external interference. The badge of freedom is variety. We all have pride in our different family, cultural, social and national traditions. Why should we not continue to enjoy them? Or why should we not respect them in others? Together we have formed a homogeneous group of sub-cultures which, together, have made one of the most successful political combinations ever seen on the face of the planet. Why should we seek either to disentangle the separate strands in the pattern, or to destroy the pattern, by making them all of the same shape, colour and size? I do not think we can disentangle them, and I do not understand why we should attempt to do so. My wife's family came from County Galway. My grandmother was a Graham of unmixed Highland origin. My father's family came, presumably, from the Lowlands of Scotland via Northern Ireland. Lord du Parcq, one of the finest judges of English law of my younger years, was from the Channel Islands. The wife of the Lord Chief Justice of England is Manx. Lord Justice Russell, the third of a generation of judges of English law, is a member of the Catholic community in Northern Ireland. Of twentieth-century Prime Ministers, Asquith, Attlee, Edward Heath and Mr Wilson were English, Lord Home and Lord Balfour Lowland, and Mr Macmillan and Ramsay MacDonald Highland Scots, Lloyd George Welsh, Churchill half American, Bonar Law Canadian, Baldwin half English and half MacDonald. What a pity it would have been if separatism rather than diversified unity had been the philosophy of the United Kingdom. At all events I will have nothing to do with separatism and nothing to do with uniformity. All this has been prominent in my thinking throughout my public life, and this kind of thinking sustained me throughout my Party Chairmanship and sustains me now.

27

Science and Technology

After the election of 1959 was over, and before the result was known, I crept round the Law Courts in the Strand to see what was going on. My reason was quite simple. I wanted nothing so much as to get back to the business of my profession and be rid of the incubus of politics for ever. I was exhausted, bruised and unhappy as the result of my two years' Chairmanship, and during the three months previous to the election I had felt, rightly or wrongly, that I had become personally distasteful to my leader, although I was conscious of no shortcoming on my part towards him, either from the point of view of personal loyalty or from the point of view of professional competence. I never attempted to enquire of him personally what, if anything, I had done wrong, and as he subsequently showed his confidence in me by seeking to make me his successor in the leadership of the party, it would be unprofitable now to pursue the question whether I was right in my belief and, if I was right, what the reasons for it may have been. To understand my feelings at the time, however, it is necessary to stress that my one desire was to escape, although I knew perfectly well that it was not likely that I would be allowed to do so.

I spoke of my troubles to Oliver Poole, but he was determined to return to the City and told me plainly that I would be failing in my duty if I returned to the Bar. I accepted this view, and awaited my interview with the Prime Minister with fatalism. When I received my summons it was to learn that he offered me the choice between a return to the Education Ministry or the new and rather amorphous Portfolio of Minister for Science, which I was to combine, in order to provide for my salary, with the almost complete sinecure of Lord Privy Seal. I chose the latter option, in the main because I was disgusted with the whole life of politics. I believed that in this politically minor but intellectually exciting field I would find some consolation for having to stay, against my inclinations, in public life.

My appointment was greeted with some degree of scepticism by the Press. Was it mere window-dressing by the Prime Minister? Why was he seeking to put the bell-ringer, the bather, the arch party propagandist in charge of Science and Technology? Was it suitable that someone with a double first in Classics, Philosophy and Ancient History, literate, perhaps, but not, it was thought, numerate, in a position of this kind? I do not know what animated the Prime Minister in making the suggestion to me, or whether he expected me to accept the option rather than my old love, the Education Ministry.

As a matter of fact, however, I regarded myself as exactly suited to the job, and although, outside the office, there were many miserable and testing times ahead, which I did not at this moment foresee, my years there were, in their own way, among the most happy and rewarding in my life before I became Lord Chancellor, and I believe that I was a success, a view which I think I am entitled to hold, because ten years after I demitted office I was honoured by being made a Fellow of the Royal Society which, as it was the first honour ever bestowed on me, almost overcame me with pleasure.

Since, however, this is not a memoir but a description of the development of my general ideas, I will simply give my reasons for what I have just written and explain why the experience of becoming the first Minister for Science in the world was so exciting and rewarding from my own point of view.

Nothing has ever disgusted and irritated me more than the talk, which was current at the time, of the two cultures, the literate and the numerate. I had always regarded the corpus of knowledge and culture developed in western Europe as a single whole, a spectrum certainly, but never a duality. It has, of course, become so large in bulk over the last two centuries that it is impossible for any human mind to cover the whole field. The age of the great polymaths is over, and to some extent the specialist reigns supreme. The best specialists of every kind are those who do not allow their general culture to wither, but use their specialty to develop their own contribution to general culture. The so-called two cultures are constantly enriching and cross-fertilizing one another in peace and war. Carbon 14 is coming to the aid of classical archaeology. Among the best code-breakers of the last war was my old friend and fellow-scholar of Christ Church, Denys Page, sometime Regius Professor of Greek in the University of Cambridge. I had myself obtained at School Certificate level distinctions in Advanced Mathematics and other scientific or numerate subjects as part of my general education. Moreover, professionally speaking, all practising members of the Common Law Bar, even including those who have specialized in crime, know a very great deal about applied science in a number of specialized fields. How else can they present a case involving medical or engineering questions or the niceties of forensic science? Or how can they advise clients or examine or cross-examine expert witnesses if they cannot master the intricacies of scientific evidence?

Moreover, my experience has been that all the best specialists are prepared to discuss their specialities in terms which the educated general public can understand if they have the intellectual equipment and curiosity to apply their minds. It is a second-rate scientist and, I would add, a second-rate lawyer, who treats his specialty as an arcane mystery, only capable of being divulged to fellow initiates. The man who cannot attempt to explain or justify the occupation to which he has devoted his working life is the man who has not thought about it enough himself. The truth is that the republic of learning is not open to everyone. To acquire or even to retain its citizenship requires years of self-discipline and study and constant alertness of mind. But, once inside, it is, as I have already said, a single world, a true democracy in which there is neither privilege attached to birth or wealth nor equality of esteem or merit.

A second fallacy which always annoyed me is the belief that the results of science could, as it were, be commanded to yield positive results, much as Moses, by striking it with his stick, is said to have commanded the rock in the Sinai desert to yield water. Nothing excited my intellectual contempt for the present leader of the Labour Party so much as his famous speech about the white heat of the tech-nological revolution, and nothing would have been more repugnant to me when I accepted my new appointment than to introduce the techniques of the Party Chairman, the bell-ringing and the bathing, into the administration of science and technology. What I sought to bring to bear was a clear analytical brain trained to absorb and apply abstract ideas, and to explain them in the councils of the nation whenever and wherever I thought it appropriate. As a matter of fact, by far the best equipment one can bring to bear in order to understand the intricacies of nuclear physics from the outside is the kind of philosophical equipment one acquired in Greats.

There are two more heresies to be scotched. The first is that scientists are necessarily mutually intelligible to one another. This is not so. Occasionally a figure arises like Solly Zuckerman, or William Penney, or Alexander Todd, who, with a scientific training, can bring to bear a truly scientific intellect on the totality of scientific problems. But to some extent they are the exceptions rather than the rule. The biologist does not necessarily know a great deal about electronics or physics. The engineer does not necessarily know much about physiology. There is a real sense in which there is no such thing as science, but only sciences.

The second heresy is that the politician can get results from science simply by pouring a pot of gold over what he is pleased to call research. If we knew exactly what to research into, this would be true. But you do not identify a suitable subject for research simply by pointing to a known human need. If we could identify the right questions to ask, research would be easy and, in many cases, unnecessary. The research which is really worth doing is a very difficult subject to identify. We all, for instance, would like to know more about cancer, disseminated sclerosis, or asthma. But the amount of money that it is appropriate to spend upon it does not depend simply upon the urgency of the need. Since all true scientific results are, or should be, public, it depends on what is being done elsewhere all over the world, and not what is being done in any one country. It depends upon the existence of hopeful leads. It depends too upon the availability of first-rate brains interested in the problems raised by those leads. There is nothing easier to waste money upon than research, and the biggest fallacy of all is to assume that because a human need can be identified, a politician can win a reputation for himself by spending money on the subject in the probability of getting quick results. In the absence of suitable leads, research money will be wasted anyhow. If second-rate human material is employed, not merely will the initial money be wasted, but it will continue to be wasted, for the second-rate material will recruit more second-rate material to assist and succeed it, and will lack the power to audit its own activities so as to bring them to an end when they have ceased to be useful.

All this adds up to the fact that, in the higher fields, research ought to be selected and administered by scientists, and cannot become simply a function of government. This does not mean, of course, that politicians or civil servants should know nothing of science. On the contrary, in my view, every spending department, like all big business, should recruit scientific advisers and employ some researchers as part of the normal business of administration. There is no other way of applying the results of science to practical life. Moreover, in a mature democracy, all politicians should seek to acquire some knowledge of science, and cultivate social relations with scientists. But the central organization of science should be independent of departments, and looked after by a mature politician without close departmental responsibilities.

I was particularly anxious during my period of office to cultivate my relationships with the engineering bodies and faculties. As often as not it is the engineer who puts the results of science to practical use. Moreover, whilst the scientist may be the intellectual of the numerate world, the engineer is the artist. All design, like all policy, is a compromise between divergent requirements - safety and cost, mobility and strength, speed and reliability, and so forth. It requires a touch of artistic genius to get the balance right. This is the function of the design engineer, whether he is producing a bridge, a motor car, a radar station, a military aircraft, or a safety razor.

When I took on the office, the professional engineers were badly organized into excessively numerous and rival institutions, insufficiently appreciated in the older universties, and perhaps at that time even in the Royal Society and in industry itself. I made it one of my main objectives to correct this, and up to a point I succeeded, partly through the efforts of a committee chaired by Dr Feilden, and partly, after I had resumed the office of Lord President of the Council, by my direct contacts with the Chartered Bodies.

The net result of my activities over the years was to widen my circle of friends and renew my intellectual speculation about the nature of the world, which to some extent I had allowed to lapse during the years of labour at the Bar, in the army, and in politics. I believe I gave scientific work a fillip by procuring more money, increasing at a faster rate than ever before. I also believe that the interest I showed in the well-being of scientists, and the nature of the work in which they were engaged, bore lasting fruit by improving the relations between science and government. I did not seek immediate credit for myself. That is the way, in politics, to achieve the best results.

I am sorry to say that some, though not all, of the work that I attempted to do has been spoiled. This was due to two, I believe mistaken, decisions taken by the first Wilson administration after the 1964 election. They are now irreversible but, nonetheless, I believe that their results have been harmful.

In my time, government spending on science was already divided between Defence and Civil Science, and by very much the biggest patron of science was defence. I did not myself see how this could be avoided, and I do not myself complain of the division now. My own portfolio was concerned solely with civil science, though the knowledge I acquired of atomic physics and of the nuclear bomb was considerable, since the Atomic Energy Authority spanned both fields and was my responsibility. Incidentally, this knowledge stood me in very good stead when I negotiated the Test Ban Treaty in 1963.

But the subdivision of Science between Industrial and Pure Science, and the subordination of the former to the Department of Industry and of the latter to the Department of Education, dates from the Wilson administration and is wholly wrong. The motivation was misguided, that is, an attempt to gain short-term political advantages in a false endeavour to command quick results in applied science. The total effect has been to weaken the influence of scientists on government, which I had sought to foster, and to make the pure scientist the Cinderella of the educational machine instead of a separate force with an independent influence, bringing pressure to bear through a separate Minister, with individual contacts with industry, universities, the Atomic Energy Authority and, not least, the Royal Society. The mistake of Mr Wilson has always been that he has never endeavoured to understand a subject before making it a political instrument, and the mistake of the Labour Party, which remains, in its upper reaches, authoritarian in outlook, is to think that the politician can command the scientist by the power of the public purse rather than be advised by him as to the proper appropriation of public money in the interests of pure and applied science and industrial development. However, government scientific endeavour, and the Chartered Engineering bodies, most of which have admitted me to their fellowship, have never looked back from the impetus acquired during the period of my responsibility, and, if we hear less now about the two cultures, it may be partly due to the intense trouble I took to expose the fallacy underlying this unprofitable dualism. So far as I was concerned, my contact with the scientists was personally enjoyable, intellectually exciting and spiritually enriching.

28

The House of Lords

Ever since my father accepted a peerage in 1928 on becoming Lord Chancellor for the first time, I have been interested in the House of Lords as an institution. My friend the second Lord Birkenhead who, as a young man, enjoyed embellishing amusing stories about his contemporaries which were often taken more seriously than they deserved, invented a series of myths about my reception of the news, and my reasons for it. The sober truth, that I was in fact in France when his decision was made, is now recorded by Mr R. F. Heuston in his sketch of my father's life contained in his book about twentieth-century Lord Chancellors, and duly verified by the contemporary documents.

But the fact is that my father did discuss the matter with me before I went abroad, since Lord Cave, the reigning Lord Chancellor, was known to be dying, and Baldwin had made it clear that he wanted my father to succeed him. I had urged him not to accept, since I felt sure that this was the advice which would have been given by my mother, then dead only three years. The fact was that Baldwin had told my father, as was the case, that there were only two candidates as possible successors to the leadership of the party. One was Neville Chamberlain. The other was my father. I wanted my father to stay in the race as, not unnaturally, I believed that he would make a better Prime Minister than Neville Chamberlain. I did not know then, of course, that in 1936, before Baldwin in fact retired, my father would have had his first stroke and would have been incapable of succeeding to the leadership. It is therefore quite impossible to gauge whether my filial loyalty was justified or not. However, my desire for my father to become Prime Minister became, in Freddie Birkenhead's version, an ambition to become Prime Minister myself. At the age of 21, although ambitious for myself, I was not quite so absurd as that.

Nevertheless there is some truth underlying the myth. I was anxious to enter politics by way of the law, and the fact is that it is, or before the Peerage Act 1963 was, a very great handicap for a young man harbouring such ambitions to be the heir to a hereditary peerage. It is not only the office of Prime Minister which is closed to him, but most of the main portfolios, including what is most attractive to the political lawyer, the two prime posts of Attorney and Solicitor-General. Apart from their intrinsic desirability, these offices are passports to a lucrative practice when one's own party is not in office and offer, or rather then offered, the virtual certainty of a high judicial appointment at the end.

I did not wish to become a hereditary peer. It seemed unjust that I should have this fate thrust upon me and my whole career distorted because of Baldwin's temporary embarrassment, in the genuineness of which I did not at the time believe, in finding a suitable successor to Lord Cave, especially when the alternative, as I thought wrongly, was that I might one day see my admired father hold with distinction the highest office under the Crown. I have no doubt my father genuinely believed that it was his patriotic duty to accept the Woolsack. I did not. But my father's opinion naturally prevailed. In reaching it he was fortified by the strong support of my stepmother whom he was then on the point of marrying.

I should make it clear that, while I always supported the creation of life peerages and the right of disclaimer in eldest sons, I have never been a supporter of the more grandiose schemes for House of Lords Reform, which have been proposed from time to time notably by the late Lord Salisbury, who was an enthusiast, and more recently under Mr Wilson's first government by Lord Carrington and Lord Jellicoe. The truth is that there are two ways in which constitutional government can develop. In one form, the more usual, internal forces create a revolution, as in the American War of Independence, and produce a constitution which may or may not prove lasting. In the other, indigenous and traditional institutions adapt themselves by evolutionary methods to the changing needs of the time. The former type of constitution needs to be rational, or at least as rational as contemporary ingenuity can make it, and all its institutions must be justifiable on some ascertainable principle of rationality. But traditional institutions can never be rational or capable of justification on these lines any more than a tree can be rational. Like trees, traditional institutions are natural growths and, if their continued existence is to be justified, they must be justified not on the basis that they are rational, in the sense that the design of a motor car or the American Constitution is rational, but on the ground that they are useful and produce valuable results. If the former is the case the tree is allowed to continue in the garden because it provides shade or blots out an eyesore, and an institution, say the hereditary monarchy, continues to exist because it provides the best focus for national feeling and is above politics, decorative, a tourist attraction, and solves a number of otherwise difficult constitutional problems. But it is there primarily because it is useful, and one of the main reasons why it is useful is that it has always been there.

I had therefore then, and have now, no fundamental objections to a hereditary house of legislature provided it served a useful purpose. I happened to think, and think now, that the usefulness of the system of the descent of peerage by male primogeniture, which was geared to a particular system of land tenure, will not last indefinitely. But at the moment I have no doubt that the House of Lords does a great deal of good and relatively little harm. When it does go, if it ever does, I believe its functions will have to be taken over by other bodies which, for want of a better name, I will call a Senate and a Supreme Court of Appeal, but when, and if, these arrive they will have to be justified not merely by their potential utility but by their being composed on some rational principle.

About a year after the beginning of Mr Macmillan's second administration, the Prime Minister sent for me and told me that the then leader of the House of Lords was about to be appointed Foreign Secretary and would then give up the leadership. I was his deputy and rather assumed that I would be asked to succeed, but the Prime Minister told me that this was not his intention. I could not blame him for this. I still believed that, in some way not known to myself, I had given him personal offence. Moreover, I felt sure that he had been taking advice as to the suitability of a successor from a source which I regarded as timid and over-cautious. However, personal decisions are taken with the heart rather than the head, and I told him that in that case I would resign and return to the Bar, which was what I had always wanted to do ever since October 1959. I said that I would make it as easy for him as I could by refraining from any kind of reproach, and pointed out that I had been serving the public now ever since 1956 at the derisory salary of £5000 without any parliamentary allowance, when my age and maturity, and the responsible tasks I had undertaken, would have enabled me to earn more than four times that sum elsewhere. I meant what I said. But, rather to my surprise, after a period of reflection, he told me that I was to stay in the government as leader of the House of Lords and Lord President of the Council. I therefore remained a senior member of his administration throughout its last phase, through the Vassall and Profumo affairs, and finally during the leadership crisis of 1963. Again, I regarded my continuation in office as a sacrifice on three fronts, financial, professional and personal, because I was finding that the prolonged deprivation of the pleasures of family life and personal privacy were telling on my nerves and doing my family no good.

The task of leading either House of Parliament is about as different from being Conservative Party Chairman as anything which can be imagined. The only point it has in common with the Chairmanship is the need to possess the capacity to influence one's fellow-men. It involves making friends with one's colleagues and the back-benchers on one's own side, and not antagonizing the main figures on the Opposition front bench. As the leader of the Opposition was at that time the pugnacious and formidable Albert Alexander, and included at least one former Prime Minister in Lord Attlee, this was no light matter for one who had been so recently Party Chairman. On the whole, I think I succeeded, with the exception of a terrible brush with a former leader, Lord Salisbury, when he made what seemed to me a wholly unjustified attack on my Cabinet colleague, Iain Macleod. I was much distressed by this breach in what had been our amicable relations, and I was happy when I was Lord Chancellor to pay a heartfelt tribute to Lord Salisbury on the occasion of what turned out to be his last appearance in the House of Lords.

A good deal of misunderstanding exists as to the present usefulness of the House of Lords. This does not depend principally upon its legal powers of revision or delay. These powers are both necessary and useful for two reasons. In the first place it would not be possible to induce self-respecting persons of the required eminence to attend or governments to pay attention to what they said when they did attend unless there were some positive powers behind their right of admonition and advice. In the second place, the judicious use of these powers has in practice compelled successive governments, Conservative and Labour, to pay more attention than they otherwise would to deeply felt movements of public opinion, particularly in matters affecting the environment and respect for law, than they otherwise would if all they had to contend with was their own machine-made majorities in the House of Commons.

But the real value of the House of Lords at the present day is as a forum and focus for specialist and informed opinion. The basic difference between the two Houses is not, as is generally thought, the hereditary or official character of most peers, lay, legal, or spiritual, but the fact that members of the House of Lords are summoned individually by the sovereign and therefore attend as individuals, and on occasions when they feel that their presence represents a personal contribution or service. On the other hand, the Commons attend as representatives and, in modern days, represent a cause, a group and, when supporting a government, an administration.

During Lord Jellicoe's leadership of the House of Lords I was astonished to hear that the daily circulation of the Lords' Hansard was actually significantly higher than that of the Commons' Hansard. My surprise diminished when I began to reflect on this, at first sight paradoxical, piece of information. The fact is that, apart from the four front bench speeches, some part of which is not seldom lost in uproar, much of the rest of a Commons debate is often a dreary mass of ill-informed and almost unreadable verbiage. By contrast, a debate in the House of Lords on an important subject, let us say economics, will contain, apart from the speeches from the front benches, contributions from three and possibly four ex-Chancellors of the Exchequer, two or more trade union leaders of experience, one or two chairmen or ex-chairmen of nationalized industries, and several industrial chiefs in the private sector. A similarly impressive array of experience and talent can be brought to bear on Foreign Affairs, Defence, Industrial Relations, the Environment, Education, Law, Local Government, Aviation, or any other major topic of controversy or public interest. There are, of course, eccentrics and bores, as there are in every other deliberative assembly in the world. But there is no uproar, no disorder and, by and large, there is civilized and well-informed discussion. It is quite unfair to describe it, as my friend Lord Beaverbrook once did in my hearing, as a House of Make-Believe. On the other hand, it is vital that it should never forget that what it is there to exercise is influence rather than power. Power rests with the Commons. But by virtue of the high authority and quality of the individual and collective opinions expressed there, particularly from the back benches, the Lords continue to exercise considerable influence. The wholly irrational composition of the House is in fact a hidden asset of great value. It is an absolute guarantee that they will never be tempted to exercise functions which can only be performed by the elective chamber.

While their main value is as a deliberative and advisory assembly, the legislative activities of the Lords achieve a great deal of detailed work which would either have to be done in the Commons or which, if not done there, would never be done at all. The great limiting factor in the modern House of Commons is the chronic shortage of parliamentary time. More cannot be provided without placing Members in an impossible position in relation to their constituents or their families. Sometimes there is a move to improve procedure in such a way as to facilitate the passage of business at a more rapid rate. But this could only be achieved at the expense of the legitimate rights of the Opposition or other minorities. In an institution governed by the vote of a bare majority, and that majority more or less in the control of the Government Whips, the power to impose delay in the passage of government business is the one effective protection which minorities and individuals possess in order to enforce the rational consideration of their points of view. If this right were taken away, Parliament would cease to be an instrument for the preservation of freedom and become an organ of tyranny and oppression. There is no limitation on the powers of Parliament such as that exercised in the United States by the Constitution and the Supreme Court. In addition to this, the power which rests with the Prime Minister of the day to advise a dissolution at any moment at which he thinks it convenient to do so makes the freedom of our own constitution one of the least protected in the free world. The shortage of parliamentary time, inconvenient as it undoubtedly is, is thus a most important constitutional safeguard, and it therefore follows that any government which has business to transact must use the House of Lords, sometimes ruthlessly, to tidy up legislation insufficiently discussed in the Commons, to perfect legislation which the Committee and Report debates in the Commons have left defective, and to introduce legislation which has no very controversial content in order to tidy it up before reaching the Commons and so ensure it an easy passage.

The House of Lords is thus a useful instrument of public opinion, and it has become more useful since I first became a member when my father died in 1950. When I first came there, the average daily attendance was about fifty, which was far too low to enable the House to perform its proper function. At the present time it is running at something like 250, which may be more than is strictly necessary. The Life Peerages Act and the daily attendance allowance have combined to effect this blood transfusion, and the right of disclaimer, though far from always exercised, has relieved heirs from an unmerited injustice and a great handicap. There may, of course, come a time when the House of Lords gives place to a Senate elected on some regional or provincial principle. It will then have ceased to be a traditional institution and, indeed, will no longer remain the House of Lords as we know it. But until that happens, it serves many purposes which could not, under our present arrangements, be achieved by any other means, and its venerable antiquity and continuous tradition possess a certain mystique which tends to support our other traditional and evolving institutions. The so-called 'built-in' Conservative majority is more of an embarrassment to Conservative Governments, which it seldom hesitates to defeat, than an aid to Conservative Oppositions, who quite rightly will never use it to defeat a Labour Government unless it believes that the public will support them. Speaking for myself, I hope it continues during the remainder of my lifetime. If it is ever abolished, I hope that it will be succeeded by something equally useful. I would never have willingly joined it until I became Lord Chancellor, and I bitterly resented having to go there against my will in 1950, when Mr Attlee refused me what a Conservative majority subsequently accorded to Mr Benn. But when I went there, I tried to do my duty as a hereditary legislator. I made it clear, however, that if I were ever permitted to escape, I would take the first opporunity to do so. In fact, I have been consistent in this matter. So soon as I had an honourable opportunity I disclaimed my hereditary peerage and offered myself for election to the Commons which, in my view, I should never have been compelled to leave.

29

Morality and Hypocrisy in Public Life

If this were an autobiography it would now be necessary to recount my part in the declining years of the second Macmillan administration, and the short and not very happy interlude under Sir Alec Douglas-Home. In particular, I should have to describe the extraordinary sequence of events which led to the sudden resignations of the Lord Chancellor and the Chancellor of the Exchequer, and the Vassall and Profumo affairs in 1962, and the change in leadership in 1963. Fortunately I feel under no such obligation, and I shall only make such observations about each as are necessary for the purpose I have in mind, which is to expose and develop those ideas which I have had from time to time about the conduct of public affairs. Briefly, therefore, I will only say at this stage that, from 1962 onwards, having expected that I should be one of the first casualties in any government reshuffle, I came to realize that I occupied a renewed position of confidence in the Prime Minister's estimation. By the beginning of 1963 my new role became more marked. I became a sort of trouble-shooter and the recipient of unusual assignments. I was invested successively with the foundation of the Ministerial responsibility for Sport, then for dealing with the serious unemployment which had developed in the north-east of England, and the forward planning which this entailed, and finally, in the summer of 1963, for negotiating the Test Ban Treaty. The culmination came when, after the passage of the Act which enabled peerages to be disclaimed, I was sent for by the Prime Minister and told unequivocally that he wished me to succeed him in the leadership of the party, and therefore of his public office. Until he avowed the fact himself in the course of a recent television programme, I did not feel myself at liberty to disclose the fact in defence of the part I played in 1963, although Randolph Churchill somehow got hold of it, presumably from Mr Macmillan himself, and published it in the course of his book on the subject. I was later informed that Mr Macmillan had revealed his preference for me to his intimates as early as February 1963. But, if so, he certainly said nothing to me about it until the eve of the Conservative Conference at which his resignation was announced.

In retrospect, both the Vassall and the Profumo affairs were badly mismanaged. I have nothing particular to say about Vassall. I thought myself that the Press had behaved very badly both towards Tam Galbraith and still more towards Lord Carrington. I thought also that the two journalists who were punished for contempt acted wrongly when they refused to disclose their sources to the tribunal. So far from regarding them as martyrs, I believed, rightly or wrongly, that they had no sources to disclose which would have justified what they wrote, and that, on being ordered to do so by the tribunal, they should have put their cards frankly on the table. They could hardly have had any information which would have got their sources into serious trouble. I thought that the Prime Minister was mistaken in accepting Galbraith's resignation, and I believe that his realization of this fact after it was too late led him into an opposite error of judgement when it came to dealing with the Profumo affair shortly afterwards.

There remain, however, a number of extremely difficult issues about morality in public life which can appropriately be discussed in the light of these extraordinary events, and some others which have happened later. I write with a certain amount of hindsight. Since the Profumo affair we have had a far worse scandal to deal with in the shape of the prosecutions which followed the Poulson bankruptcy. We have also seen a President of the United States brought down only about two years after a landslide victory by reason of defects in his personal ethical standards. Mr Heath's government was saddened and two valuable political careers of different degrees of distinction prematurely curtailed by the resignation, connected with one another, but in widely differing circumstances, of Tony Lambton and George Jellicoe. Mr Maudling's distinguished career as Home Secretary was seriously interrupted, and it may be permanently affected, by the reference to him made during Poulson's public examination in bankruptcy, without proof of anything on his part more serious than a certain want of judgement in selecting his business associates.

Obviously, therefore, the question of morality in public life shows signs of becoming once more a matter of public discussion. I am not sure that this is more than a coincidence. Every generation has usually managed to provide a clutch of public scandals. The Dilke divorce, and the Baccarat case, the Parnell divorce and several other cases in the Victorian age, including even the circumstances leading to the resignation as Lord Chancellor of Lord Westbury, were potentially every bit as explosive. When I was a small boy, my father was professionally engaged in the Select Committee investigating the Marconi affair, which, after all, affected the public honour of a reigning Chancellor of the Exchequer and a Law Officer and future Lord Chief Justice. Behind all these there must have been a vast array of other incidents in previous years which never came to light.

I am afraid that as the result of a television programme in which I appeared with Bob McKenzie, I have acquired the reputation of being a bit of a prude about sexual morality. This is far from being the case. For myself I accept and seek to practise and inculcate the full Christian doctrine. But you cannot practise at the Common Law Bar for more than forty years and be easily shocked. Moreover, while I was serving in the Lebanon I was ordered by my general, Jumbo Wilson, to defend every officer tried by court-martial for sexual offences since I was the only officer qualified by experience to do so in the whole of Middle East Command who was not already disqualified by being in the Judge Advocate's department. So far from being prudish in sexual matters, I am sadly aware that I have been coarsened by my profession into being insensitive on a number of situations when decent folk are still properly shocked, and that, though not quite as bad as Richard Nixon's or, even in translation, Khrushchev's, my language and conversation sometimes give legitimate offence.

What, however, is the standard of morality to be expected of our public men? From the outset it must be clear that there is an element of sheer hypocrisy which is unavoidable. In no system of society do political leaders rise to the top as the result of an investigation into their private morality, whether in matters of sexual morals, personal honesty, or anything else. In democracies, at least, any such investigation before they enter into public life is rightly discouraged. When I was Party Chairman, I got to know a good many seamy stories which never came to light. It follows from what I have said that politicians are in fact a more or less random sample of the community in respect to private morals. But, of course, they are more likely to be found out than anybody else. To begin with, they are news, and to go on with, there are more people interested to discredit them. In the Vassall affair there never was any real security point or any other point to his discredit about Tam Galbraith, who was wholly innocent of any wrong of any kind. Nor was there ever any real evidence of a Bank Rate leak of the kind which led to the enquiry affecting Oliver Poole. This proved, in the event, a complete mare's nest. Though Profumo was Secretary of State for War at the time, I never regarded the so-called security aspect of this case as having any reality. From the start it was a somewhat discreditable ploy to justify the involvement of a prominent politician in a sexual scandal. The same was equally true of Lambton, while Jellicoe, if one disregards the purely ethical aspects, was the victim of pure bad luck, since what he did had no relation to his public career. In all these cases, the politician is not only more likely to be found out than anyone else, but when he is found out he suffers a penalty disproportionately high. So long as his activities are not public property, even though in a restricted circle his reputation may not be of the best, nobody whispers a word. But when his misdeeds become public property, everyone utters cries of moral indignation and, when the hunt is up, as it was, for instance, about Edward Kennedy over Chappaquidick, every newspaper and television network in five continents feels free to put a pack of private bloodhounds on the track if they believe they can interest their viewers or their readers. This means, in effect, that we have two standards of morality - one for Mr Everyman, including the politician who is not found out, and one for the politician who is under scrutiny or whose sins are discovered. There is, therefore, an immense amount of hypocrisy involved.

I suppose that in one way this is inevitable. When I was talking about education I wrote that there is a sense in which every teacher is a teacher of morality just as every teacher is a teacher of English. This, alas, is inevitably true of politicians, and a large number of other people in the public eye, including judges and magistrates. About all of these, unfortunately, the penalty attaches not to the commission of the offence but to the fact that it is brought to light, and the standard of morality is to a great extent arbitrary. It is not the same as the morality we learn at school, or in church, or as we develop it in the course of a life's experience. Nor is it the same for all. The Cabinet Minister who was suspected of serving dinner in a pair of leopard-skin drawers during the Profumo business would have been ruined had he been guilty. The anonymous offender who was identified as being the person actually involved during the Denning enquiry, so far as I know, has never suffered at all. The Cabinet Minister who was accused of being the 'headless man' mentioned in the Argyll divorce had to prove his innocence in a particularly humiliating fashion. No one else but a politician would have been subjected to such degrading treatment. We may as well face the fact that the public imposes on politicians an arbitrary standard of morality which is not its own and which it enforces only in arbitrary manner when chance of suspicion or malice prompt enquiry and bring about discovery. But a politician who enters public life may as well face the fact that the best way of not being found out is not to do anything which, if found out, will cause his ruin.

There was, however, a real moral issue in the Profumo affair, just as there was later in Watergate. A politician must be trustworthy, and if he is found out telling a lie or if he is discovered in even a small financial dishonesty he can only bow himself out of public life. Although the Ellsberg burglary was indefensible, the original Watergate break-in may have been very little worse than a thoroughly discreditable undergraduate prank. I would have even felt some sympathy for President Nixon if, out of a mistaken loyalty for his subordinates, and on the assumption that he did not authorize the original break-in, he had simply sought to protect his subordinates by concealing their guilt. His real and much more serious offence was that he lied and lied consistently over a period of time. It became obvious to me after a bit that he was lying and from that moment onwards I knew that, if the lie could once be established, that would be the end of him, and this is what in fact happened when the last tapes were actually extracted. It was this element in the Profumo affair that I endeavoured to point out to Bob McKenzie, and why anyone ever thought that I was saying anything else I have never at all understood.

There are people, of course, who try to say that lying and dishonesty is one thing, and sexual morality something quite different. In a logical world, of course, this would be true, but logic argues without the elements of sheer malice and hypocrisy to which I have drawn attention, malice in political enmity, and hypocrisy among the public. If Chappaquidick, or the Lambton, Profumo, or the Jellicoe affairs have any message, the moral is clear. If you are found out, you are for it. If you are suspected, your enemies will see that you are found out. If there is a danger of your being found out, your friends will not be able to protect you, unless you lie. If the matter is purely one of sexual morals, and you are tempted to say that your private morality is nothing to do with anyone else, your enemies will point out that, things being what they are, you are a security risk, because you are vulnerable to blackmail owing to the penalty of being found out. If you are a security risk there will be statements, or innuendoes, in the House (as in the Profumo case) which you will be called upon to deny, or else you will be faced with a public or semi-public enquiry when you will be called upon to answer under oath. You will then be faced with the alternative of telling the truth (as did Jellicoe) or lying (as did Profumo). But in either case you will be made to leave public life in an atmosphere of humiliation in which your family will be hurt as much as you are hurt yourself.

Corruption is, of course, another matter again. But even here there is a great deal of hypocrisy. When I was Lord Chancellor, like the Lord Chief Justice and the Attorney-General, I was the yearly recipient of a bolt of the best black broadcloth customarily given to these officials from time immemorial by one of the City companies. Of course, this is entirely innocent, but it is probably worth not much less than the silver coffee pot which caused all the fuss in the Poulson bankruptcy, and when a Minister's wife launches a ship, as they often do, she is almost invariably presented with a piece of jewellery worth, perhaps, several hundreds of pounds. The general rule is that you must not accept anything which puts you under an obligation. But who is to say what puts you under an obligation? A civil servant, or a local government officer who gets a turkey for Christmas from someone who has had business relations with his department is probably in the clear, and so very likely he would be if he got a bottle of whisky. But what about a case of whisky? And what if, after he retires, he is offered a consultancy or a directorate or something even more substantial? Corruption is not easy to define, and although Gibbon is credited with the statement that corruption is the mark of all free societies, my own experience has been that, although most free societies are corrupt, societies which are not free are usually a good deal more corrupt.

As I say, corruption is, itself, extremely hard to define. But it is much harder to detect, and almost as catching as smallpox. Once a decent firm has been done out of a valuable contract by one that is corrupt using corrupt methods, the temptation to use corrupt methods is well nigh irresistible, particularly when the firm is operating in the export field, and the crime, if it be committed, is committed abroad and is not amenable to the British courts. In some countries, if a bribe is not paid, contracts are quite simply unobtainable. I remember once having to advise a very reputable engineering firm which had paid a bribe to get a contract in one of the Third World countries. By the time that payment had become due, another government had come into power and pleaded the corruption as an excuse for refusing payment under the contract. The new government was quite as corrupt as its predecessor. I was so distressed that, being a junior, I called in one of the most eminent leaders then in practice to advise me. But the answer was only too plain.

Corruption is so difficult to detect that, when it is detected, it should invariably be prosecuted. A mere public enquiry is not good enough, since the price you pay for such an enquiry is that those who appear as witnesses cannot be prosecuted. I was Lord Chancellor when the public examination of the debtor in the Poulson bankruptcy occurred, and there was an immediate demand for a public enquiry both in Parliament and by the Press, notably *The Times*. I could sympathize with the motives underlying this demand which, politically, was hard to resist. Nevertheless, I verily believe I might have resigned had my colleagues yielded to it, since it would have dealt a felon blow to the possibility of law enforcement in this immensely important, but extremely difficult, field. If an enquiry had been granted in that case, none of the trials could have followed, even if more of the facts had been established which is by no means certain, and every one of the offenders would have got away scot-free, at least as far as the criminal law was concerned.

Incidentally, I believe that in recent years too many enquiries have been held. It is such an easy thing for a government which is, in fact, innocent of any wrongdoing to grant an enquiry on the ground that it has nothing to hide, and wishes to be seen to have nothing to hide, and because it is told that public opinion demands it if only in order to be reassured. I think, in one way or another, I have been concerned with, or at least have studied, almost every enquiry since the Budget Leak enquiry before the war, which disgraced Sir Alfred Butt, and ruined poor old Jimmy Thomas. No doubt that one was necessary. But nonetheless I do not remember a single case in which, when the enquiry was over, there was not a well-justified outcry against the injustice which its inquisitorial method inevitably involves. The evidence only comes out bit by bit, and the allegations or the suspicious facts, almost invariably, are published and head-lined long before the innocent, and rather less reportable, explanations appear. I well remember the misery of Oliver Poole, and even the equally innocent Miss Chataway, then aged 18, during the Bank Rate enquiry, and of Carrington and Galbraith during the Vassall enquiry. Moreover, whenever the enquiry has a political basis, there is a real danger that interested parties will impugn the honour of the judge who held it. Even the Lord Chief Justice was attacked in this way when, at immense personal inconvenience and self-sacrifice, at my request he agreed to hold the enquiry into the Londonderry shootings. A foolish American professor, who had not even seen the witnesses, chose to gain momentary notoriety by attacking his integrity on the basis of reading the printed evidence. A similar fate overtook Chief Justice Warren of the USA as his reward for under-taking to open investigation into the death of Jack Kennedy.

Incidentally, when will people begin to realize that it is usually not possible to re-try a case years after the event, when memories are dim and witnesses are not available, merely by reading a transcript of evidence given and arguing for a conclusion different from that arrived at by the tribunal? Occasionally this is possible, as for instance in the recent case of Mr Docherty who was convicted of shoplifting in Newcastle when he had manifestly been on an outing to Whitley Bay at the time of the alleged offence. But this, and the ultimate vindication of Oscar Slater and Adolf Beck, are the exceptions rather than the rule. At one time the writing of books to prove the innocence of convicted persons threatened to become something of an industry. The trouble is that no one can make money out of a book proving that an enquiry or a trial revealed the truth and nothing but the truth. No one ever made much money by saying that the Warren Commission was right. The most you can get by that is a review or an article by the Warden of All Souls placed in *The Times Literary Supplement*.

I am glad, on the whole, that in general we have abandoned the Select Committee of the House of Commons as a means of arriving at the truth about accusations against public men. Occasionally the Select Committee does useful work, as did the Privilege Committee in the case of the unfortunate Garry Allighan, and, as more recently, the Judiciary Committee of the House of Representatives did ultimately in the case of President Nixon. But there is always the danger that a political body will divide on party lines, and in this case, even if it comes to a correct conclusion, it is a conclusion which carries no conviction and offers the public no reassurance. As a means of probing the conduct of public men, the Select Committee was, I hope, finally discredited by the Marconi case. Where such enquiries are necessary, they are better chaired impartially, and in most cases by a High Court Judge, supported by impartial and experienced lay members, and held under the Act of 1921, which was largely inspired by memories of the Marconi case.

One method of enquiry which has nothing to commend it is the type of enquiry presided over by Lord Denning at the time of the Profumo case. This was a private enquiry in which informers were encouraged and only the results published. No blame attaches to Lord Denning for agreeing to hold it. A judge is put in an impossible position if he is asked by the Prime Minister or the Lord Chancellor to put his expertise at the disposal of the public in order to reassure public opinion. It says a good deal for Lord Denning's shrewdness that worse did not befall. But if two of my colleagues, who had to appear before him, are to be believed, they got off by being in a position to prove their innocence and not simply because they were not proved guilty. One had been the victim of what was, in effect, blackmail, and the other of malicious rumour.

Incidentally, I do not regard it as appropriate that the Lord Chancellor of the day should be charged by the Prime Minister with investigations of this kind, as happened to Lord Dilhorne, Lord Kilmuir and Lord Gardiner. There is nothing in the character or qualifications of a Lord Chancellor which fits him for the role of inquisitor, even if his function is limited to making up his mind whether there is a prima facie case for further investigation. The most he should be asked to do is to read a dossier of papers in order to advise his colleagues as to the appropriate course. If a crime is suspected, the matter should be directed to the police or, in the case of commercial law, the Department of Trade. If a security leak is suspected, the Security Service should be used. If there is to be an enquiry it should normally be held under the Tribunals of Enquiry (Evidence) Act. But such an enquiry should not be held if it will bar prosecutions, or unless there is a strong prima facie case, either that some impropriety has been committed or that some natural disaster or accident demands an enquiry in order to establish the truth, prevent recurrence or, perhaps, reassure public opinion. It is very much for argument whether, in any given case, the evidence should be published when it comes out, or whether it would not be better if the report and the evidence could be published together. Whichever course is taken there will be criticism. The Act says that, prima facie, the enquiry should be in public throughout. But I well remember that when, exceptionally, this procedure was applied to the Trident disaster, the government was exposed to savage criticism for allowing it. It is true that that enquiry was held under another Act. But the arguments would have been exactly applicable to any enquiry under the more general Act, for instance the enquiry into the Aberfan disaster.

In the end, the public will get the kind of public men it deserves. Since politicians are not selected for the high standards of their private morals, they will in fact reflect the standard of private morals which is more or less current among the general public at the particular time. If they want something better, they will receive

it only if they are prepared to raise the general level. In the meantime, politicians had better realize that if they are found out doing
something which is in fact wrong they must expect harsher treatment than they would receive elsewhere. This may seem unfair and
hypocritical, but then, of course, they did volunteer in the first
place.

30

Sport and the North-East

The idea of a Minister of Sport has always appalled me. It savours of dictatorship and the nastiest kind of populist or Fascist dictatorship at that. I abominate the kind of sporting Chauvinism which relates the value of a country, or a school, or a college or university to prowess in organized athletics of any kind. It is a fact of life, and a very important fact at that. But it is one of the many facts of life which I view with distaste, though I must admit that when my own school, college, university, country, regiment, or county wins some important sporting contest I experience the same sense of emotional or spiritual uplift as anybody else, and a corresponding sense of gloom when 'we' are defeated. So there may be something good in this kind of idealism in spite of my distaste. All the same, I cannot bring myself to applaud it.

Moreover, I am not a man who enjoys 'watching' sport, and ever since I got rid finally of the incubus of compulsory games at school, I have carefully eschewed almost all forms of sport or game which depends on a marked-out ground, a racetrack, a swimming bath, a pitch, or what have you, to enable it to be carried on. At one time I used to play tennis. But I abandoned that after the war owing to trouble in my ankles.

Although clumsy and unathletic I am strong and robust. Before I lost the use of my joints I liked mountain-climbing and walking, almost to idolatry. I enjoy swimming in seas, and lakes and rivers. The little hunting I have ever done I found wildly pleasurable. I continued to scull up from Eton Rafts to the Queen's Eyot Club in a racing outrigger until well after the time my younger son went to Eton. On my father's estate and my own farm I enjoyed walking through woods and fields with a gun and a dog and, in more recent years, the generosity of my friends, and their tolerance of my bad marksmanship, has enabled me to join in that supposedly aristocratic and Tory pastime of organized pheasant, partridge and grouse shooting. But I suppose that nothing has surprised me more than being appointed our first Minister with responsibility for Sport, the more especially as quite unwittingly I talked myself into the job.

It occurred during a Cabinet meeting in which government responsibility for Sport was being discussed. It was being said that, properly speaking, responsibility for sport was being shared between quite a number of departments and authorities, education, local government, universities, the services, and all the voluntary bodies dealing with athletics, from the Olympic and Commonwealth Games and League and Cup football at the top, to badminton, fives and even chess at the most refined and esoteric end of the spectrum. I pointed out that recreation generally presented a complex of problems out of which modern government was not wholly free to opt, and which government funds were, in fact, and were likely to continue to be, committed in one way or another in coaching, in the provision of playing-fields, in matters of safety at racecourse and football grounds. I waxed eloquent on this subject, talking of the fares for Olympic competitors, and many other topics. I suggested that there was need, not for a Ministry, but for a focal point under a Minister, for a coherent body of doctrine, perhaps even a philosophy of government encouragement. Paradoxically, I thought, there was in fact a kind of analogy in the way in which I had tried to administer government science, making use of independent expertise, but not seeking to impose regulation or central administration. My eloquence had its effect on the Prime Minister and, before I knew where I was, I was left to organize the first government unit of this kind under Sir John Lang, who had been Secretary of the Admiralty when I was First Lord. As in most of the other things I have done in public life, except the Party Chairmanship, I always strive to work through other people with the minimum of fuss, as I find that this is the best way to get things done. This particular activity was a minor matter, and I thought comparatively little of it at the time since it occurred at a period when other things were preoccupying my mind. It was, however, the first of a series of special functions entrusted to me in Mr Macmillan's second administration which indicated to me that whatever it was, if there were anything, that had come between me and him in the summer of 1959 had begun to pass away.

Far more important, and correspondingly more exciting, was my mission to the North-East of England, which meant, in practice, Northumberland, Durham and the North Riding of Yorkshire, the so-called 'Land of the three rivers', including Berwick-on-Tweed. It did not include Cumberland, Westmorland or the North-West (although I had carried out a minor mission there when I was still Party Chairman), and it did not include Hull or Humberside, although it might have been well if it had.

The conception of the scope and purpose of the mission was my own in origin, and it was a novel experiment in government. It is for this reason that I include some account of its purpose here. For the first time since the war, the North-East was beginning to suffer from widespread unemployment and oppressive fears of a return to the hungry thirties which had produced the Jarrow march. Again it was not a matter which any one department could handle. The Board of Trade, no doubt, could offer grants and loans, and try to channel new industry from the booming South with a careful use of Interim Development Certificates and other devices. The Employment Ministry could do a very great deal in retraining and could offer advice on the trade unions concerned. The local authorities, and the Local Government, Education and Transport Ministries, could spend public money on various construction projects. Defence Ministries and other spending departments could place orders. But there was no one authority with money to spend, local or national, which could view the problems of the region as a whole. Moreover, there was no adequate focal point at which efforts could be co-ordinated regionally on the spot. Such government departments as had regional offices had few lateral contacts with one another, and their relations with the local authorities, of which there were about fifty altogether, were entirely separate, and in some cases almost mutually hostile.

My idea was to use the power of the Prime Minister, with some help from the Chancellor of the Exchequer, not to create a separate office but to remedy these weaknesses. This would be done by bringing a miniature Whitehall to the region, containing effective representatives of a number of departments in a single team, under a separate Minister, with special responsibility, formulating a plan and leaving at least a skeleton of the team behind to see that the plan was carried out. The success of the scheme would depend on a number of factors, including the goodwill of the employers and the trade unions, the co-operation of the local authorities in all their variety and at all levels, a rapid improvement in local morale, and a very careful and clear-sighted use of the limited money which was available. I was anxious to avoid competition with the other special areas of high unemployment, notably Scotland and Wales, and I undertook special engagements there to underline the point that, though I had special responsibility for the North-East alone, I was to some extent fighting a battle which was common to them all. Once more, I found that my arguments were persuasive and that I had talked myself into a job.

At the time I was appointed I had an important engagement to fulfil in the United States, and the first problem which I had to solve was whether to keep it. I decided to do so. From the point of view of public relations, the stupider media would, I knew, and in fact they did, exploit the fact that almost my first action on being appointed was to leave the country altogether. But, in truth, the visit to America was very much a blessing in disguise or, rather, I used it deliberately as an aid to my plan.

There was a tendency on the part of the press and in Parliament to demand immediate action by a Minister armed with specific powers. For reasons I will develop as I go along, this would have been fatal. With the backing of the Prime Minister and the Chancellor of the Exchequer, I needed no powers which my native intelligence could not provide. Without that backing, no powers would have prevailed.

There was also a danger, which proved to be a very real one, that the press or the Opposition would caricature my efforts as a public relations exercise by the old bell-ringer designed to win votes without producing results, and this in turn would lead to the difficulty that I would not be able to achieve co-operation with the Labour movement on the ground. Such co-operation was absolutely necessary to the success of my enterprise, since most of the local authorities were controlled by Labour majorities, and the trade unions in the North-East, as elsewhere, were heavily Labour in sympathy.

In the nature of things, the operation must fail unless it were very scientifically planned. What I was attempting was something which had not been seriously attempted since the Domesday Book. It was nothing less than a clear-sighted and detailed look at the resources and potentialities of a region obviously dependent very largely on three traditional industries then in decline, coal, steel, and ship-building, and suffering very much from the obsolescence of much of its social capital. The object of the enterprise could only be achieved if every member of the team could be inspired with exactly the purpose which I had in mind. This was nothing less than an im-provement of the whole quality of life in the region, and not simply the propping up of dying concerns, like the railway wagon works at Darlington, or some of the smaller Durham collieries, or the provision of specific jobs.

The danger of being treated simply as a public relations exercise was all the greater because public relations certainly formed an essential part of what I was trying to do. There was a danger that the region itself would talk itself into a slump with the aid of the media by evoking, with suitable photographs and TV scenes, memories of the thirties. This very nearly happened later. In the meantime it was midwinter. I carried out a lightning reconnais-sance, collected my team and harangued them, put them into action, and went away to America, at the price of only one fatuous, if not wholly unfriendly, TV programme from *World in Action*. The object of this preliminary exercise was to place my team on the ground, work out a programme of action, arrange for second and subsequent visits to the area, and lay down a timetable by which a report would be ready by the autumn. The report was ultimately produced after the change of leadership, when Mr Heath had assumed the responsibility. It was essentially and in detail the work of the Civil Service team. But I think I may claim it as my legitimate offspring as it owed everything to my original idea and was written under my supervision and to my prescription.

When my main visit took place in the spring, I was particularly anxious to arrange the public relations and planning aspects of the scheme to be in harmony. More than anything else I was anxious to be rid of the atmosphere of stagnation and failure which the media were only too eager to imprint once more on the area. I tried desperately hard not to be photographed against a background of the Newcastle Bridge (symbolic of the technology of the twenties) or to be seen 'chatting to the unemployed' or visiting derelict or dying concerns. On the contrary, I tried to be seen visiting the new trading estates, the new towns, looking at modern architecture, modern shopping centres such as that at Jarrow, new universities, technical colleges and schools, or even visiting natural beauty spots. The idea was to give the impression of a part of the world which was, or could be made, pleasant to live in, with a real hope of future prosperity. On the whole, I succeeded, but with one mishap. I always wear a bowler hat when on business. When I arrived in Newcastle on one of my earlier visits the bowler had been left behind. I do not now remember whether it had been left in the train or in the official car in London. The wind was blowing cold off the North Sea, and it was clear to me that I must have something to cover my head. Needless to say, bowler hats in Newcastle are not easily come by, and I do not like, or wear, soft hats. Being a countryman, I do wear cloth caps. So I sent my secretary to buy one of these useful articles, which was easily obtained. I reckoned without the malice and stupidity of the political world, which will always look for a devious and, if possible, discreditable motive for the simplest actions. The cap was publicized. The story was put about that I had bought the cap in order to identify with the working folk of the district. Apart from the fatuousness of such an attempt, the cloth cap image was about the last thing I was trying to promote for the North-East. Some people praised, but rather more ridiculed this supposedly symbolic gesture on my part. Nobody suggested that what I really wanted was a comfortable head-covering which I could afterwards wear out on my farm. But this was the sober fact out of which the legend grew.

I found the actual work, both in the North-East and in Whitehall, extremely interesting, but difficult and stimulating. I made it my business to begin with the communications, the railways, the roads, the civil airports, and the seaports, viewing the last from the point of view of the depth of water and their ability to accommodate the latest tankers and bulk carriers. Of the potential civil airports,

Middleton St George was in the hands of the RAF, and Woolsington was threatened by the Coal Board who wished to mine the coal beneath the runway. Of the roads, the A.1 passed through the region, of course, and there were first-class rail links to Darlington and Newcastle. But equally important to the life of the district were the A.19, which was then a driver's nightmare, and the commuter services. I also had to try to site a college of advanced technology.

It was necessary to write off somewhat brusquely various concerns which could not have survived as viable entities. The only rough treatment I received was at Darlington, where the wagon works were due to close. I also received a poignant letter from a North-umberland vicar pleading for the survival of an uneconomic coal-mine. In all such cases I had to harden my heart. It was absolutely vital to support only what could survive if it were given help, and to plant only that which could continue to grow naturally after the preliminary aid had been exhausted. Looking at the subsequent efforts of some of the Ministers who have succeeded me in the difficult field of promoting employment, I cannot help thinking that they would have been wiser to deploy their necessarily limited resources rather more cautiously and on the same lines. Neither a policy of refusing all help to lame ducks nor one of heaping largesse on hope-lessly uneconomic concerns proves in the end to be in the interest of the work force in an area.

Although my territorial responsibilities were limited to the land of the three rivers, I was at great pains to seek to promote in other parts of the country projects which would increase the demand for the local products of the North-East, power stations on the Thames Estuary which would burn North-Eastern coal carried in North-Eastern ships, and bridges over rivers which would use North-Eastern steel. In all this I was careful not to specify the area from which the steel or the coal should come. It seemed to me of great importance that I should not antagonize those who were carrying out similar work on behalf of other areas like Lancashire, Wales or Scotland.

On the ground, I not only promoted the development of existing new towns, but sought to plan the location of fresh ones, and fresh trading estates. I also tried to interest local authorities in the renewal of urban centres, notably in Newcastle itself, where plans were al-ready fairly far advanced. For the first and only time in my political life, I enlisted the churches on my side, and called meetings of the clergy of all denominations in each of the dioceses concerned. I tried to explain to them what I was about. I asked them frankly to call upon the people to pray for the success of my enterprise. I believe myself in the efficacy of prayer. But even on the purely natural and psychological level, I felt convinced that, if people pray for a thing, it helps to put heart into it, and to identify their individual purposes with that of the enterprise as a whole. I see nothing wrong or cynical about this. At the deep level at which prayer operates, there is no contradiction between the natural and the divine.

My own part in the enterprise was completed before midsummer. But I intended the activity to have two results which have not, I think, borne all the fruit I had hoped. I regarded my own voyage of discovery as a pilot experiment to promote not only the well-being of the North-East but regional planning throughout the country. Only in Scotland was this challenge fully accepted. In the second place, I had intended that what had started as an empirical approach to a problem of regional development should end by becoming the foundation for a policy of regional devolution on a scale and of a type never before seen in this country. Perhaps if the Macmillan government had lasted, or the change of leadership had gone differently, these two thoughts might have gone further than they did. In the meantime, two new ordeals awaited me before 1963 was over, the negotiation of the Test Ban Treaty and the disclaimer of my hereditary peerage. Each deserves some measure of notice.

31

The Test Ban

The first time I ever heard of the potentialities of the atom was on the occasion of a Commem. Ball at New College when I was at Oxford. Three things happened on that memorable night. There was a total eclipse of the sun which did not prove very exciting as the sky was totally obscured by cloud. Frank Pakenham met Elizabeth Harman for the first time, and that led to one of the fruitful matrimonial partnerships of our time. Somebody split the atom, but despite an announcement in the marquee by John Maud, who seemed in some sense to be in charge of the proceedings, it failed, then, to blow up the world. Indeed I am told that, at an earlier stage of his experiments, Rutherford had remarked blithely that the investigation on which he was engaged could, he was glad to think, have no practical application whatever.

The next time I gave the matter a thought was in 1945 when I was joint Parliamentary Under-Secretary for Air – almost the last man to have been appointed a Minister in the Coalition Government. Mere Under-Secretaries were, of course, not entrusted with the really secret stuff. But somehow rumour reached me of an atomic bomb. I do not believe for a moment, I said, that it would work. But it did work, some months later and life has never been quite the same again. The morality of war is something which quite frankly I do not often discuss and do not care to think much about. But I do not believe there is much difference between what we did to Hamburg and Dresden and what the Americans did to Nagasaki and Hiroshima. If the true story were told of the old sackings and burnings I do not suppose there is much difference between these modern horrors and what took place at Maiden Castle some centuries B.C. or what Cromwell did at Drogheda. The morality of these things may vary enormously with the moral climate of the time, the state of international law, the necessity for what has occurred, and the objective justice of the cause. But mere scale in mass or indiscriminate killing is not by itself quite the relevant factor which it is represented to be.

Viewed simply from the point of view of humanistic utilitarianism I have no doubt that, to date, the existence of the nuclear bomb has been a blessing rather than a curse. Its use at Nagasaki and Hiroshima may well have allowed the Japanese to get out of the war with fewer casualties and in a shorter time than would have been the case had it been fought to a finish with conventional weapons, and, of course, American and Commonwealth casualties were immeasurably fewer. Since 1945, though there has been fighting on a significant scale somewhere in the world ever since, I am quite sure that the fear of nuclear war has kept the great powers from fighting as nothing else could.

But can a Christian look at it quite so cold-bloodedly, and if he can, and indeed must, unless he accepts, which I do not, the entire pacifist position, is this really the end of the argument? I do not think it is. Unless we can devise some adequate means of political change without war, the gradual head of accumulating injustice building up over the years, in a world of no war and no change either, will surely lead in the end to some mighty explosion. We were closer than most people know during the Cuban crisis of 1962. As, every evening, I came back from my work to visit my wife in the nursing home, where she had just given birth to our youngest daughter, I kept looking into the cradle and wondering whether I should not baptize the infant myself secretly, lest a disaster overtook us before we met again. Superstitious, you think? Yes, I suppose it was, but the fact that I entertained the thought shows how seriously I took events which were taking place before me and which I felt powerless to influence.

Quite apart from the danger of conflict between the great powers is the danger of proliferation. I have never doubted but that India and Israel would get atomic weapons by one means or another if they wanted them. The fact is that all uranium reactors produce plutonium as a by-product of their nuclear chemistry as surely and steadily as our own lungs produce carbon dioxide, and the problems of assembling a critical mass of fissile material and delivering it through any defensive system are not all that difficult if a power is willing to spend enough of its resources in doing so. It used to be the case that the diffusion plant necessary to produce enriched uranium was sufficiently large to be detected and monitored from the air or by satellite. I do not think this would be true of a centrifuge, and in any case, despite all precautions, it should be possible to obtain fissile material by other means than making it at home. Obviously, the possession by a number of powers of atomic weapons, and the means of delivery, multiplies the danger of atomic and nuclear war by a factor that is impossible to calculate. If a nuclear war broke out on any scale, the resultant pollution can only be guessed at, because it would depend on the type and number of weapons used, the duration of the exchange, and the targets on which, and the manner in which, they were employed.

At the time of which I am writing, that is in 1963, public opinion was sensitive about the testing of nuclear devices in the atmosphere. It was evident to me that the danger of this was very heavily exaggerated, and over-emotively discussed. I have never quite understood why public opinion should be so heavily apathetic about 50,000 odd lives every year lost unnecessarily from cigarette smoking and other pollution and so extremely sensitive about the minute quantities of strontium 90 and other isotopes procured by an atomic or thermonuclear explosion. Whilst it is undeniable that these must cause some danger, the quantities involved were so minute, even at the height of the American and Russian tests, that it has, so far as I know, proved quite impossible to relate any single human death, still less any single human deformity, to atmospheric fall-out. Nonetheless, by the summer of 1963 American and Russian tests in the atmosphere were increasing in scale. The effects are, of course, cumulative, since the life of strontium 90 is relatively long and it was obvious, therefore, that if they went on indefinitely, sooner or later a point would be reached when significant damage would be done. By that time, of course, owing to the long life of the pollutant, the damage, if not permanent, would be persistent and continuing, and little could be done about it. Moreover, since the degree of contamination bears a relationship to rainfall, the British Islands, and particularly the western half of them, would be particularly affected. At the end of the day, I am bound to say that I was more worried about an outbreak of atomic war in the Northern Hemisphere than I was about atomic tests in themselves.

However this may be, it is clear that, if nothing else stood to his credit, Harold Macmillan's influence in bringing about the negotiation of the partial Test Ban Treaty would entitle him to be treated as one of the great benefactors of this generation. Obviously praise must also go to the Russian authorities, and to Jack Kennedy, whose handling of the Cuban crisis also won my intense admiration. But the main credit goes to Harold Macmillan. He it was who saw that the time was ripe, and the parties were willing, and I do not myself believe that, if Britain had been absent from that table, a viable agreement would at that time have been negotiated, since Russian relationships with the United States were far less relaxed then than now.

That I was the Minister selected for the task of leading the British team has always been a matter of surprise to me. It is the one important international negotiation which I have ever undertaken at that level, and I was at pains to warn the Prime Minister of the risk he was running in entrusting this delicate matter to inexperienced hands. I also reminded him that the reputation that I bore, though I believe unjustly, was not that of a tactful man in the sense that I was good at flattery. I was assured that all these things had been taken into account and fully discounted and that the choice was deliberate.

A barrister, however, is not necessarily a bad diplomat. Of course, his professional success largely consists in winning his cases but, in civil litigation at least, a great deal of his time is spent in negotiation and settlement. A good counsel is one who senses the point of time at which his case appears to be at its strongest, even perhaps stronger than it really is. If he chooses that moment to close with a favourable offer, he is worth much money to his client.

In order to prepare myself for the event, I underwent an intensive course of preparation, both as to secret and non-classified matter, and as to international factors governing the event. On the British side, we were all anxious to conclude a total test ban agreement, which would have brought all testing to an end completely. Not surprisingly, but disappointingly, this proved impossible in the

event. The Americans required a measure of inspection facilities
which proved unacceptable to the Russians, who showed themselves
hypersensitive to the danger of espionage on Russian soil. I offered
Penney as a scientific mediator, but the offer was refused and he
went home. I was myself satisfied that both sides were fully determined to go on testing underground and, having reached this conclusion fairly early on, I went all out for a partial ban.

On the personal side, we held a briefing meeting at Birch Grove.
Kennedy was there and it was my only meeting with him. He was
assassinated before Christmas. I found him a captivating human
being, quite unlike any other politician I have known, and I was
moved to tears at the news of his death. He also seemed to me to
stand head and shoulders above anyone else on the American side.
The others seemed all to be taking up positions dictated by their
departmental responsibilities. He alone appeared to me to be aware
of the world-wide importance of what we were attempting, and to
be capable of grasping the subject as a whole. He had selected Harriman as my opposite number on the American side; unlike me Harriman had vast experience, and especially of the Russians, whom he had
dealt with on and off since 1943. There is no 'H' in the Russian
alphabet, and I was, and am, puzzled by an apparent anomaly which
appeared the moment we arrived in Moscow. Harriman was always
known to the Russians as Mr Garriman (as in the well-known
Shakespeare play *Gamlet*). I was known, equally consistently, as
Khailsham. No one was able to explain this to me.

I do not even now feel at liberty to discuss the course which the
negotiation took. There were ups and downs and each national team
had many opportunities to display their peculiar characteristics.
Every morning we would spend hard at work. After the morning
session we would then leave the lawyers and other experts to hammer
out a text of what we had agreed during the morning. In the evening,
the American and British teams would meet alternately in each
other's embassies to compare notes and agree a plan of action for
the next day. At the time we were negotiating we were well aware
that concurrent talks were going on with a Chinese delegation. It
was, I think, the crucial moment of the parting of the ways. It may
or may not have been significant that our own agreement matured
after the Chinese had disappeared in dudgeon. I remember quite by

chance meeting Mr Suslov standing morosely by himself when I had left a reception in one of the main buildings. I understood him to be the great doctrinal expert in political theory, and he had, apparently, been in charge of the Chinese negotiations. The last time I had met him was at a reception in London when he rebuked me for anti-Soviet utterances.

I was left very much with the impression that, although we were by very much the smallest of the participants, our presence at the table did act as a catalyst. Obviously we would never have reached agreement if the two Great Powers had not basically wished for one and, within limits, thought it to their interest to conclude one. But again and again there seemed to be an emotional block between the two sides which prevented agreement being come to. This was all the more difficult because the Americans, at that time, had not the advantage of the same degree of communication with their base in Washington as we had with London by virtue of our reciprocal arrangements with the Russians. The final act of the agreement was negotiated with the President himself in the White House over an open line from a part of the Russian Foreign Office. A strange memory occurs to me of a New York telephone operator failing to understand Harriman's urgent request to be put through to the White House. She claimed she did not know what he was talking about. When the deal was through, the British delegation gave me dinner at their hotel. I was immensely gratified our mission had been successful. It was not, as I had hoped, immediately followed by a détente between East and West, and the Test Ban itself has not been accepted by France or China. But it was the biggest step forward in international relations since the beginning of the Cold War, and it has always been a matter of great satisfaction to me that I played my part in it. It is also the last time that Britain appeared in international negotiations as a great power.

32

The Leadership

If I were asked to describe the many odd things which have happened to me at one time or another, I would have to say that one of the oddest of all was that at one time I was within measurable distance of being Prime Minister, so close, in fact, that I was even designated by the previous incumbent as being his favoured choice.

Since 1928, when my father became Lord Chancellor, and I the heir to a hereditary peerage, I had always assumed that the highest offices of state were closed to me. I had made a brief, sincere, but totally ineffective attempt to escape from my destiny when my father died in 1950. Mr Attlee, then Prime Minister, chose to misunderstand what I was asking for, I was asking for no special privilege for myself. I was asking for a general law, of the kind which was ultimately accorded to Mr Benn by a Conservative Government. I could not carry things to the lengths he did because it is against my philosophy to defy the law. Fortunately the temptation to abandon my principles was small. Being Conservatives, my Oxford constituents would not have allowed me to carry things to the lengths pursued by Mr Benn. After my protest, I accepted membership of the House of Lords and sought to do my duty in it. By the curious sequence of events I have described, in spite of my desire to pursue a judicial career, in 1963 I was Leader of the House.

At this stage there were two very plain facts to be seen. The first was that Harold Macmillan's days as leader of the Conservative Party were numbered. We did not then know, as we know now, that he was a sick man. What was obvious was that, though he was occasionally at his superb best (as, for example, in his timing and superintendence of the Test Ban), he was not seldom not at his best. His handling of the Vassall and Profumo affairs is open to criticism, and the 1962 reshuffle which, to my surprise, I had survived, was clumsily, and even not kindly, done, although some of the casualties I thought were not ill-chosen. The second fact was that there was no obvious candidate to succeed him. The main alternatives seemed to be R. A. Butler, who would have been acceptable to me, but not to many right-wing and middle of the road Conservatives, and Maudling who, at that stage, although I admired his qualities, seemed to me to combine most of Butler's disadvantages without all his distinction. At this stage of the proceedings two significant events occurred. The first Lord Stansgate died and was succeeded by his heir, the Hon. Anthony Wedgwood Benn, MP. The second event was that, after it became apparent that legislation to exonerate Benn from the handicap of the peerage was probably going through in some form, Oliver Poole visited me in my office in Richmond Terrace and told me that I ought to consider myself as a potential successor to Harold Macmillan. I now think that, directly or indirectly, Harold Macmillan's preference for myself was probably at the bottom of this approach. I did not treat Poole's suggestion seriously at the time. On the other hand, I had always made it plain that I would stick to the resolve I made at the age of 21 in 1928 and, if a chance occurred to me to escape from the House of Lords, I would take it, if only to prove that I had been sincere and consistent all this time in what I had said about reluctant heirs. It must have been about now that I talked to Alec Home about the situation. He was my predecessor as Leader of the House, and the reigning Foreign Secretary. He told me that he had no thought of disclaiming, and I told him, and we both agreed, that it was not in the public interest that we both should do so. At that stage I was only concerned to disclaim myself. It did not occur to me that either Alec or I were potential Prime Ministers.

I cannot now remember the exact stage that the Stansgate business had reached at the time I went to Moscow over the Test Ban and, as my intention is to write this book as I remember events, I am not going to verify the references. What I do remember, however, was the course of events which was slowly unrolling before Parliament. The result of Benn's by-election had been a Select Committee, a joint Select Committee and, by the time I went to Moscow, unless I am vastly mistaken, there was a Bill before the House, which had come up from the Commons to the Lords and was later sent back to the Commons with a Lords' amendment which was actually passed against the government whilst I was negotiating the Test Ban in Moscow.

The Select Committee, whose report gave birth to the Bill, had been sitting since 1962. I had given evidence before it twice, and my second piece of evidence changed the course of events. Both memoranda are published. There was always a strong lobby, at least amongst the Conservatives, which wished to make it as difficult, even as humiliating, as possible for a peer to disclaim his title. I was not one of these. Once a change was to be made, my argument was that the only principles worth pursuing were the public interest and justice for individuals. These principles, which were enshrined in my first memorandum, proved to be meat too strong for the taste of the committee. By the beginning of the Long Vacation of 1962, a friend told me that the committee had virtually concluded its work and was about to report that no peer who had in fact taken his seat was to be permitted to disclaim. In other words, Benn, who had refused to perform his constitutional duties, was to be released. Other peers, who had duly performed their duties, even when, as in my case, they had performed them under protest, were to remain prisoners for life. I was outraged, and sat down at the Leader's desk in the House of Lords to pen my second memorandum, pointing out the injustice of this. The memorandum was considered at a reconvened meeting of the committee after the vacation, and my memorandum carried the day by one vote. The Conservatives were divided, but by a majority voted against me. The Socialists, unanimously, I think, were in my favour. If I had not taken my second stand, neither Alec Home nor I would have been permitted to disclaim. Either Maudling or R. A. Butler or some dark horse would have become Prime Minister in 1963. As it was, Alec Home was Prime Minister as a result of the solid Socialist vote in the committee and my own second memorandum.

There was still a further hedge which was surmounted by a mere chance. The original Bill, as it was proposed in the Commons, provided that the first opportunity to disclaim was to be at the end of the current Parliament. The Labour Party sponsored an amendment, supposedly for the immediate relief of Benn at Bristol, to provide an immediate opportunity to disclaim. It was called the Gordon

Walker amendment, from the name of its sponsor. It was beaten in the Commons. But as I left for Moscow, I learned that it was to be proposed again in committee in the Lords. Had I not gone to Moscow it would have been my duty if possible to see that it was defeated in the Lords. As I had to leave, I had to depute the task of resisting it to Lord Dilhorne. Whilst I was in Moscow, I learned to my satisfaction that the Lords had beaten the Government, and the amendment was inserted. There was no prospect of the Bill passing without it, and the Government capitulated in my absence. Had they not done so, either Alec Home would have become Prime Minister in the Lords, or he would have had to dissolve Parliament immediately on his appointment, or else someone else would have succeeded Harold Macmillan. On such slight chances do human fortunes depend.

All this, however, is leading up to the events of that strange Conservative conference at Blackpool in 1963. It was known that Macmillan was not well, and on the Monday he sent for me and told me that he wished me to succeed him if he retired. I say 'if', because he had not then determined to do so, and was in any event talking about retiring, if he did, at Christmas. I had already privately made up my mind to disclaim. Indeed, I had never contemplated any other possibility since 1928. But so long as Macmillan was in the chair, it was manifest to me that I could not do so without an act of disloyalty towards him, and this, I felt, would be a betrayal on my part, indefensible in any event, but particularly so in the light of his confidence. Nevertheless my disclaimer was largely anticipated. I addressed a trade union meeting in Bloomsbury in the morning of the Tuesday, and followed it with a public meeting at Morecambe in Ian Fraser's constituency. At that meeting I was offered the seat in unequivocal terms, one of at least four seats which were to approach me. It was not, however, until later in the week, on the immediate eve of the important C.P.C. speech, that the news of Macmillan's resignation reached the conference. Both Julian Amery and Maurice Macmillan urged me to act. It was clear to me that I was free and, after speaking to Butler, who was clearly affected, I decided that, when I came to reply to the vote of thanks that evening, I would declare my intention to disclaim. I do not regret this decision. To have done so after the result of the leadership issue had been decided would have looked like an act of pettiness or pique. After the leadership issue was decided I was approached many times both by people I loved and people I revered urging me to change my mind. I rejected this advice. It does not seem to me to be decent, after one has staked one's chips on the gaming-table and lost, to pick them up again and walk away whistling a merry tune. But there was a deeper reason than this. Ever since 1928 I had intended to take this step, and I had said so again and again. The chance had come late. But it had come at last. Everybody believes that I disclaimed my peerage 'because I wished to become Prime Minister'. The fact is otherwise. I did not disclaim until after Alec Home's appointment, and after the new session of Parliament had begun. I had always wished to return to the House of Commons. I disclaimed after any chance of the leadership had gone.

Others have written about the politics of the change. I shall not do so in any detail. But I must make one thing absolutely plain. Once it was clear to me that the lot was not going to fall on me, I did my level best to secure Butler's appointment, and to prevent Home's. That it did not happen that way was due entirely to Butler's own choice. I had spoken my mind clearly to Home on the Saturday morning as we walked back together to the Imperial Hotel on Blackpool front. I did not think he possessed sufficient experience on Home Affairs. I told him that, if appointed, he would not remain there long. I like and admire Alec as much as any man alive, and when he retired from the leadership he was good enough to assure me that I served under him most loyally. Indeed I had, and there has not ever been a breach of charity between us. But I regarded his appointment as a mistake, the product of the tendency of the Conservative Party to play safe instead of taking a calculated risk. It is not always the wisest or the safest thing to do. For a brief moment, after my ploy to secure Butler's appointment had failed, I was in some doubt whether to go on. It became clear to me, that for me at least, resignation was not an honourable course at this stage, and I not only determined to continue myself but urged Boyle, who was equally in doubt, to change his mind and continue, and in fact he did so. Iain Macleod remained outside, and so did Enoch Powell. I shared, I suppose, their premises. But I rejected their conclusion.

There is a second thing I must say on my own behalf. I did not myself expect to succeed and, to tell the truth, I was not over-anxious to do so. I have seen too much of the office of Prime Minister at close quarters to have any illusions that it brings happiness to the recipient. I would not have allowed my name to go forward at all had it not been for Oliver Poole's conversation with me in the summer, and Harold Macmillan's express invitation on the Monday. I knew the Conservative Party too well to suppose that I would be readily acceptable in all quarters, though I fancy the constituencies would have welcomed me with open arms. But one thing I did, and do still, occasionally resent. There is nothing discreditable in almost being selected, after a lifetime of service, as the leader of a national party. Whilst I was in the running and after I had failed, for almost eighteen months I was assailed and attacked on every conceivable ground, both publicly and behind my back, as if I had done something discreditable.

As regards what would have happened had the chance gone differently it is rather difficult to say. As the White Knight remarked in *The Looking Glass*: 'I do not say it would have been better. I only say it would have been different.' On the whole, the circumstances of the contest, and the differences which it aroused, would have made it difficult for anyone who had succeeded Harold Macmillan to have survived the defeat of 1964. It follows, therefore, that my only chance of leaving a favourable mark on history would have been to win that election. Under Alec, the party very nearly won. Would the odd 250,000 votes have come our way with me as Prime Minister? We shall never know.

The wounds have healed. But they have left a scar. That they have healed has been due very largely to Willie Whitelaw, our Chief Whip after the change, and my gradual acceptance by a younger group of colleagues. I am grateful to them all. The scar is not felt at all unless, for some reason, I relive the experiences of that fortnight when I feel a momentary stab of pain. Only one permanent mark remains on my character. From 1940 until 1963 I used to write verses regularly as a form of self-expression. From 1963 onwards, whatever little rill of inspiration there ever was has dried up. I have written poetry no more.

33

Return to the Commons

I greatly underestimated the difficulty of returning to the Commons. I had expected to be welcomed as an old friend, and so I was, by some individuals. But the House is something altogether different. It never gives an easy reception to those who have an outside reputation. Moreover, there was no opportunity to play myself in quietly. There was the business of disclaimer to be gone through and, though it was done deliberately, I found it painful. Though the Hailsham title is not an old one it represented the life and work of a kind father and a good man. I did not hesitate about going on with it, but there was something miserable about it, and though I was convinced I was doing right, it was disagreeable even to seem to cast the smallest slight on my father's memory.

Then there was the business of the by-election. I had hoped in the heat of conflict to recover energy and strength. Of the various safe seats which were offered to me, Marylebone was my own choice. Three generations of my family had lived there; indeed, I had done so before my first marriage. It had been my father's constituency for seven years. At one end of it was the Regent Street Polytechnic with which I have been associated all my life. At the other end, up the Finchley Road, were the Quintin and Kynaston schools bearing the Christian names of my grandfather and my godfather, the late Sir Kynaston Studd. I was therefore no carpet-bagger, and my predecessor, Wavell Wakefield, had, so far as I was informed, long wished to retire.

But a London constituency is not like Oxford. There was no heat of conflict, and only a massive apathy, punctuated by personal attacks from my own opponents. By and large, the people who work in Marylebone during the day do not sleep or vote there, and those who sleep and vote there work elsewhere. Twenty per cent of the votes in the constituency at any one time will be gone before twelve months elapse. Public meetings are not attended and, as I was to discover later, if people want to see their MP they just take a bus or underground to the House of Commons. They do not attend 'surgeries'. After I discovered how to work the constituency I became extremely fond of it, but by-electioneering in Central London in December is not much fun, and the list of grievances, from the rates to the potential use of the coal-yard for Marylebone Station, was formidable. Happily it was a safe seat, and I did not suffer the humiliation of Gordon Walker at Leyton.

I then had to face the House of Commons and made a terrible mess of my first speech. I had greatly underestimated the form, and should have come out fighting. As it was, I tried to make an anodyne speech and flopped badly. I do not think I really recovered until after the 1964 election when I was spokesman on Home Affairs on the Opposition front bench.

It is generally supposed, and often said, that opposition is more agreeable than government. In fact it is difficult, unrewarding, and depressing. There is no Civil Service to prepare your brief. Facing you are the embattled forces of the government, superior in numbers, certain to beat you in the division lobby, and dependent upon your defeat in argument for their future employment and influence. The art, of course, is to keep up your spirits and oppose outright as seldom as possible. The flank attack is far more effective than a frontal assault, since the latter invariably unites the forces of the enemy, superior in numbers and, with the Civil Service behind them, usually in argument. The secret is to divide the forces of the government as often as possible. If they are faced with irresponsible opposition from their own extremists, sympathize with them for having such short-sighted supporters or, equally effective, sympathize with the supporters for having been betrayed by their own front bench who abandon their principles once they are confronted with the facts of life. Probably the most effective leader of opposition in my lifetime was Baldwin, which may explain why he had so little of it. But he had left the House before I entered. The best opposition spokesman I remember was Oliver Stanley. He utilized wit and gaiety, mocking his opponents rather than condemning them, and overcoming their taunts with indefatigable good humour. As a matter of fact, the most effective opposition often comes from the back benches or below the gangway. Aneurin Bevan was about the only effective House of Commons critic during the Coalition. Iain Macleod made his very considerable reputation as a result of a single attack on Aneurin Bevan, after Bevan had floored one Conservative Privy Councillor after another. All the same, opposition is a wearisome and thankless task unless one is conscious that at last one feels the groundswell of public opinion beginning to carry one forward. On the whole, oppositions tend to fall apart and quarrel amongst themselves. Governments tend to stick together, and close their ranks, particularly when an election is thought to be approaching.

34

Race Relations

Of the period of 1964 to 1970 I need say little. I tried to play a full part in the affairs of the party and the House. To the surprise of most people, except my clerk and myself, I managed to re-establish myself at the Bar so far as my parliamentary duties would allow. But the only thing which stands out in my mind in my parliamentary career worthy of general comment, which affected me closely, is the dismissal of Enoch Powell from the Shadow Cabinet.

Except in the immediate post-war period when I favoured re-settlement of displaced Poles and other refugees from eastern Europe, I have myself never favoured massive immigration into this country. This conviction has not much to do with race, although racial, religious, or linguistic differences tend to accentuate any difficulties there are for other reasons in any society. My reasons were twofold. In the first place there are enough people in the habitable parts of this country anyway. In point of fact, ignoring moor and mountain, it is one of the most densely populated countries in the world. In the second place, immigrants tend to congregate around the least desirable jobs. Many of these ought to be automated. Where they cannot be automated, it is undesirable to fill them with an easily-identified minority of underprivileged people. The result was that throughout the Macmillan and Home governments my voice was always used quietly but firmly on the side of those who wished to move towards restriction. But one thing I never thought honourable. If, for reasons of our own, we choose to admit the immigrants and, as we did, at least until 1962, even invite them, we have no right whatever to curtail their rights, depreciate their status or discriminate against them. Nor, taking every precaution against malpractice and evasion, should we encourage a situation in which families are split, irregular unions formed, or young men kept in artificial isolation. I do not think that in this I am being particularly idealistic or soft-hearted. I believe that this corresponds to natural justice, international obligation and, incidentally, enlightened self-interest. By the time, however, that we were in opposition a large population of immigrants had appeared, at first of West Indians and then of Asians. Some, particularly transport workers and nurses, had been more or less actively recruited. The name of the Minister of Health during part of the time was Enoch Powell, and, although I may be doing him an injustice, I do not remember him actively protesting. He certainly did not resign or, so far as I know, discourage the importation of Jamaican or Indian nurses. Nevertheless, before the end of Mr Macmillan's administration in 1962, we had partially closed the door by the Commonwealth Immigrants Act. We passed this Act in the teeth of bitter opposition from the Labour and Liberal parties, and from some Conservatives. I myself regretted it was not far tougher than it was and done earlier, and it would have been tougher but for the bitterness of the parliamentary opposition which came from all quarters, though in different proportions.

The Labour Government, however, passed two Acts of Parliament in 1965 and 1968 dealing with race relations. I found neither intrinsically attractive. I hold the view that in general race relations are better not made the subject of Acts of Parliament. What need to be protected are the rights of minorities of all classes and of individuals as such. If these are properly looked after, other questions can look after themselves. At Common Law, incitement to racial hatred could have been dealt with under the law of sedition, and what really needs doing is to bring a number of old laws like forcible entry, treason, sedition, and the like, up to date and within the ambit of a penal code. In practice, the 1965 Act, has proved wholly ineffective as I always thought it would. It was nevertheless less objectionable than the 1968 Act, and, although I was not then the official spokesman, I gave it a cautious welcome, on the basis that it did little more than strengthen the Public Order Act which was passed in 1936 under a Conservative Government to deal with Mosley's Fascist movement.

It was the passage of the 1968 Act which was much more troublesome, and by this time I had become the spokesman of the Shadow

Cabinet responsible for our parliamentary tactics and our official utterances. Both the Shadow Cabinet and the party were split three ways, and all of them threatened to adopt irreconcilable public attitudes which would make us look ridiculous as a credible political force. On a much deeper level, I was greatly concerned about the growth of racial tension in the country. If party warfare had broken out in Parliament between the Government and the official opposition on the subject I could foresee bitterness and a threat to public order on a scale quite incommensurate with the value or demerits of the legislation as such. I was determined at almost all costs to prevent either a permanent split in the party or an outbreak of a bitter dispute on party lines.

In contrast to the 1965 Act, which was virtually an extension of the Public Order Act, the 1968 Bill proposed by the Labour Government was an attempt to enlist civil law procedures in order to eliminate racial discrimination. It was very heavily sold by its enthusiastic supporters, who included members of all parties. Their propaganda was largely based on American research and experience. Of this I myself was more than a little sceptical because the whole basis of the American racial problem has very different historical roots from our own, American attitudes to race are very largely to be interpreted on inherited viewpoints derived ultimately from Negro slavery, the Civil War of the early 1860s, and the period of 'reconstruction' after it. Our own racial problems are of a very different kind, and stem from the importation of Jamaicans and other West Indians during the 1950s and early '60s, and a later influx of immigrants from the Indian subcontinent or of Indian or Pakistani origin. Both of these groups have characteristics and inherited memories very different from the American Negro, and I had grave doubts how far American experience could be said to be valid here.

The main idea of the Bill, which has since passed into law more or less in the form in which it was proposed, was to start with a blanket prohibition of discrimination, followed by particular provisions against advertising, and special prohibitions against discrimination in particular fields, like housing and employment. There was to be an enforcement agency in the Race Relations Board, operating through the County Court and by way of sanctions seeking declarations, injunctions and, in some cases, damages, where conciliation failed, and a Commission which, rightly or wrongly, I regarded as little more than a piece of window-dressing.

I was myself more than a little sceptical of the value of this legislation and, if I had been Home Secretary, I doubt whether I could have been induced to introduce a Bill of this type at all. If I had, I would have limited its provisions at the outset to large-scale housing and employment. These were the only fields where I believed there was at least a theoretical case for legislation dealing specially with race and nationality as such, and there was at least some evidence that, at least in the USA, such legislation had done some practical good. The point was that large-scale employers and large-scale landlords are sometimes terrorized by their workers and their tenants into refusing to engage or promote perfectly qualified black workers, or to let flats or houses to perfectly suitable black tenants. They can be assisted in their need to resist these pressures by the existence of an express prohibition against racial discrimination which compels them to do so. Outside this particular field, there is very little relevant evidence supporting this type of legislation. Where the danger of a serious social problem exists, means are found of evading it unless it possesses the support of those who are expected to observe it. On the other hand, where the support is available, there is as a rule no serious social problem, and legislation tends to be enforced and drafted in such a way as to excite ridicule and bring the law into disrepute. This has already happened under the Labour Act, where it was discovered some time ago that you may not advertise publicly for a Scottish cook who can cook porridge and haggis, a Chinese who can make sweet and sour, or a French teacher who can speak with a native French accent. I had predicted all this during the passage of the Bill. My own view is that law should be rational, simple and practical, and I did not and do not find the Labour Act of 1968 to conform with this prescription. Moreover, I doubt the advantage of special law enforcement agencies where they can be avoided. Such bodies tend to proliferate and operate inconsistent standards and, when they find that the problems they are asked to deal with remain unsolved, they tend to ask for new and more formidable powers instead of recommending their own demise, or the amalgamation of their functions with another body. I was therefore not enthusiastic about the proposed Race Relations Board, and am not surprised now that they are running true to form and demanding extra powers on the ground that their existing powers do not give them sufficient rights.

I was therefore no particular friend of the Labour Bill. It could not be written off as altogether bad. It was based on the defensible principle that before the law all persons should be equal. It also covered a limited field in which enforceable legislation could be justified but was hardly necessary. But my immediate problem consisted in the difficulty of presenting a cool approach to it without irreparably destroying the unity of the Opposition. There were in our parliamentary party, and in the Shadow Cabinet itself, elements which seemed at all costs determined to adopt attitudes which appeared to rest more on emotion than on sound legislative principles and common sense. Some of these favoured the Bill more or less whole-heartedly. The more powerful body of opinion, not in the Shadow Cabinet equally numerous or articulate, but common on the back benches and well representative of party workers, was as emotionally opposed to the Bill as the first party were enthusiastic in its support. They feared or hated the appearance of a large number of black faces in the streets to the point of total rejection and a degree of blindness to the dishonourable character of discrimination. I could understand this point of view. As I say, I have never regarded this island as underpopulated and was completely opposed from the first to any large-scale additions of a permanent kind. But I was sure that the great mass of immigrants had come here legally, some of them actively encouraged, that they possessed a legal status and rights under the British Nationality Act of 1968, upon which they were entitled to rely, that they could not be got rid of without a gross breach of natural justice and international usage, and that any act on our part to countenance, or worse, encourage, discrimination against them would lead to social conflict which it was our bounden duty to prevent if we could. I therefore regarded the second opinion which, had I adopted it, would have led me into direct opposition with the Labour Government as, potentially, the more dangerous. I therefore pursued a policy half way between the two extremes.

The left wing were, as I thought at the time, the more unreasonable of the two. They were a distinct minority, and therefore on any show of strength they would be beaten, and their defeat in open conflict would mean the victory of the right-wing element which was what they most detested and feared. Yet they went out of their way to make a cautious policy difficult by making it plain, not merely that they could make no concessions to appeals from the front bench, but that they would vote with the Government every time that a division occurred, and even join forces with the fanatics of the other side in trying to force the Government into even more extreme attitudes. As the Bill proceeded, this made the conduct of the Committee and Report stages of the Bill almost impossible, since without command of a united party in the lobby I had almost no bargaining strength, to enforce my own point of view or even counsel moderation to the two wings. I believe I succeeded in carrying out what was technically an extremely difficult parliamentary task, at the cost of only one temporary lapse of my calm, in the early hours of one morning at about five o'clock when I was subjected to hostile barracking at the hands of some of the right-wingers. Since this was on third reading it came too late to do any harm.

In the meantime, the problem I had to deal with first was our attitude on the second reading, and the first hurdle I had to surmount was the division within the Shadow Cabinet itself. I succeeded in carrying my middle of the road attitude with two exceptions, although it was still clear that when it came to a division the party in the House would be split three ways. We were in the recess, and Parliament would reassemble for second reading on the following Tuesday. There was one man, who so far as I was concerned had remained silent throughout, neither tendering criticism nor offering advice. It was Enoch Powell. I therefore asked him, after we had left the room, if I had explained the situation fairly. 'You could not have been fairer,' was his reply. That was all he said.

My holiday plans involved a week-end visit to Willie Vane, Lord Inglewood, in the Lake District, with my son James. The boys were to climb. I was due to spend the day walking separately with Willie. When I got home, the younger of the Vane boys, who had either not gone climbing or had returned, asked me if I knew about a speech by Enoch Powell. 'He has been saying some very odd things about immigration,' he said. 'You had better listen to the news.' It was nearly six o'clock, and there was just time to switch on. At that time the two bulletins came out within about half an hour of one another, and I was in time for the first. Featured as the principal item was Enoch Powell's speech about the 'Tiber foaming with blood', with Enoch Powell before the cameras actually delivering it before a somewhat unsuitable audience. He had not even informed me that he was intending a speech of any kind within my area of policy, and he had gone so far as to withhold his text from Conservative Central Office, with the result that I was completely unprepared. I was outraged. The speech obviously rendered my position the following Tuesday, already difficult, almost impossible. I badly needed advice as to what to do. I fully intended to resign from the Shadow Cabinet if my own estimate of the speech was correct. I did not then appreciate that my own was the majority view.

Fortunately Willie Whitelaw lives only a few miles away from Willie Vane, and I was able to contact him on the phone before the second bulletin appeared. I did my best to sound conversational and matter-of-fact. I did not wish to prejudge the issue. I simply asked Willie to switch on his television and tell me what he thought. My intention was to let him, as Chief Whip, know that I could not continue my responsibilities if colleagues were to be allowed to invade my area at a critical moment without so much as informing me of their intentions. But I reserved this for a separate conversation. It might be that my first impression was wrong. I have always been accused of being headstrong in my political actions. I do not plead guilty to this charge. In matters of importance, like the Thorneycroft resignations, I believe I act swiftly, but with circumspection. In fact, the sequel of my conversation was that Ted Heath dismissed Enoch from the Shadow Cabinet without awaiting, as he was entitled to do, the advice of his colleagues at the next Shadow Cabinet, at which it would have been my intention to confront Enoch with his conduct and force a choice upon my colleagues. I have always regarded Ted Heath's action on that occasion as honourable in the extreme. I would, however, have taken the responsibility myself, as I feared that it might well lead (as in fact it has done) to a permanent rift in the party, to save which I was quite willing to sacrifice my own position.

After that episode, coming as it did after his part in the Thorneycroft resignations, and his refusal to serve in any capacity under

Alec Home, I began to view Enoch in a somewhat less favourable light. I was sorry about this since his talent and his intelligence are truly amazing. When we were in opposition I sometimes used to sit next him capping Greek quotations. I was always the originator, starting from my humble store of carefully garnered learning. He never failed to beat me on my own ground. He remembered the rarest of things. He had it instantly available. It was always exactly in point. Add to this that he reads German virtually bilingually (my own is of the Grimms' Märchen variety), has taught himself Welsh, reached interpreter standard in Urdu (which presumably means knowledge of the Arabic script) and, I have no doubt, is competent in French, Italian and Spanish. Observe also the width of his learning as revealed by his works, and the immense variety of topics, scholarly, political, economic, philosophical, religious, on which he writes with ease and authority. I admit frankly that in none of these matters do I hold a candle to him, apart from philosophy (at which I was a specialist) and law, of which he knows nothing, although he has more than once given his own imperfect, inexpert and offensive opinion, even venturing to suggest that the reigning Attorney-General was deliberately not telling the truth. But look now at his record. Show me the issue upon which he has not patently changed his mind. Show me the cause to which he has been consistently true. Show me the colleague to whom he has not been disloyal. Remember his treatment of his own constituency association in 1974. And do not forget the curse of Reuben. 'Unstable as water, thou shalt not excel.' *Corruptio optimi pessima.* In the shrine of Apollo at Delphi there were two texts of oracular wisdom inscribed. The first was Mêden Agan, nothing to excess, which I ventured once to translate as a counsel of moderation in all things. The other was gnôthi seauton, know thyself, which being translated might be construed as 'Beware of your own subconscious'. I do not doubt that Enoch thinks of himself, and is thought of by many, as Aristides. But while he shows much of the talent, he displays also some of the failings of Themistocles, who died in the Persian camp.

35

Ulster

At the time I was in opposition, Ulster was part of the multifarious responsibilities of the Home Office and, as the Shadow Home Secretary, I was therefore opposition spokesman on Ulster, in addition to law and order, Criminal Law, the Police, Civil Defence, Immigration, Drugs, Gaming, the Death Penalty, British Nationality, the Children's Act and, in the House of Commons, Magistrates. Of all my parliamentary activities, I have singled out only the topic of immigration, but my one connection with Ulster also stands out in my memory.

Mine is an Ulster family and, like others of Irish extraction, we have never forgotten our origin. Some time shortly after the Boyne two brothers of my name set out for Ireland from the port of Liverpool, and by 1722 they were established in the North. They were Quakers. They were presumably Scottish in origin, since my cousin Oliver Hogg, who has made a life study of the subject, assures me that all Hoggs come originally from Galloway, and the persistence of certain family names, such as James, is at least not inconsistent with the view that they are in fact connected. Among the Jameses was the Ettrick Shepherd, a famous Governor of Texas, and my own great-grandfather, Sir James Weir Hogg, Bart. (last Chairman of the East India Company), and there have been many others called James, including my own younger son. Incidentally, the word Hogg, as any reader of the agricultural columns of the Border press can certainly assure you, does not mean the same thing as Hog. Hogg is a sheep. Hog is a pig. Down the generations the subject has been the occasion of numerous black eyes given and received at school, since yearling sheep do not like to be called pigs, particularly castrated pigs. Some years ago I went down to parents' day at Sunningdale and an irate mother complained to my wife that my son James had blacked her darling's eye, and she pointed out the *corpus delicti*, a proper shiner. 'He should not have called my son Piggy,' was my only apology. I knew at once what had happened, and it had.

The Hoggs remained Quakers until one direct ancestor of mine ran away with a Church of Ireland parson's daughter, called Rose O'Neill. At that time, Quakers were not permitted to marry outside the Society and he was disowned, which was their way of saying excommunicated. My branch of the family has been Church of Ireland or England ever since. In other words, but for the Scottish origin of most of my forebears, I would be what the Americans call a WASP, or White Anglo-Saxon Protestant. But I am not Anglo-Saxon. My O'Neill ancestors were presumably native Irish. My grandmother was Highland, a Graham, with some traces of Gaelic a generation or two back. The Hoggs were, I expect, probably British. In spite of the fact that for many centuries Galloway has been English-speaking, the older local place names seem to me to bear marks of the P-Celt language.

At all events, all through the alarms and excursions of 1914 we were Unionist, and proud of it. But the Union then meant union between the whole of Ireland and Britain. A Unionist meant that one believed in a single Parliament at Westminster, and Carson was the most prominent exponent of that view. A Home Ruler, like Redmond, meant that one wanted a single Parliament at Dublin uniting North and South, but still under the British Crown. Neither Carson nor Redmond got what they wanted, and I suppose neither would have approved what they got, though Carson obviously regarded it as second best and, at least until recently, was worshipped consubstantially with King William in the present North.

I have never ceased to regret that Parliament at Westminster has never really come to terms with federation, or even devolution. The old Stormont was, of course, the mutilated fragment of a semi-federal devolution preserved unnaturally, like a fly in amber, from the abortive federal settlement with the South in 1920, and grafted on to our own unitary state. Whether Gladstone's reforms of the eighties and nineties would have worked, I do not know. My father, who was alive at the time, thought not. But if they had worked, the world would have been a better place today. The Union with Scotland succeeded for two hundred and fifty years, despite the continuance of a legal system incompatible with the Common Law, and still persists. But it was formed at a time when government was a far less complex thing than now, and we are faced with nationalist movements both in Scotland and in Wales. Can they be bought off with something less than independence? Or will compromise, as so often, feed the fires of separatist demands and destroy the complex unity which has proved one of the most successful political institutions of all time?

For myself I have no doubt where I stand, and have always stood. I stand for the unity of the British Islands, allowing the maximum degree of diversity within the unity, and therefore the maximum degree of devolution compatible with safety from foreign invasion and economic prosperity. Though I regret it, we have lost the Republic of Ireland for the foreseeable future. We must keep our bargains at all costs, and we have admitted their complete independence. But we are their co-partners in Europe. If ever there came a time when they would be prepared to rejoin the family of British Islanders in a sort of loose confederation I would rejoice with a joy wholly disproportionate to the importance of the change.

I believe that Ireland missed her destiny in 1921. Before that there was an Irish people. Since then there have been two communities in one Ireland, mutually tolerant up to a point in the South, mutually antagonistic, where the Protestants are in a majority, in the North. It is, however, all very well to speak of the tolerance shown to the Protestant minority in the South. Before the break, about fifteen per cent of the population of the twenty-six counties was Protestant. The figure now is about five per cent. They have voted with their feet, in the case of many of the Southern Irish Protestant gentry, including my parents-in-law, under threat of murder and arson.

In the North of Ireland a different regime has prevailed. It is fashionable in left-wing circles to deride and condemn the Stormont regime in unmeasured terms. It is arguable that they are wrong. It is, at least, arguable that the basic trouble has been the refusal of the Catholic minority to recognize the Northern authorities in any way, that they have refused to rise for the National Anthem, to participate in government, to join the police or the Civil Service. Their reason for doing so is at least intelligible, though I believe it to have been profoundly misguided. They think themselves Irish, for the very good reason that they are Irish, though many of them, particularly in the urban areas, are immigrants from the South a generation or two back. They see no reason why the majority in the North should claim the rights of a majority, since from the point of view of the whole island, which is the only entity they recognize, the Protestants are a minority. They overlook the fact that there is no longer an Irish people. There are only two mutually antagonistic communities occupying one territory, like Turk and Greek in Cyprus, or Jew and Arab in Israel. In such a situation there is no right and no wrong, no solution, only an urgent need for a *modus vivendi*, and recognition by both sides of the need for co-existence despite their incompatible aims. Such a *modus vivendi*, however strongly supported by a longing for peace, and a mutual understanding of each others' qualities and defects, however securely buttressed by a new ecumenical understanding within the body of the Christian Church, will have to rest, like all human society, upon a modicum of force, if need be severely applied.

Such a modicum of force existed under the old Stormont regime, in many ways unattractive as some of its exponents were, and in spite of occasional outbursts of fanaticism on both sides, and of a number of grievances of various degrees of importance. But life went on. There were occasional outbreaks of violence. But these died down. There was every reason to hope that slowly, inch by inch, the barriers of prejudice and bigotry could be broken down, that the Protestants would cease to regard all Catholics as Fenians, and that the Catholics would come to realize that, whatever their ultimate aspirations for a United Ireland, their immediate duty was full participation and their ultimate choice might well be for the wider vision of the multinational community which is Britain.

Then came the Civil Rights movement with its provocative marches and clashes in the summer of 1969. Then came the riots and burnings, and the Westminster government intervened with British troops. At that stage Ted Heath sent me to Northern Ireland on a so-called fact-finding mission and a mandate to speak to the Conservative Conference about it.

I had not viewed the Civil Rights marches with any degree of favour. The grievances they were supposedly designed to remedy were not manufactured. They were genuine. But they were trivial in comparison with grievances which exist by the million elsewhere in the world. The O'Neill government was as enlightened as any the province had ever seen, and sincerely determined to lead the province forward as fast as the situation would permit, and it was against the O'Neill government that the Civil Rights movement had aimed its demonstrations. The Chichester Clark regime which had followed it, and was in office at the time of my visit, was being hurried along too fast in the wake of the Hunt Commission. It was also suffering from want of that sympathy on the part of the British Government which it deserved.

Still, there was no getting away from two facts. Parts of Belfast and Londonderry were barricaded off, and when I was permitted inside the Bogside to speak with the defiant committee, I had to leave first my hosts, and then my army guide, and enter unprotected and alone the citadel of what was in effect a community in complete revolt. The second fact which it was impossible to deny was that, although there had been riots and burnings on both sides, about eighty per cent of the burnt-out houses in Belfast were Catholic homes. The advent of the army had been necessitated by Protestant rather than Catholic violence, and unless one was prepared to see hundreds, and probably thousands, embroiled in further disorders its continued presence was necessary.

It would be idle to deny that I was moved by my visit. I thought at the time my speech to the conference had succeeded in its object. But it did not please the Protestants, even Robin Chichester Clark, who had been my host, and this greatly distressed me. It may be that I was throughout too preoccupied with the danger of provoking a new 1914 situation in which the two major British parties confronted one another on purely party lines, the Conservative opposition playing the Orange card, and the Socialist government with an eye on their Irish constituents in Manchester, Glasgow, Liverpool, Birmingham and London, the green one. I had one over-mastering desire, to prevent blood flowing as the result of anything I might say, and to promote so far as I could some degree of charity and understanding between the two communities.

I had, like all Conservatives, in a sense condoned the Unionist domination of Stormont over fifty years, reluctantly, but nevertheless without doubting that it was a lesser evil than the bloodshed I foresaw only too plainly if it were suddenly removed. But it is one thing to acquiesce in the continuance of an unjust situation as the lesser of two evils. This is clearly morally right. It is another thing to attempt to restore it and then fail. I was convinced, rightly or wrongly, that any attempt to restore the *status quo* would fail. I have yet to be proved right, since, as I write, the surrender of Mr Wilson's third administration to the Ulster Workers' strike may have, as its ultimate result, the total restoration of Protestant ascendancy. Nevertheless I harboured a juster, and I still think, a nobler ideal. I hoped that Ulster would develop into a normal democracy, with both communities participating in government from time to time, the Unionists tending to become a Conservative party based on a prosperous and public-spirited middle class, and their opponents, based on the interests of the wage-earner, tending to recruit a number of Protestant working-class leaders, and to break the stranglehold of communal hatred and substitute normal and healthy political conflict. Also with an eye to the Republic to the South, I had hoped that a growing reconciliation between the communities north of the border, and their adhesion to the Common Market structure in Europe, would combine to destroy the *malade imaginaire*, sick-room atmosphere of Dublin, preoccupied with a border which ought never to have had much economic or political significance, and to drive the three interested parties, Britain, the North and the Republic, together in policies of practical co-operation which, over generations, would heal the wounds of past antagonism. I tried to put all of this into my speech at the conference. I spoke for forty-five minutes without a note, and held, and I believed moved, my audience. But beyond that immediate effect I clearly failed. When I visited the North again as Lord Chancellor in 1971 I went there as an old rifleman to give support to my regiment in the Falls Road and on the borders of the Bogside and the Creggan. Things had gone from bad to worse, and they have become much worse since then. Although I recognize the intractable nature of these problems which have reproduced themselves in many areas of the world, I close this melancholy chapter with two rather bitter reflections. The first is that nothing will overcome my sense of shame as a Christian and Englishman of Irish origin that two communities, each brought up with much genuine piety into two different but legitimate interpretations of the Christian religion, cannot with our help create a just society on peaceful lines and that the British Islands should tolerate this misery in their midst. The second is that I can find no charity in my heart for Englishmen who go over to Ireland without this feeling in their bones, and make speeches stirring to even greater hostility the passions which are already deep enough to plan the shedding deliberately of innocent blood. There are those on both sides of the political fence who have done this. For all my failure in this field, when I would dearly have liked to bring the land of my fathers to a lasting state of peace and justice, I am at least guiltless on this score. At least no innocent man, woman or child has died or suffered injury as the result of hatred stirred up by me.

36

Lord Chancellor

My career has been, as I have endeavoured to show, a series of totally unexpected events. Nothing has gone as I planned it to go. But no culmination of my career could have been more unexpected than that, in 1970, the very year which I had named in my incautious and almost frivolous prophecy to the pressman twenty years before, I should become Lord Chancellor. The appointment was not wholly without preliminary indications. Lord Gardiner, at least, had told me plainly on one occasion that, of all possible Conservative candidates, he would favour my appointment. I had been both flattered and surprised but did not see how much could come from that quarter. I now think that there had been a good deal of consultation with the judiciary, and Willie Whitelaw had dropped at least one pregnant hint. Nevertheless, I had prepared myself to become Home Secretary and, when I was summoned to Downing Street in the wake of the 1970 election, the offer of the Woolsack came as a surprise. The Home Secretary's place, I was told, was already filled by Maudling. I was offered the Woolsack, and I accepted, knowing that I must now go back to the House of Lords and that this might well be the last opportunity I should have of public service.

The functions of the Lord Chancellor are not perfectly understood and, as I shall show, the actual boundaries of his office are imperfectly and not very rationally defined. Nevertheless, he is a key figure in the working of our constitution, and if, for any reason, he ceased to exist as a separate entity, we should be less free and less lawfully governed than we are.

Montesquieu, as is well known, divided the powers of government into three branches and, basing himself on the English or British constitution, as it was then understood, stressed the importance of the separation of the powers of the three elements in government as it was then understood. This doctrine became the established orthodoxy of the founding fathers of the American Republic and, in consequence, the separation of powers is an established part of the Constitution of the United States. But Montesquieu wrote before the development of Cabinet government as it is understood today, and when the founding fathers deliberated in the aftermath of the War of Independence, they viewed Cabinet government as a new-fangled abuse and an instrument of tyranny to be corrected and not to be copied. Therefore they returned to an idealized form of the Constitution as they believed it existed under William III, with an elective king, called the President, who was to control the Armed Forces and the Executive Branch, a Congress whose business was to legislate and control finance, and a Supreme Court which was there to keep the other branches in order, and even able to declare Acts of Congress illegal if they exceeded their powers.

The genius of the British Constitution is wholly different. If America is a monarchy with an elected King, Britain has become a Republic with a hereditary Head of State. Parliament is supreme, and no judge can declare an Act of Parliament void, not even, strictly speaking, under the 'Common Market' Act. The British Cabinet is not, as in the United States, a collection of random characters assembled by the elective William III from outside Congress. It is a committee of leading members of the legislature chosen from the ruling party, and though they are selected by the Prime Minister, they remain in Parliament even if they resign and cease to serve. No Haldemans, Deans, Erlichmans or Mitchells can exist here.

On the other hand, the importance of an independent judiciary is not less but all the greater when judges have to serve under an all-powerful Parliament dominated by a party Cabinet, and concentrating all the powers, and more than all the powers, of the executive and legislature combined in one coherent complex. The tenure of office of the judges is maintained inviolate by the Act of Settlement but, in theory, the Act of Settlement can be repealed, and as we saw recently in the case of Sir John Donaldson, the House of Commons at least can try to exercise political dominion over the judges by public insult and covert threat. Even under the Act of

Settlement, the two Houses can combine to remove a judge, though this has never actually been done. It is clear that the pressures on the independence of the judiciary are increasingly great. The nineteenth-century judges were seldom called upon to chair enquiries into politically sensitive topics. The litigation over which they presided largely represented actions between private litigants. They did not have to administer, as they do now, a general supervision over the administration of a growing body of Statute Law which increasingly reflects aspects of social policy, and is seldom devoid of contentious implications. The criminal trials were largely of the traditional offences, and the criminals very often persons whose actions did not come in for much political comment except by way of a general condemnation of criminal behaviour. All the changes which this summary implies and, since we live in an age of revolutionary change, much more, makes the preservation of the integrity, independence and impartiality of the judiciary a work of increasing importance and responsibility, and the sheer volume of litigation before the courts an increasingly onerous task of administration. It follows that the appointment of suitable judges and the preservation of the rule of law is now a major constitutional responsibility, clearly to be distinguished and divorced from 'law and order', that is, law enforcement in the ordinarily accepted use of the term. On the continent of Europe, the problem is partly solved by making the judiciary part of the Civil Service. A promising youngster joins the judicial service when he leaves law school at, say, age 27. He is promoted by seniority and merit, and finally departs at retiring age without experience either of advocacy or of the interior of a solicitor's office. The judiciary is a separate profession. By contrast, the Common Law countries appoint their judges in middle age from successful advocates. No doubt both systems have their merits. I am quite clear myself that ours is the better, whether from the point of view of recruiting suitable material, or from the point of view of appointing persons with a wide experience of social conditions. In addition, in England and Wales we have imposed on ourselves the duty of appointing and supervising a body of 21,000 or more lay magistrates, most of whom have no professional qualifications as lawyers, and who dispose of 98 per cent of the criminal cases which come before the courts, and apart from these have important licensing functions and matrimonial jurisdiction.

It is obvious that, where the constitution does not limit the powers of Parliament, and Parliament itself is largely under the influence of the executive, the preservation of the integrity of the rule of law has to be entrusted to a man and not a legal instrument. In Britain that man is the Lord Chancellor. In some countries the Lord Chief Justice or his equivalent has executive functions. This has the merit of impartiality, but it completely by-passes the responsibility of Parliament for public expenditure and efficiency in administration and overlooks the necessity of having a voice in the Cabinet itself dedicated to the administration of justice and the rule of law. Having seen the system and discussed it, I am satisfied that it is not satisfactory. Some other countries employ a functionary called a Minister of Justice who is responsible to the Lower House. This tends to lead, at the very best, to political appointments to the bench, and to interference by Members in the administration of the courts. Moreover, all too often the Minister of Justice is also responsible for the prosecution of offences, and sometimes for the penal treatment of offenders, and even the police. These functions should be divorced from the function of supervising judicial appointments and from the administration of the courts. It is very important indeed, incidentally, that prosecutions should not be subjected to political influence. With us this is secured by ensuring the professional independence of the Attorney-General and his divorce from the Home Office. It could not be satisfactorily maintained by combining his functions with those of the Lord Chancellor or with some mythical Minister of Justice.

It is vital that the man entrusted with judicial appointments and court administration should not merely have the confidence of the Cabinet, but also of the judiciary. For this purpose he must be a professional lawyer of the highest quality and not simply a politician or a political lawyer. We achieve this by swearing in the Lord Chancellor as a member of the Judicial Body and making him sit from time to time in the judicial committees of the House of Lords and the Privy Council. When my father was Lord Chancellor he sat judicially practically every day during term. This was possible because the House of Lords did not sit in its political capacity until a quarter past four in the afternoon, the judicial sittings taking place in the Chamber of the House of Lords between ten-thirty in the morning and four in the afternoon. This was changed during the war because, to beat the blackout and the air raids, the House sat during the daylight hours from eleven o'clock onwards. This is the origin of the Appellate Committee which now hears most appeals on the committee room floor, adjourning to the Chamber only for the purpose of delivering and perfecting their judgements. This practice has continued since the war, as the House has never gone back to its old hours of sitting. It sits politically at two-thirty in the afternoon, with the result that the Lord Chancellor cannot be in two places at once. Recent Lord Chancellors have therefore sat less frequently than their predecessors. I regard this as a pity but inevitable in the light of the vastly increased administrative duties of the Lord Chancellor's office. I nevertheless attach very great importance to the continuance of the judicial functions of the Lord Chancellor, and I managed to sit often enough to make this plain. Once you give up the function of sitting judicially, it will only be a matter of time before a Prime Minister appoints to the office a politician who does not match up to the professional requirements of the office. Once this is done the confidence of the judiciary and the profession will be lost and a most important balancing factor of our constitution will have been destroyed.

The Lord Chancellor is, of course, Speaker of the House of Lords as well as Minister of Justice and President of the highest tribunal of appeal. His actual functions as Speaker are really mainly ceremonial and formal. Unlike the Speaker of the House of Commons, who is elected, the Lord Chancellor has always been a Crown appointment. The result has been that, whereas the House of Commons has thought fit to delegate many of its powers to its Speaker, which is how he obtains the very considerable authority with which he keeps order, the House of Lords has never delegated its powers to the Crown appointee, who sits on the Woolsack. The Lord Chancellor has no power to keep order, to control the order of speeches, or to rebuke recalcitrant members. These powers are exercised by the House itself, normally under guidance from the Leader of the House, but occasionally at the instance of back-benchers or the Leader of the Opposition. In revenge, the Lord Chancellor has no obligation to be impartial in the political debates. He has nothing to be impartial about, and he plays his full part as a member of the Government, making partisan speeches on their behalf. But he is not allowed to make these speeches from the Woolsack. When the House is in Committee he speaks from the Government front bench. When the House is in session, the Lord Chancellor notionally speaks from the position in the House assigned to him by King Henry VIII. This is from what is now the Liberal Front Bench, theoretically known as the Earls' Bench or sometimes as the Dukes' Bench. In practice, when he wishes to make a speech, the Lord Chancellor simply moves two paces to the left from the Woolsack which brings him opposite the place from which notionally he must have risen.

At first sight much of this must seem, like other traditional uses, immensely anomalous. But traditional offices and customs are to be judged by their utility and not by any intellectual theory. The value of having the Lord Chancellor both a member of Cabinet and of the Higher Judiciary I have already stressed, and now that I have held the office for more than four years, I must say that I am more impressed with this than ever. It is vital that the independence of the judiciary and the rule of law should be defended inside the Cabinet as well as in Parliament. The Lord Chancellor must be, and must be seen to be, a loyal colleague, not seeking to dodge responsibility for controversial policies, and prepared to give to Parliament a jus ification for his own acts of administration. His ceremonial seat on the Woolsack ensures that he should be in the House of Lords and not in the elective chamber. In practice, although members of both Houses can challenge the day-to-day administration of this office, this does protect the administration of the courts from a good deal of political interference. A certain remoteness is beneficial without being inconsistent with full parliamentary responsibility.

When I became Lord Chancellor there were one or two preliminary dispositions that I made. Some of my predecessors, including my immediate predecessor Lord Gardiner, had complained of overwork. This was partly their own fault. David Maxwell Fyfe, for instance, spent hours and hours speaking at relatively minor political functions in the country. I cut out all this almost entirely, and did the minimum of political speaking. Gardiner spent a great deal of time in the House on the actual Woolsack. With his complete concurrence,

I arranged that, after the House had passed from questions to its main debate, and unless I myself had a part to play, the Woolsack should be taken by a succession of Deputy Speakers, nominated by rota, under the captaincy of the Lord Chairman of Committees. A modern Lord Chancellor has far too exacting a task to allow him to spend the working hours of the day simply listening to debates in which he has no inclination or duty to intervene, and over which he has no powers of discipline or control.

I also arranged with the Prime Minister that normally I would not either preside at, or attend, the multitude of Cabinet committees which had previously been demanded. Previous Lord Chancellors of both parties had tended to allow themselves to become a sort of inter-departmental housemaid, sweeping up the debris after some kind of mess or scandal had occurred. Fortunately we had few of these, but these few I managed, in my opinion wisely, to avoid. I made the resolution when I accepted the ancient and honourable office of Lord Chancellor that I would concentrate on being as good a Lord Chancellor as I knew how, and would, so far as possible, do nothing else. It is for others to say how far I succeeded in my endeavours. But I am sure that both the office and the Government were strengthened by my resolution. Moreover, rightly or wrongly, I assumed that my appointment was, in a sense, a signal from my younger colleagues that the more political aspects of government policy should be left to others. I was grateful, and took the hint.

I have said that the exact boundaries of the Lord Chancellor's responsibilities are a little unsatisfactory. This must necessarily be so with an office of a traditional character. The Lord Chancellor's is the most ancient lay office in the kingdom. It is older than Cabinet Government, older than Parliament, older even than the Norman Conquest. The earlier Chancellors were the nearest thing that a medieval monarch possessed to a Prime Minister. Becket, Wolsey and Thomas More all belonged, in their different ways, to this breed, of which the last, born out of his time, was probably Clarendon. The eighteenth-century Chancellors, who usually outlasted several governments, were in some ways royal confidants, not at all unwilling to intrigue with the sovereign against their colleagues, and take what would now be regarded as an undesirable part in Cabinet-

making, and unmaking. Thurlow, Eldon, and possibly even Hard-
wicke, were Chancellors of this type. Until comparatively recently,
Chancellors had to sit at first instance to decide equity cases. I am not
sure who last performed this role. None sat regularly, I am sure, since
the Judicature Act 1873, though Lord Birkenhead sat at first instance
in 1921 in the Divorce Division to teach the Divorce judges how to get
rid of the backlog of undefended Divorce after the First World War.
He was the last Lord Chancellor to sit at first instance in any Division
of the High Court, except for the annual and purely formal opening
ceremony on 1 October which takes place both in the Chancery
Division of which the Lord Chancellor is notionally President, and
in the Court of Appeal.

By contrast, the administrative work of the Lord Chancellor's
office has steadily increased. It was already considerable in my
father's day, but it had multiplied exceedingly by 1970 and during
my Chancellorship it multiplied again as a result of my assumption
of responsibility for the administration of the new Crown Court,
which took over the functions of the Assizes and Quarter Sessions.
Lord Gardiner has more than once expressed the view that the Lord
Chancellor should assume responsibility for the training and administration of parliamentary draftsmen, who at present live in a
sort of Arcadia of their own under the nominal tutelage of the Prime
Minister. If ever a Chancellor attempted to add this province to his
empire, I fancy he would have a fight on his hands. Those wily men
vastly prefer King Log to King Stork.

I think I am also right in ascribing to Lord Gardiner the opinion
that the Lord Chancellor should also assume formal responsibility
for law as such. This would involve taking over Criminal Law and
Procedure, and Criminal legal aid from the Home Office, and
Mercantile Law, including Sale of Goods, Hire Purchase, Bankruptcy, Company Law, and perhaps restrictive practices, from the
Ministers who exercise the functions of the old Board of Trade. This
is a somewhat tall order, since there are points at which law merges
imperceptibly into social policy with which the main Executive
Ministries must primarily be concerned. Granted that the Lord
Chancellor could usefully be consulted, and listened to more often
than he is, I doubt whether such a drastic change is either possible
or desirable. The Lord Chancellor should hold a watching brief for

the general rationality and workability of legislation and law. But I question whether he ought to have higher general ambitions than this.

There are, however, a number of minor, but still important, fields where, in common with most recent Lord Chancellors, I would think that an addition to the Lord Chancellor's direct responsibilities could usefully be made. As I view the function of a modern Lord Chancellor I would assess his real responsibilities as follows. First and foremost to see that everyone gets a fair trial in court. For this purpose he must defend and preserve the independence and integrity of the judicial proceedings of all kinds, civil and criminal, including modern judicial tribunals and enquiries. This is his main function, but for this purpose it is necessary that he should be responsible for the administration of all courts, that is, the physical provision and location of court-rooms, the organization and protection of the clerical and administrative staff, the appointment of judges, and the method of listing cases. He should also be responsible, not indeed for the substantive law, but the procedural law and the law of evidence and legal aid as much in criminal as civil cases. His present responsibilities stop short of this and the result is that in a number of matters there is no adequate movement towards efficiency and reform. For instance, although the Crown Courts and the County Courts are increasingly better housed, located and administered, the Magistrates Courts are controlled by four separate authorities, the local authorities, the Magistrates Courts Committees, the Home Office and the Lord Chancellor's Office. The result is that the petty sessional courts are badly sited, badly designed, invested with various anomalous jurisdictions, some of which, particularly that in matrimonial cases, are patently absurd, possessed of inadequate procedural rules, and an insufficiently attractive career structure for the staff.

So far as criminal law is concerned, I would leave the responsibility for substantive law where it is, with the Home Office, and the responsibility for initiating prosecutions either where it is or with a reformed public prosecutor. But from the moment the accused man enters the court and is asked to plead, to the moment when he leaves it, either a free man or under some kind of order, responsibilty should not rest, as it does, with the Home Office, but with the Lord Chancellor's Office, which means, in effect, with those, including the

Judiciary, who are principally concerned with the provision of a fair trial. The Home Office's responsibility for criminal procedure is usually incompatible with their police and law enforcement functions, and theoretically, though not in practice, with the independence of the Judiciary. Likewise, I see no justification for the present division of responsibility for the provision of legal aid, by which civil legal aid is the responsibility of the Lord Chancellor, and criminal legal aid that of the Home Office. As I tried to point out in an earlier chapter, the rule of law means something much wider than what is generally comprehended in the phrase 'law and order'. Law and order is certainly a matter for the Home Secretary. But the rule of law, an increasingly sophisticated idea, ranging from the way in which tribunals and local enquiries should be conducted, through the Magistrates and County Courts, to the High Court, the Crown Court and the Court of Appeal, is essentially a province for an official with a foot in both camps, a sworn judge as well as a sworn Privy Councillor, with an independent duty towards the judiciary and the legal profession.

37

Judges and Judge Making

One of the most important functions of the Lord Chancellor is the exercise of judicial patronage. In theory, the highest judicial posts of all, those in the Court of Appeal, the House of Lords, and the Lord Chief Justice, are, under the Crown, in the direct gift of the Prime Minister. It would be wrong to suggest otherwise. But in practice the Lord Chancellor greatly influences his decision. In making appointments to most other judicial appointments in England and Wales, and in Northern Ireland, the Crown acts on the formal advice of the Lord Chancellor alone. In practice, however, none of these appointments are arbitrary acts, and since the practice is not generally known, I had better set out what is done. In all appointments to the High Court and Court of Appeal there is a meeting between the Lord Chancellor and the Heads of Division, that is, the Master of the Rolls, the Lord Chief Justice, the President of the Family Division, and the acting head of the Chancery Division, now known as the Vice-Chancellor. A number of names is always discussed. There is never a vote, but a consensus is usually arrived at, at which, not unnaturally, the President of the Division in which the vacancy has occurred carries more weight than the others. While the last word rests with the Lord Chancellor, who takes formal responsibility to Parliament in all cases where the Prime Minister is not actually involved, I never remember a case in which the decision, when made, was not in fact a collective one. In fact, meetings with the Heads of Divisions, or one or more of them, occur very much more often than the above would imply. Whenever a problem affecting the Higher Judiciary occurs, a Lord Chancellor is wise to take these high judicial officers into his confidence. In turn, they each consult the group of judges with whom they are particularly associated.

Appointments to the County Court Bench are less formal, although amongst others the Heads of Divisions are usually consulted as to appropriate names. It is a convention of the Bar that no one can apply to become a High Court Judge. But appointment to the Circuit Bench is on application, and the Lord Chancellor keeps an elaborate card index of applicants for silk and all other appointments. As it is customary in most of these cases for the applicant to give references, and for the Lord Chancellor to seek opinions, a very large mass of information about individuals is acquired over the years.

Although these appointments are made from the Bar or, in the case of Recorders, the Bar or the Solicitor's professions, it was certainly my practice to encourage applicants to sit judicially as a Deputy Judge or Recorder before giving them a full-time appointment. The reason for this is apparent. It is very rare to find a good all-round advocate who makes a bad judge. This is because, in order to conduct a case, you must be able to see the strong and weak points of it, and because some of the most responsible and difficult work at the Bar consists not in fighting cases but advising clients, where the work is not radically different from judicial work, except, of course, that the strain of presiding in court and hearing conflicting evidence is absent.

Nevertheless, in appointing judges, there is a definite personality hazard. Lord Hewart was a very great advocate indeed, but I doubt whether he will go down in history as a great, or even a good, judge. I doubt whether Patrick Hastings would have made a good judge. There are counsel, like Dick Crossman's father, who, whilst they were good counsel, find the responsibility in making decisions too much for them when they get on the Bench. This can lead to various troubles, slowness being one. It can also lead to improper attempts to force a settlement on the parties. There are judges, popular and effective at the Bar, who, on the Bench, become subject to judges' disease, that is to say a condition of which the symptoms may be pomposity, irritability, talkativeness, proneness to *obiter dicta*, a tendency to take short-cuts. Some previous experience of a judge's showing is therefore desirable in the interests of all parties, not least of the judge himself, before making an irrevocable appointment.

When I first went to the Bar something like half the Common Law Bench had at one time or another been in Parliament. A number of these, although a decreasing number, were, in the worst sense, political appointments. Since 1945 I do not know that any appointments to the High Court Bench have been criticized on this score. The great majority of judges who were former MPs became good Common Law judges, and some of them were among the best. This is because experience in politics and Parliament can broaden the mind and knock some of the angular corners off it. I regard it as a sad thing that I was unable to appoint a single High Court Judge from among members of the House of Commons, although I was able to maintain the principle of giving recorderships to members of the House of Commons. This is partly owing to the fact that the exacting duties of parliamentary life make Parliament an impossible burden on members of the Bar with a busy practice. But it is also partly the fault of Selection Committees in the main political parties. In the old days a silk of eminence in his profession was a sought-after candidate on both sides in politics, and if he found difficulty in securing a seat for himself could count on the good offices of party managers. Nowadays the reverse is true. After they had lost their seats during the first two Wilson administrations, at least two QCs among my friends had great difficulty in finding another constituency. One at least is now a very highly regarded figure indeed. In a number of cases they were not even short-listed, and in others younger and far less able men were preferred. I regard this as very much to be deplored. Parliament has need of able lawyers, and the Bar and Bench both need members with political instincts and experience. It is a great mistake to suppose that the possession of definite political ideas or the experience of having contested elections constitutes a slur on a judge's impartiality. Indeed, it is arguable that the opposite may be the case. Simonds, Maugham and Goddard were far to the right of most Conservative Members of Parliament, and unless I have misjudged him, Lord Gardiner is politically far to the left of Roy Jenkins, Lord Elwyn Jones, or the late Mr Justice Donovan. Impartiality does not consist in having no controversial opinions or even prejudices. The Bench is not made up of political, religious, or social neuters. Impartiality consists in the capacity to be aware of one's subjective opinions and to place them on one side when one enters the professional field, and the ability to listen patiently to and to weigh evidence and argument and to withhold concluded judgement until the case is over. I found no difficulty in advising Harold Wilson professionally in a matter of libel when I was in opposition. I was proud to be asked to do so, and I fancy he had no reason to complain of the quality of the advice or representation he received.

On the whole, I have no doubt that judges are much better educated, more polite and more patient than they used to be. When I first went to the Bar some of the County Court judges were holy terrors, especially to young Counsel, litigants in person, and solicitors when they appeared as advocates. I did not especially mind this since, if one knew one's job and how to look after one's self in court, it made solicitors less inclined to award briefs by favouritism or family relationship. But it was not in the public interest, and I am glad to think that in the present generation of judges this kind of conduct is very much the exception.

Every Lord Chancellor receives a stream of letters, some of them from MPs who should know better, complaining of individual decisions of the courts. Often these are accompanied by allegations of perjury by witnesses, trickery by Counsel or solicitors, or even corruption of the judge. In almost every case the only answer one can give is, that if you do not like a decision, the only remedy is to appeal. A Lord Chancellor cannot interfere. But in a number of cases, although I seldom told the complainant that I had done so, I showed the complaint to the judge concerned. I thought it good for him both to see what was being said about him from the other side of the court, and how perhaps a lapse of manners or a momentary impatience could undermine confidence in his decision. Some of the complaints I got related to press accounts of judicial proceedings, especially in the case of criminal sentences. These are seldom sound guides. By the time sub-editors have done with the case, the report, necessarily truncated, and sometimes of only one day's hearing in a long case, bears little resemblance to the material on which the judge decides. Still, I very often showed the judge the comment, and I got some very interesting replies.

One sometimes reads criticisms in the press to the effect that judges who are appointed to the Bench have insufficient knowledge of social conditions. I doubt whether this can be so. Before the war it was certainly true that High Court Judges had often relatively little recent experience of serious crime before they were called upon to pass sentence. This is almost certainly untrue today. Of course, some judges are appointed to the High Court Bench because of some particular specialist experience, say in Revenue work or Patent Law. But these are not those who are usually asked to try serious crime and, when they do sit, they have almost always had judicial experience in easier crime before they try a serious case.

It would be difficult to imagine young men and women who have a wider view of the causes, social and otherwise, of human unhappiness than those who go to the Common Law Bar at the present time. They have studied in detail crime, sex, matrimonial cases, road accidents, factory accidents, disputes between neighbours, landlord and tenant, hire purchase, sale of goods. The claim that they should have a wider spectrum of knowledge tends to be geared to the belief that they should be impregnated with some specific social doctrine or would benefit by the real or supposed advantage of study under one of the newer disciplines in the universities. On the whole I doubt whether this would reduce their prejudices or improve their reputation for impartiality. When they get to the Bar they will have ample opportunity of contact with every kind of opinion about these issues by conferring with and examining or cross-examining expert witnesses and appearing on opposite sides in particular classes of case. The real test of a good judge is not the personal knowledge he applies to a case so much as his capacity in assessing and being influenced by the experience and views of others, where these are relevant and given in evidence or can be referred to by advocates. This is the expertise in which, if he is to be a good judge, a man must ultimately excel.

38

The Lay Magistracy

Ninety-eight per cent of the crime in England and Wales is tried summarily by magistrates, and very nearly all of this, except in London, is tried by magistrates who do not possess a legal qualification and are legally advised only by a qualified clerk. All of these, except those who are within the area administered by the Chancellor of the Duchy of Lancaster, are appointed by the Lord Chancellor and are removable by him in case of misconduct or incapacity. This system has no parallel in Scotland or Ireland or, indeed, elsewhere in the world, except perhaps in Western Australia. It was not copied in the United States or in most of the Commonwealth. In Europe, the facts are greeted with incredulity, as is also the extremely small number of our professional judges which, of course, is a corollary of the system. It is an incredibly cheap method of trying cases, but by itself this would be a small recommendation in a civilized country. Justice is the first of the social services, and it behoves a wise nation to provide good justice and not cheap justice. But the truth is that the lay magistracy survives because it gives satisfaction, and on the whole it gives satisfaction because it dispenses justice of a high quality.

The key to the whole system is the method of appointment, and this has survived the scrutiny of successive Royal Commissions and Lord Chancellors. The modicum of training now rightly insisted upon is of much smaller importance. The important thing is to get the right people.

Unlike the professional judges, the lay magistrates are not necessarily politically neutral. Indeed it would be impossible to recruit them if they were. Some of the best magistrates come from local authorities or are prominent in local politics, and this nowadays almost always involves identification with a political party. What is important is not the views they hold, but the way in which they hold them and the extent to which they can be taught to leave them outside the court when they sit on the Bench.

Although I myself at least glanced at, and in many cases read carefully, every nomination form submitted to me, it would be impossible for any Lord Chancellor or any central Civil Service organization to find or vet suitable candidates for the lay magistracy. This is the function of local committees, usually presided over by Lords Lieutenant, whose business is to identify, screen and interview potential candidates. For many years the Lord Chancellor has never appointed candidates who were not so recommended, but I did not always appoint those who were.

By far the most important factor a Lord Chancellor has to examine in making appointments to a Bench is social and political balance. In some parts of the country it is only too easy to get Benches consisting of nominations in themselves perfectly suitable but, coming as a whole from one class or one political party, to the exclusion of all others. In some parts of the country it is the Conservative, and in others the Labour, Party which has this predominance. Moreover, as good magistrates remain in office until they reach retiring age, or leave the district, the search for young blood, magistrates from minority groups, and women suitable and willing to serve is almost continuous, and the newer parties always tend to be under-represented.

Although membership of a political party is no bar, it is not necessarily an advantage. I would never allow an agent or candidate for Parliament to sit within his own district. Sometimes one has slipped by in the past. For twenty years or so before I became Lord Chancellor and found out about him, one old friend of mine had, I believe, been a magistrate within his own constituency, I understand to the general satisfaction. But how important it is to be on one's guard against these things I found out very early. A Member of Parliament brought improper pressure to bear upon me to retain the services of a magistrate whom Lord Gardiner had directed to retire on account of deafness. He even went further and advised him to sit, despite Lord Gardiner's and my warnings. It was only later I discovered that he was the MP's own part-time election agent. The MP later had the gall to raise the matter on the adjournment in the House of Commons, accusing me of political bias when I removed the magistrate for misconduct. Apart from candidates and their agents, the main persons excluded are the near relatives of existing magistrates, the police, the probation service and local solicitors and, of course, their wives. This is not a reflection on their suitability, but on the compatibility of the functions, or their identification with husbands and wives exercising functions incompatible, while they last, with judicial work.

The real price one pays for a lay magistracy is, of course, undue lenience. This seems to me a small price, and worth paying in the case of minor criminal offences. The more serious offences should be sent to a higher court with a professional judge. Occasionally one finds an aberrancy, as in the case of a now deceased Chairman of the Wealdstone Bench who is reported once to have said to a motorist before the war, 'In this case the Bench consider that there is a doubt. We do not intend to give you the benefit of it.' After I ceased to be Lord Chancellor I read of a case before the Divisional Court on appeal from a magistrate who said, 'In cases where it is word against word, I make it a rule to believe the police.' Having appeared a great deal before lay magistrates and stipendiaries, I wonder how many of both kinds in fact observe such a rule but are not naïve enough to admit it. On the whole, by far the bitterest complaints I received as Lord Chancellor were about professional judges and magistrates and not about lay magistrates. The great saving grace of a lay bench is that it consists of more than one in any case, and that the rota ensures that the bench is differently composed from day to day. Stipendiaries in London have such an immense load of cases to dispose of that it is almost inevitable that they occasionally become irritable or appear perfunctory or even cynical. One remedy for this is to try to ensure that they have a change of diet, by inviting them to sit as deputies in the Crown Court, or even, where they have the necessary experience of civil proceedings, in the County Court. An abiding trouble has been that their salary scale is not, as it should be, identical with that of a County Court judge.

Another problem of the lay magistracy is that they may find it more difficult to withstand local pressure, or may even themselves yield to political prejudice. This is one of the things which has made it impossible to operate a lay magistracy in Northern Ireland (where even the professional judges in the lower ranks are not always immune). I did have a little trouble in Wales during the language cases. But it all passed off happily in the end, apart from one lady who chose to disregard a warning and reprimand from Lord Gardiner, and who could not be permitted to offend again when she threatened to do so.

For some years now the task of a magistrate has become increasingly onerous. He has to sit at least twenty-six times a year. He has to undergo a compulsory course of training at the outset, and is encouraged to take courses of one kind and another during his period of office. Too often I would receive political representations from various bodies or MPs demanding the appointment of individual constituents as if the addition of JP after your name was either a reward for public service like a sort of junior OBE, or as if the lay magistracy were something which was given as a right to representatives of a particular point of view, so that a particular party or body could nominate their representatives. They could only be told that this was not the case and that, although a record of public service was a recommendation, and a constant search was going on for suitable candidates from all walks of life and shades of opinion, the ultimate tests were suitability and availability, and acceptance of these qualifications by a local committee.

Of course, in a body of 21,000 men and women a few cases occur every year where magistrates are asked to resign for misconduct. Where these cases involve moral turpitude, there is no difficulty. The Caesar's wife principle must apply to those whose duty it is to administer justice, however sad the application may be in individual cases. The difficulty arises in relation to motoring suspensions and matrimonial troubles. In these cases I was compelled to operate harsher sanctions than my private conscience really would have urged. The breathalyzer cases do not, in my judgement, involve moral turpitude; they are far more in the nature of disciplinary proceedings of the kind which, in my youth, were strenuously applied to boys when they were allowed to handle a shot-gun, a far less lethal weapon in my opinion than a motor car. Moreover, it is not possible to apply the same severity to the professional bench as to the lay magistracy. I was able to relax the rules at least to the extent of viewing each case on its merits. I was also able to relax the rules about matrimonial troubles so as to bear some relation to the facts of life in modern society. I was shocked to the core when I learned that a most experienced magistrate, who had been deserted cruelly by her husband, had been asked to resign from the juvenile panel on that account because of the pendency of her divorce proceedings. No doubt magistrates should not sit while they are subjected to any form of acute personal worry or scandal, because in such circumstances they cannot give proper attention to their cases. Nor should they be allowed to sit when their own conduct has given rise to local feeling. But it is difficult to lay down general rules for this.

One thing is certain. If it were not for the lay magistracy it would be impossible to man the judicial bench in England and Wales. We have an extraordinarily small legal profession, and I regard this as thoroughly beneficial to society. Lawyers should be few, of unblemished reputation, and very highly qualified. There are too few at present, as the poor rewards in comparison with other professions allowed the numbers to sink dangerously low after 1945, and to make a mature lawyer ripe for judicial preferment, or to take a senior partnership in a solicitor's firm, or conduct high-grade litigation as an advocate at the Bar, takes at least seven to ten years of active practice, apart from the preliminary training and examinations, so that any deficiency can only be made up slowly. We are at the moment suffering from such a deficiency, which is accentuated by the increasing volume of work and, in particular, by the volume of crime. However, I would rather have too few lawyers than too many as in the United States. Lawyers are indispensable to any civilized society, but they have limitations and weaknesses and should not be too thick on the ground.

39

The Legal Profession

The most remarkable thing about my legal career, at least to me, consists in the number of times I have had to begin again at the bottom. Every successful member of the Bar has to begin twice, once when he is called, and once when he launches out again as a newly created silk. I have had to endure two additional beginnings, one in 1945, after the Conservative defeat in the General Election, and one in 1964, after a similar defeat. On the first occasion I returned after seven years, on the second after eight. On the first I had to contend with complete oblivion. I was completely forgotten, except by two solicitors, Mr George Pettefar of Wisbech and Mr Herbert Baron of Queen Victoria Street. On the second, my difficulty was exactly the opposite. Instead of complete oblivion I had to contend with excessive notoriety, but in another field; everybody knew me, but nobody at first believed that my intentions at the Bar were serious. On both occasions I was advised by knowledgeable friends against making the attempt. No one, they said, had succeeded in returning to the Bar after so long an interval, and I believe they were right. On the second occasion there was the additional practical difficulty that I had to refuse almost every case likely to last over a fortnight on the ground that it was incompatible with my front-bench duties. Nevertheless, I persevered, and I succeeded. Had I not done so I could not have become Lord Chancellor.

In effect, this struggle was a blessing in disguise. Most of my predecessors on the Woolsack have been really fashionable counsel for years before their promotion. I had been so recently, and so often, amongst the struggling rank and file that in some ways I was able to sympathize with any who came my way better than if I had reaped for myself and my family a more abundant harvest.

The legal profession is not one of the Lord Chancellor's responsibilities, and he has no authority over either branch of it, except in relation to solicitors' conveyancing fees, where the Lord Chancellor presides over a small statutory committee although he exercises but a single vote. Nevertheless, he possesses a good deal of influence, and ought not, if he is to succeed in any branch of his work, to disinterest himself in the well-being of any branch of the profession, which now includes the important class of teachers of English law.

The English legal profession is organized on a traditional basis. It is therefore to be judged by its utility and not by the intellectual or conceptual symmetry of its structure. In this it is not alone. Apart from Scotland and Ireland, where the profession has developed on rather similar lines, the French legal profession, for example, was, at any rate until recently, divided into four or five quite separate groups, the judiciary (organized as a sort of judicial Civil Service), the *avocats*, the *avoués*, the *notaires*, and the *huissiers*. Apart from teachers of law, we are divided into solicitors and barristers.

The ignorant often say that this involves additional costs and unnecessary duplication of work. But in this they show themselves unaware of the practical economics of the business. The solicitor carries the heavy overhead costs of an expensive office with numerous staff, files, papers and records, rent, maintenance, correspondence, and a minimum of two bank accounts. By contrast, the barrister has practically no overheads. He writes few letters, keeps no accounts other than those necessary for income-tax, and now VAT, does not hold other people's money, act as a trustee, speculate or invest in local property, or generally act at all as a man of business. To keep himself afloat financially, the solicitor must be at his desk, deploying his staff, interviewing clients, dictating letters and so forth virtually throughout the day. The barrister must hold himself free to appear in court wherever he is needed, to be consulted, to research his opinions, and to keep very much up to date with the increasing flow of new law. The one is a man of business, the other, to some extent, an artist and a scholar. If anyone doubts the utility of the division, I refer him to an excellent essay published two or three years ago in a symposium and written by my predecessor Lord Gardiner. Since nowadays it is possible, without much difficulty or practical disadvantage, to transfer from one branch to another, there is little point in the constant talk about fusion. One of my pupils at the Bar is now a most experienced and respected solicitor. The present Lord Chief Justice was originally admitted as a solicitor and not called as a barrister.

Nevertheless, all is not well. Before legal aid was introduced, the Bar was allowed to fall to a dangerously low level, and the evil effects of this are still with us. It takes about four years from call to make a competent, and about seven to make a really mature, advocate able to cope with every emergency within his field, and the leading members of Bench and Bar at any given time reflect the intake of between ten and twenty years before any given date. Moreover, the actual accommodation available for barristers' chambers is concentrated in a few precincts and is there largely limited to the accommodation which was in use some years ago. Expansion is therefore a difficult and painful operation, and since a set of chambers requires a range of counsel with a wide variety and range of experience, expertise, from the most mature to the latest pupil, the development of new sets, either in London or the provinces, is a difficult matter. For different reasons, the solicitor's branch at the moment is still more seriously undermanned.

Almost as soon as I was Lord Chancellor, I was confronted with a series of meetings with professional bodies, raising a number of difficult problems of what I might call internal professional politics. One of these was the internal organization of the Bar which was developing a wholly undesirable tension between the practising members of the profession, represented by the Bar Council, and the governing bodies of the four Inns of Court which, traditionally, are four separate collegiate institutions, ruled from their respective high tables, with governing officers changing, like the Roman Consuls, every year. Some years before I became Lord Chancellor, Lord Pearce, to whom the profession owes much, had encouraged the formation of an embryonic university institution, the Senate. The internal politics of the Bar now largely revolve around the development of this, the traditional independence of the Inns, and the growing sense of frustration in the Bar Council.

Another problem concerned itself with the remuneration of solicitors. With the aid of Aubrey Jones's Prices and Incomes establishment and Lord Gardiner's Treasury colleagues, during my predecessor's reign bad blood had developed between the Lord Chancellor's office and the Law Society. After a good deal of trouble, I put an end to this with the help of three successive Presidents of the Law Society, two of whom, fortunately, were very well known to me before our official relations began. I always thought that much of the bad blood was caused by the custom of fixing maximum scales of conveyancing remuneration by reference to the value of the property concerned and then forbidding practising solicitors from charging their clients anything less than the scale fee so calculated so that the maximum became a fixed price. This may or may not have been a sound practice when the value of property was more or less stable, but with prices rising rapidly at different rates in different parts of the country it had become absurd. Moreover, although I was compelled to interest myself in the matter by statute, it seemed to me to be altogether wrong that, apart from legal aid, the economic rewards of solicitors could be decided by a committee on which the Lord Chancellor (who might or might not be under instructions from his Cabinet colleagues) and two eminent members of the judiciary had a permanent majority. In the end I had my way, so far as the statute allowed, and instead of rigid scales it is now established that the cost of conveyancing was to depend on the fair value of the work. This became possible when the solicitor's profession was induced to abandon their restrictive practice preventing price competition. All this was not done without a certain amount of anguish, and I received some pretty abusive letters from some country solicitors, and even from some Conservative Members of Parliament. As in many other reforms, however, so soon as the change was made, and it was seen that the new basis was fair and even rational, the storm subsided. There remains, and will continue, the problem of solicitor's remuneration in contentious litigation. This cannot be left solely to a private bargain between solicitor and client, since, under our system, the unsuccessful party has to pay part of the cost, and a bargain to pay only if you win, the so-called 'contingent fee', which is common in America, is excluded here as being subversive of professional ethics.

Much more difficult, though far less directly within the Lord Chancellor's duties, is the problem of legal education and professional training. Who is to pay for it? Medical education is virtually paid for by the State, student grants and all. Legal education is not.

Until recently, entrance to the Bar was more or less self-financing, being supported partly by the Inns of Court and partly by fees obtained from students, many of whom were entered from Commonwealth countries fired with an ambition to become 'barristers-at-law' at one of the four Inns of Court. This system has ceased to be economically viable. The question then arose as to what the future system should be. What should be the nature of the academic course necessary for call to the Bar and who should mount it? In most other countries the only entry to the legal profession is by way of a university law degree, but in England the two professions themselves had mounted academic courses, slightly more vocationally orientated, and these have proved invaluable for foreign entrants, students who had not the benefit of a university training, or students like myself who had preferred to read a more humane course of study at the university and treat law more as a vocational training than an academic study. Side by side with the academic qualification was the traditional professional apprenticeship, pupillage for a barrister, or articles for a solicitor. This is absolutely necessary in both cases if a newly-fledged graduate is not to be a public danger in his first years of practice. For various reasons it had become necessary to mount a practical course, either in addition to or instead of pupillage. These problems have not yet been resolved in spite of the very able report of the Ormrod Committee. As I am yet, even in opposition, involved in their resolution, I shall say no more about them now.

I have always had doubts about the value of a law degree as a general education in the absence of a more general course in history, literature, philosophy, mathematics, or science. Whether my doubts be well-founded or not, it is clear that some degree of academic legal knowledge is necessary to a wide range of occupations outside the legal profession. This range must include accountancy and banking, town planning, architecture, and estate and business management. This means that there will be an increasing demand for law teaching both in the polytechnics and the universities. But it would be a shame if entry to the professions were limited to those who had obtained some sort of a degree in their vocational subject. The professions have always been the gateway to advancement for those who have not had the advantage of training at a university. Moreover, it would be a pity if those who wished to enter a profession felt themselves bound to study their professional subject at university to the exclusion of a more general course. This would ensure that the professions were manned by over-specialized and under-educated people drawn from too narrow a social range. There must always be room in the legal profession for those who have missed a university degree altogether, and for those who have had a university education but have chosen to study for their first degree a subject other than law.

40

The Costs of Litigation and Legal Aid

When I first became Lord Chancellor a rather pompous document appeared under the imprint of the now defunct Consumers' Council. I do not wish to discuss its particular provisions because they are largely irrelevant to what I have to say here, and because, quite independently of the report, I had set about doing my best to deal with the very problems they were discussing, namely the disproportion between the cost of fighting litigation, especially for small claims, and the meagre results obtained at the end of it, if, that is, it is contested to the last, which is true of only a small minority of cases.

As much of my life has been spent in dealing with litigants, actual and potential, I believe I have something to say which people ought to understand before they propose remedies. The report I have referred to clearly did not understand it, and in several broadcast programmes in which I have participated recently neither the interviewer nor the other participants seem to have grasped it either. Yet it is something which is both obvious, when you come to think of it, and has been said since the earliest days.

All litigation is an evil, and being an evil it cannot be made agreeable even to the winner. There are a few, relatively few, fairly friendly disputes where people cannot agree, let us say about the construction of a document, and wish to get an impartial ruling from the courts. Even these, or the great majority of them, would be better settled by agreement. There are also things like divorce, or the proof of a will which can only be got by going to court. But the great mass of litigation is caused by people doing what they ought not to have done, or leaving undone that which they should have done. In the great majority of cases, when the chips are down, the wrongdoer has to perform his duty without fighting in the last ditch or the blackmailing claimant has to abandon his claim without taking it to judgement. All these cases are relatively cheap to decide, provided that, in the background, there is an adequate system of justice to be appealed to with reasonable certainty of getting the right result in the end. Of the hundred thousand, or several hundred thousand, writs issued in the High Court every year, scarcely one in a thousand lasts the course to a decision after a contested trial and, no doubt, the situation in the County Court is not all that different. Behind all these claims is a much vaster number of disputes which never come to court at all. In most of these cases there is relatively small cost, though in most of them the party who is in the right only obtains satisfaction after foregoing part of that to which in the strictest language of the law he might have been entitled. But at the end of the day, all contested litigation is an evil and cannot be made otherwise. It remains, however, a necessary evil, because until the end of time people will go on demanding things they are not entitled to have, will continue to omit to do that which in justice they ought to have done without any pressure brought to bear.

The State has an interest in litigation because, of its very nature, it must claim a monopoly of force, and it cannot allow disputes to be settled by a resort to force. The only principle according to which the State can afford to determine disputes, when an appeal to it is made, is the principle of justice; justice, that is, as defined by the ordinary law of the land. It must constantly be concerned to see that this law corresponds as closely as possible to the demands of public conscience. It can never do so precisely because the public conscience is never precise, and always in process of change. But it must do the best it can.

In order that justice may be brought to bear on a dispute, even where the law is certain and manifestly just, the facts must be accurately known. Unfortunately the process of ascertaining facts, identifying the relevant ones, and then identifying and applying the relevant principles of law is never easy and cannot be made cheap. You have to cope with human prejudice, self-deception and fallibility, weakness of memory and, in a significant minority of cases, conscious fraud and deception. A case is not necessarily easier to solve because the amount in dispute is small. The facts may be as difficult to disentangle in a small case as in a big one, and the legal principles in a small case may be as difficult, and very often as important, as in a big one. I am using the words 'small' and 'big' in what is perhaps a misleading way, in accordance with the question whether the amount in dispute is large or small. I can remember that, in two criminal cases which came my way to adjudicate upon as Lord Chancellor, one related to the presence of a single cooked caterpillar in a tin of peas, and another to a demonstration by students and others in which none of the defendants had been, or should have been, punished in any way at all.

Nevertheless, the State cannot afford to make mistakes in the cases which come before it for decision, whether they are small or large. It cannot afford to make mistakes about facts, and it cannot afford to apply the wrong principles of law. No system of justice is, or can be made, perfect, but every decision which is wrong about the facts, or applies misguided principles of law, undermines the system of justice itself because it casts doubts upon its reliability.

The State and the parties to a dispute are thus faced with a task which is both necessary and impossible. The State cannot decline interest in any case, large or small, which has been properly brought. The innocent parties to a dispute cannot afford the cost of litigation. Like all other questions of policy, a line, or rather a series of lines, far from straight, must be drawn in an attempt to reconcile requirements which are, in both, incompatible with one another if pushed to the ultimate limit.

Every legal adviser knows that the only advice to give to intending litigants is to steer clear of litigation if you can. Many people are shocked by this advice when they receive it. They say they are entitled to justice or 'their day in court'. Their neighbours, they say, have encroached on their side of the fence by as much as, say, six inches. The neighbours, meanwhile, are telling their advisers that they claim the six inches as their right. Both parties may be acting in good faith, though this is not always so. Six years later, and many hundreds of pounds the poorer, and bitterer and sadder than words can describe, both sides may wish they had taken when they had received it the advice that they would find that litigation, fought to the end, produces only Dead Sea fruit. More probably they will ascribe their dissatisfaction with the results to the rapacity of lawyers, the incompetence of the judge, or the obliquity of their opponents. But the advice has been honest and, in nine cases out of ten, a lawyer knows that it is right.

There remains, however, a large number of cases which cannot be settled, because one or both of the litigants basically want something which cannot be obtained without recourse to litigation and will not accept less. You want a divorce, the custody of a child, the proof of a will not executed in due form, compensation in a motor accident, or in employers' liability cases where the facts are disputed. It may be that someone is knocking down your house or holding on to it when you want possession, will not pay for goods he has bought, is making a blackmailing claim against you, has irreparably damaged your reputation. In all these cases much money must be spent if the matter is pursued to judgement, and the client simply has not got the money to spend. In practice, in many of these cases he has no choice but to start out on the road, believing that the system will be reliable enough to produce a reasonably satisfactory result sooner, one hopes, than later.

Gerald Nabarro, when he was acquitted, of the criminal charge which had been laid against him, did much harm to the system of justice by suggesting that it could be bought by the expenditure of money. Contrary to what is frequently thought, in private litigation it is the poor man who often wields the whip. He chooses not to pay for goods which he receives and disputes their quality. The shopkeeper can bring his action, of course. But will he get his money? The sum may be small, but can he recover the costs if he wins? And will his business stand up to the publicity in the local press?

A blackmailing plaintiff demands heavy damages for libel from a newspaper which has exposed his activities. But what are they to do? They must be prepared to invest thousands of pounds, perhaps tens of thousands, in the case and, in the last resort, they must prove the truth of what they have written to the satisfaction of a jury which does not love newspaper proprietors, and the truth may be complex and require many witnesses and a long hearing. The plaintiff who has been genuinely injured in an accident must command every sympathy. What chance has a defendant (whom everybody knows to be in reality an insurance company) even if he knows, or reasonably believes, that the plaintiff has altered the facts or exaggerated his damage, but is backed up by several witnesses among his fellow-employees or among the passengers in his car? In every case it is the man, or corporation, with the money who will be forced, as a business decision, to pay up at least something or, as the case may be, forgo his rights or at least some of them, and the man without the money who, up to a point, calls the tune. The idea that you buy justice is, in many ways, the opposite of the truth. It is the very expense to which he can put his wealthier neighbour that gives the poor man a bargaining advantage.

Before the war, when there was no legal aid, and only rudimentary 'poor persons' legal assistance, there was an 'ambulance chasing' brigade of solicitors and counsel, sometimes assisted by expert medical witnesses and surveyors who, more or less openly, defied the rules of their profession by carrying on litigation on a contingency fee basis for impecunious plaintiffs. The 'contingency fee' is, in fact, built-in to the American litigation system, though it has always been a disbarring or striking off offence in England. It leads to many malpractices, touting for work, fabricating evidence, settling claims which ought to be fought, and fighting claims which ought to be settled. Be that as it may, short of an actual arrangement, which would have been professional misconduct, many of us advised and acted in accident cases for irreproachable firms of solicitors knowing full well that, if justice were to be done, we could not ask for money in advance, and would not have the nerve to ask our clients to pay our fees out of their poverty if we did not win.

Legal aid has changed all that. The really impecunious client is catered for, and the immense volume of work in the Family Division very largely financed out of the legal aid fund. But in the case of private litigation, legal aid has brought problems of its own. Legal aid itself has always been more or less related to the Supplementary Benefit level. Above that level, regulations, more or less stringent, compel fairly large contributions from most litigants, and above a certain level, which is pretty modest, litigation remains wholly at the cost of the parties. The availability of legal aid to one side when it is denied to the other, whose means may not be more than marginally greater, immensely strengthens the bargaining power of the impecunious litigant at the expense of his opponent, and to the detriment of abstract justice. Nevertheless, the trend is to extend its ambit. I myself caused the biggest extension since 1949 when I added assistance and advice to the services, which can be provided, and prepared the means whereby centres with salaried advisers might be set up by local authorities and others, when the financial situation allowed. There is already pressure to extend it further still to many tribunals (originally set up precisely in order to get rid of legal representatives and the supposed technicalities they create). I know of no effective pressure to curtail it.

The cost of legal aid is infinitesimal in comparison with the other social services. But it has already transformed the whole economics of the legal profession. From the real poverty which only private means prevented everyone from suffering at the outset of our careers when I was young, the qualified barrister or solicitor can now look forward to a sufficiency from the beginning. The reason for this comparative cheapness of administration is twofold. In the first place, part at least of the cost of the service in civil cases is recovered from the losers or from the property in dispute and, in the second place, the administration has not given rise to an army of civil servants, as is the case with other social service, but has been carried on, more or less efficiently, by the profession.

Apart from legal aid, much litigation, like much else in modern society, is now financed by a large hidden subsidy from the system of taxation. The wits of virtually all commercial litigation, which includes all the defendants' side in accident cases and all the plaintiffs' side in actions for the price of goods sold and delivered, can be set off against tax. I am still old-fashioned enough to regard suing for libel and slander as something of a luxury, never to be done at all if possible, and to be settled as soon as the defendants can be brought to offer an apology and a sufficiently large sum to make sure that apology does not appear to be a put-up job. Divorce is unpredictable, but as it boils down nowadays either to a dispute about money or to a dispute about the custody of children or both, it is not unreasonably paid for out of property where legal aid is not available.

There remains a residue of cases in which a private individual finds himself involved in litigation which he cannot avoid or settle and cannot afford to fight. In such cases, accident cases in the main, either legal aid should be extended or the insurance companies should do more to sell insurance cover. A middle-class man, or even a wealthy wage-earner, cannot afford to go to law over a substantial stake and fight to a finish. He never has been able to do so, and so far as I can see he never will be able to do so unless legal aid is made to cover virtually the whole of the community, or unless the risk of litigation is covered by an insurance policy. The process of fighting litigation is intrinsically expensive, and I am not one of those who think that the State should pay for the expense in which a private individual with adequate means would be advised either not to sue or to settle, because of the uncertainty of the outcome or the disproportionate cost of the proceedings compared to the stake involved in the dispute. I have done more myself than any recent Lord Chancellor, both in modernizing the law and in reducing the expense of legal proceedings, particularly in the County Court and in divorce, and in extending legal aid. No doubt, in time, more will be devised and carried out, but in the end the problem is intractable. The State cannot afford to administer a form of justice which is less than reliable, and cheap ways of settling disputes are usually unsatisfactory unless the parties co-operate voluntarily in reducing the expense. I have been proud during the course of my life to conduct a great deal of contested litigation. It is a public service provided by professionals calling for great skills and a wide range of aptitudes and moral and intellectual qualities. But at the end of the day I am sure that, if a contested battle in the courts can reasonably be avoided, the client is best advised to avoid it, and professional skill is best devoted to fighting only those cases where substantial interests are involved and a real dispute exists. There is no future, or at least ought to be no future, in the doctrine that every man who persuades himself that he has got a case ought to be advised to have his day in court, and particularly no future in the doctrine that he ought to have it at the taxpayers' expense. There is also no future in the doctrine that, if the result is to be reliable, the thing can be done cheaply at all.

41

Some Thoughts on Criminal Law

Criminal law is not the responsibility of a Lord Chancellor, and it was never the principal component in my practice at the Bar. But it has long since fascinated me, and the great increase in crime since the war both provided me with some much-needed work when I first returned to the Bar in 1964, and gave me a good deal of food for thought while I was in opposition as Shadow spokesman on Home Affairs. In office, as Lord Chancellor, I had to provide the courts, the judges and the administrative staff to prevent the complete breakdown then threatened in the administration of justice by the exponential and almost continuous expansion of criminal work. Throughout this period I am bound to say that I have not found my colleagues in the profession either as clear-sighted or as intelligent as I would have wished. Some of the most eminent and enlightened lawyers of the century are among the most obscurantist and least logical of men where criminal law reform is concerned, and the regular criminal practitioner, of whatever political persuasion, is among the most conservative creatures of all when the law of evidence and procedure is involved.

Most of us have been brought up to believe that our own system of criminal justice is the best in the world. So, in certain very important respects, it is. It is much speedier than, say, either the continental system, which is based on very different conceptions of evidence and procedure, or the American which, in some ways, bears the same relation to our own as American football bears to rugby. Our judges, and what is equally important, the great majority of our legal practitioners, are incorrupt and uninfluenced by political considerations. The rules of evidence, though open, as I shall show, to criticism, do at least ensure that a shoddy or incompetent prosecution case is thrown out, whilst an inadequate or suspect defence is not necessarily rejected. Our sentencing policy is sound, and relatively merciful. I am not competent to speak of our prison administration or our police. But I believe both to be relatively humane, despite the disgusting physical conditions in our antiquated prisons and the unjustified attacks sometimes made on our police officers. The jury system works in favour of an incorrupt profession and judiciary, and in such a way as to prevent unjust convictions, although it does occasionally result in some astonishing acquittals and an occasional wrong conviction which, under the jury system, is extraordinarily hard to remedy. If we compare our own system in its rapidity, purity and certainty to rival systems elsewhere, I suppose we have some cause for complacency.

Nevertheless, I do not myself feel complacent. There is no code of English criminal law in existence, and during my tenure of office, or just before it, the Law Commission reported that the state of our substantive law was so confused that it would be impossible to build a criminal code out of it until whole branches of the law were rationalized, as was attempted to be done in the Theft Act and the Criminal Damage Act. There is not much to be proud of in having a Statute Book and Common Law in which the law relating to the most important offences have not only not been written down in the form of an intelligible code, but cannot be so written until much of it has been radically restated in fresh language.

The fact is that, as a systematic and rational whole, our criminal law is of relatively recent growth. A lucid and intelligible system of criminal jurisprudence can only be produced on the basis of a code carefully thought out and enacted by the legislature, and a system of appeals based on a hierarchy of courts. All attempts to produce a code have so far failed, and have now been officially declared, for the time being, impossible, while our system of appeals dates comprehensively only from 1907. An effective three-tier system going as high as the House of Lords dates, except for a tiny minority of cases certified by the Attorney-General, only from the last decade or two.

I do not, however, wish to speak of our substantive law so much as of our criminal evidence and procedure. This law has very largely grown up as an almost haphazard set of rules, and some of our most treasured ideas have their origin in an attempt to guard by the wrong methods against dangers which no longer exist, or manifest the distrust which professional judges felt of the juries which it was their duty to direct.

The laws of evidence have their origin in a state of affairs which bears no relation to present-day practice at all. In order to guard against perjury at one time, no one who had the remotest interest in the truth or falsity of a case was allowed to give evidence at all. They were not regarded as competent witnesses. Thus, in the famous breach of promise case of Bardell v. Pickwick, described as taking place in the Court of Common Pleas before Mr Justice Stareleigh, little more than a century ago, Mrs Bardell was not able to give evidence of any promise of marriage, although it was her duty as plaintiff to establish one, and Pickwick, the defendant, was not allowed to give evidence to deny that he had promised marriage. Sergeant Buzfuz was thus free to weave his fantasies around the postcard ordering chops and tomato sauce for dinner and, in more sinister cases, entirely perjured, but technically competent, witnesses might be produced to swear to a totally false case which, in the nature of things, it might be impossible to disprove by competent witnesses on the other side.

The result has been that English lawyers have been haunted by the fear that, alike in civil and criminal cases, false evidence would be produced, and believed by a jury (until recently the only tribunal to try questions of fact in civil or criminal law) which would result in an innocent man being convicted of a crime or, in a civil case, found liable, like Mr Pickwick, to damages. In so far as this has resulted in our insistence on a high standard of proof in criminal cases, the influence of this absurdity has been to the good, although the battle has now been won and there is no need to emphasize the point, except to politicians when they try to alter the burden by statutes in cases in which there is a political interest in securing convictions. But it follows in the nature of things that in so far as the rules result in a tribunal of fact being debarred from looking at the real evidence, the consequence must be less satisfactory.

The danger of a false case being accepted is, of course, far higher in civil than in criminal cases, since the burden of proof is satisfied in a civil case by establishing a balance of probabilities, and tribunals of all kinds seem to have an inbuilt tendency to decide in favour of claimants. Nonetheless, over my own professional lifetime, and that of my father, civil law has very largely succeeded in getting rid of the technicalities. This is because practitioners in the civil courts have gradually come to realize that a rational tribunal charged with the ascertainment of facts must be competent to adjudicate upon the weight to be given to evidence, instead of being guarded against error by having the evidence kept from it, and that a reasoned decision, if misguided, is more easily reversed than an unreasoned verdict. This has been achieved gradually, at first by compelling the parties to state the real issues in the case before they come into court, and then by admitting evidence which would previously have been excluded on the grounds of hearsay or the like, but subject to whatever comment as to its reliability or weight the party disputing it desired to make. Apart from libel and slander actions where the continued existence of a jury stands out as an unjustified anomaly, we have virtually abolished the jury in civil cases, without any loss in the reliability of the system but at an enormous saving of time and expense. The fallibility of the single judge, which, on the whole, I would have described as less than the fallibility of a jury, is compensated for by the obligation imposed on a judge to state reasons for his decision, and by a greater availability of appeal on questions of fact. The saving in time is approximately one-half to one-third of the time absorbed in a comparable jury trial. Moreover, one of the great hazards of jury trial, a disagreement, is eliminated altogether, and an order for a new trial, frequently the result of a successful appeal from a jury, is also largely avoided.

In the light of this experience in the civil field, it remains therefore somewhat surprising that so little progress has been made in criminal law and procedure, and every step forward that has been taken has been the subject of bitter dispute, and even violent misrepresentation. Take, for instance, the majority verdict decision taken by Parliament in 1967 while Mr Jenkins was Home Secretary. This was designed to prevent the odd maverick amongst the jury from aborting a trial and thereby compelling everyone to come back for a new hearing. I promised Roy Jenkins my support from the first, and I gave it to him consistently from the beginning to the end. At the White Paper stage I enlisted the support of both John Hobson and Peter Rawlinson. But by the time the thing had developed into a clause of the Criminal Justice Bill, both had reneged, no doubt partly under persuasion from the profession, and by the end of the debate, I think I was alone among the lawyers on the Conservative side to back up the Home Secretary. I pointed out that a majority verdict might just as well be one of acquittal as conviction and, as a matter of history, the first majority verdict ever given in an English court was one of not guilty. This argument carried little weight with the profession at the time. They argued, with perfect lucidity and impeccable logic, but with, to my eyes, little practical common sense, that if twelve votes of guilty were necessary to secure conviction in the past, a provision that, in future, ten might be enough was to reduce the degree of certainty and thereby compromise the integrity of the burden of proof. The answer to this, of course, is that you could improve the integrity of the burden of proof by increasing the numbers of a jury to fifteen, twenty or a hundred, but no one really suggests that this is necessary. Except in capital cases we got on perfectly well during the war with a jury of seven, and in Scotland they have been satisfied with eight - seven majorities out of a jury of fifteen since the memory of man runs not to the contrary. No one now wishes to go back to unanimous verdicts, and eleven to one or ten to two verdicts are in practice at least as reliable as twelve to nothing.

Contrary to what has sometimes been suggested, with two minor exceptions, I would not interfere with jury trial in criminal cases. Juries have been with us since Magna Charta and on the whole they give satisfaction because they offer a barrier, though not, as history proves, an insurmountable barrier, to political prosecutions and judicial oppression. But my own view is that, if we are to preserve jury trials, we must still try to bring our laws of evidence and procedure more into line with reason. My motive in saying this is not to increase the proportion of convictions to acquittals, nor even to prevent the odd perverse verdict of acquittal. My motive is simply my belief that the more the laws of evidence conform with logic, reason and common sense, the greater the degree of respect in which the law will be held. My father, who like myself was more experienced in the field of civil than of criminal litigation, always used to say that the purpose of criminal justice must be the conviction of the guilty and the acquittal of the innocent. No doubt, like many other things which are worth saying, this is an over-simplification. Apart from anything else, it does not stress the far greater damage done to society by a false conviction than a perverse acquittal. But it does take account of the fact, brought out again and again by the Criminal Law Revision Committee, that English criminal law often loses sight of its underlying purpose in stressing the importance of correct procedure as distinct from the function of ascertaining the truth. Once one recognizes that the rules of procedure and evidence were devised at a time when the accused could not give evidence on his own behalf and was unable to appeal against misdirection, the case for a complete overhaul is almost unanswerable. This is precisely what has never happened.

The two significant limitations to the jury trial which I would be myself prepared to make are, first, in the field of commercial frauds and, secondly, in the field of motoring offences. I was able, when in office, to some extent to achieve my purpose in the latter field. In the former, it must be left to some reforming Home Secretary. There are two basic objections to the present system of prosecuting commercial frauds. The first is the length of time taken to bring a case on for trial (in the Rolls Razor case it was something like twelve years). This alone prevents the possibility of arriving at a sensible result, since the memory of the witnesses on both sides must, by that time, be defective. When the Rolls case came on it was virtually untriable and, not unnaturally, there was a sensible plea bargain which gave rise to criticism. The second is that the complication of tracing the facts through a series of double-entry accounts and sometimes two or even three inconsistent sets of books, one or more of which may be wholly or partly fraudulent, is almost impossible in front of a jury who, it must be remembered, is in theory taken at random from the electoral roll. In order to prosecute for a number of commercial frauds, it is first required that an enquiry be set up by the Department of Trade under the Companies Acts, usually consisting of a Chartered Accountant and a Queen's Counsel. They are not bound by the rules of evidence, but normally take about eighteen months to two years in preparing a report on the dossier system, stating whether, and if so what, offences have, in their opinion, been committed. The case is then handed over to the police and prosecuting authorities, who interview the defendants and prepare a case on the normal lines for a jury. There are then committal proceedings before magistrates, which may nowadays be short or long, at the option of the defence, and finally an Old Bailey trial before a jury who will have to sit for many weeks - in some cases months - and try to find out the true nature of a transaction which has taken place years before through a mass of documents (say not less than 500 or so), with the nature of which they are wholly unfamiliar, and which it has taken two professionals eighteen months or two years to sift. I cannot believe that, whatever Magna Charta may say about trial by peers, this is a sensible way of arriving at truth. I would substitute a trial before a judge and two laymen, the judge deciding the law, and the majority the facts, with a reasoned judgement instead of a curt 'guilty' or 'not guilty' and an unlimited right of appeal on law and fact to the Court of Appeal. If I am asked whether this would yield a slightly higher number of convictions, I would say 'Probably, yes'. But this is not what I am after. Maybe some people who are now acquitted, or not prosecuted, would be convicted or plead guilty. Maybe some people who are convicted or plead guilty would actually escape. This is indifferent to me, as long as the new system is more reliable in practice and more rational in theory than the old. The idea that we must preserve irrationality in our criminal procedure in order to safeguard the rights of the individual against the State is one with which I cannot at all agree.

The same principle of rationality ought to apply in the field of evidence, and pre-trial procedure, and this does involve some alteration in the so-called right of silence. Of course, it would be contrary to our whole approach to individual liberty to compel a defendant to give evidence and thus face him with the dilemma of conviction or perjury. It would equally be abhorrent to a humane society to admit evidence which was obtained in a manner contrary to the Universal Declaration of Human Rights, or the European Human Rights Convention. These forbid torture, or degrading or inhuman treatment. But our present laws relating to confessions or admissions are based on no rational principle, are immensely technical, and lead to an inordinate waste of time at a criminal trial. A jury is perfectly competent - no tribunal better fitted - to judge the weight to be given to an alleged confession, said to have been procured by some questionable device. A jury is perfectly competent to decide whether silence at a particular stage was due to a proper and prudent desire, on the part of the accused, to hear the whole case before giving his own account, or some other proper motive, or to a guilty sense that he could only blurt out a compromising admission if he spoke at all, or a desire to play for time in order to concoct an alibi from confederates. This is the sort of thing which juries are expected to understand better than lawyers, and it is perfectly fatuous to try and keep the evidence from them. Incidentally, I am myself persuaded that the artificiality of the rules sometimes leads the police to the wholly inadmissible practice of colouring the evidence in one way or another in order to comply with them, and this alone would be enough to justify a common-sense approach to the realities of a case.

Quite apart from anything else, in a long criminal trial immense time and expense could be saved by making it obligatory on the prosecution and defence to disclose in advance what were the real points intended to be disputed. This has already been done, up to a point anomalously, in the case of alibis, where the defendant is to some extent now bound to disclose his case in advance so as not to take the prosecution by surprise. But it should be a universal rule in cases likely to last some time that the defence and prosecution should appear before an officer of the court and discuss the points which are really at issue. In a murder case, is it disputed that the alleged victim is dead, and is it established what was the physical cause of death? Did he die as the result of something done by the defendant, or is it going to be suggested that it was done by someone else? Is it intention which is the main issue? Is it going to be said that there was provocation, diminished responsibility, or insanity? Was it an accident? Hours of time are nowadays wasted, and a great number of witnesses brought unnecessarily to court to establish points not really in dispute, or to challenge questions in principle not capable of challenge.

All this I have written to show that nothing really justified the chorus of disapproval and obloquy which greeted the report of the Criminal Law Revision Committee when it reported during my period of office as Lord Chancellor, and caused the government of which I was a member to conclude that nothing positive could be done. A former Lord Chancellor, Lord Campbell, wrote in the nineteenth century that Law Reform is either by consent or not at all, and I have no doubt whatever that it was at the time wholly impracticable to carry the matter further than we did. But two lessons stand out to me as matters to be learned from the fiasco. The first is that in order to secure consensus about Law Reform the practice worked out by the Law Commission is superior to that followed by the two committees on Law Reform, of which the Criminal Law Revision Committee was one. The Law Commission publishes its tentative conclusions as a Working Paper before it delivers a report, and a period of a year or two years of public discussion by the profession and other interested bodies usually precedes the final consideration of the Working Paper by the Commission. This tends to prevent the kind of hysterical outburst which greeted the report of the Criminal Law Revision Committee.

The second moral I draw from the controversy is more complicated. On the government side, I have always believed that Criminal Law and Procedure should be the primary responsibility of the Lord Chancellor and not of the Home Secretary. Since the Home Secretary has the responsibility for the police, and therefore for law and order generally, it is clearly right that he should be responsible for the substantive provisions of Criminal Law. But the function of providing a fair trial, fair, that is, both to the prosecution and the defence, is something altogether different from, and I would have thought to some extent incompatible with, responsibility for the police, for prosecutions, or for law and order generally. What happens to a man during the period in which he is before the court should be the affair of the Minister responsible for the judiciary, except in so far as it is within the province of the judiciary itself, that is, the judge at the trial, or the Court of Appeal after it. Any proposals for the reform of criminal procedure or evidence emanating from a Home Secretary are liable to be judged by the press and the profession as primarily aimed either at securing more convictions or as tending to a greater liberalization. In truth, neither represents what is wanted. What is wanted in our criminal law is a greater degree of intelligibility and rationality and not, as such, either a higher number of convictions nor a higher degree of protection for the individual. We need to be less preoccupied with the rules of the game and conceptions of fair play, cricket, or sportsmanship, and turn our attention to the real object of the exercise which is the ascertainment, not necessarily of the whole truth, but so much of it as is necessary to dispose of a particular prosecution. We are right to insist that the benefit of any possible doubt at the end must be given to an accused person. But for the most part we are clearly wrong to suppose that we achieve this object by concealing part of the evidence which is logically probative (or disprobative) of the charge. No doubt there are certain matters, such as previous convictions, which have an emotional impact disproportionate to their logical value, and are therefore rightly excluded. But the chief guide of the lawyer in the twentieth century should be rationality. It has not been our guide in the past, and it shows no sign of being our guide in the immediate future.

42

Return to Opposition

The offer of the Lord Chancellorship in 1970 entailed my return to
the House of Lords from which I had escaped with difficulty in 1963.
Having decided that, except as an ordinary member of the Cabinet,
my participation in the formation of policy would not be particularly welcome, I set myself the task of being as good a Lord Chancellor as I knew how to be. I did not attempt to influence policy at the
highest level before it came to Cabinet except in matters in which I
was directly concerned or in which I thought the rule of law was
necessarily involved. Although a member of the Cabinet is always
collectively responsible for any decisions taken by his colleagues
during his period of office, he can intervene more or less directly in
the formation of policy. If he decides to do the former he must
belong to as many as he can of the policy-forming committees or
groups. By the time things come to Cabinet it is usually too late to
do anything but exert a moderating influence, unless there already
exists a difference between members of the relevant committee. I
decided to take the second option and so far as possible to limit my
activities. This seemed to me consistent with the duties of a Lord
Chancellor. Moreover, I was 63. As I said to my friends at the time:
'The present chapter of the biography will be called the Woolsack.
The next chapter will be called "Eventide" or "Last Days".' Apart
from the fact that, so far as I am myself concerned, no biography
of myself will be written by me, I still think that this was the right
line to take. I cannot help speculating as to what would have happened if I had known, or if Ted Heath had known in June 1970, that
Iain MacLeod would die within a number of weeks, and that Reggie
Maudling would find himself in baulk before the end of the Parliament, as the combined result of these losses has been to leave us

dangerously short of debating talent in the House of Commons, a shortage which has been increased by the premature retirement of Anthony Barber and Christopher Chataway. It may very well be that, if the truth had been apparent to us in June 1970, either I would not have been offered the Woolsack or, having been offered it, I would have declined it. As it was, I accepted it as the last public service I might be able to render before retiring completely from public life, and though I had hoped for another term after a fresh General Election, which would have taken me on to retiring age or more, I knew perfectly well when I accepted the office that this was something which no power on earth could guarantee.

As it was, I spent over four years of my life in one of the most exacting, and one of the most satisfying, of public offices under the Crown, and I was privileged to watch, and participate in, one of the most important turning-points in our national history since 1948.

It would be neither right nor proper for me to attempt a history of the Heath government of which I was a member. This would involve me in the betrayal of confidences and a critique of colleagues whom I like to call also my friends. Events, however, have taken a turn since the end of that government which enable me to say one or two things about it which may be of value for the future.

The two subjects which seem to me to require treatment in this way are, respectively, the Industrial Relations Act, and the election of February 1974. As long ago as 1957, when I was Party Chairman, I had asked Conservatives all over the country to write to me suggesting possible criticisms of Conservative policy at that time. The letters, which were numerous, were tabulated, and by far the most numerous were those criticizing the Macmillan government for 'truckling to the unions'. On the whole I rejected this criticism, and so, more importantly, did Iain Macleod and Harold Macmillan. I think we were right, although the case on the other side was extremely formidable. Wage demands by the unions, supported by militancy where there was adequate industrial strength, were a major cause of inflation, and a serious brake on our industrial efficiency and competitiveness. Looking back at the matter now, when the contrast between our own industrial performances and that of our defeated enemies, or still more decisively defeated ex-allies, becomes more and more painful to behold, I have no doubt whatever that the attitude of the Trade Union Movement, and of the Labour Party with which it is organically connected, has been a major, I would say the principal, cause of our national decline. Neither can ever make up its mind whether its role is to destroy the capitalist system and its values or rescue the capitalist system from its faults, and there are far too many people in both sides of the movement who take the former view to permit those who adopt the latter to do anything of sufficient value for the country to save it. Nevertheless, in 1957 I was quite clear that, on balance, it was better to attempt to influence the trade unions by persuasion than to take measures which, however reasonable in principle, would be construed as a declaration of war and so lead the country through a period of industrial strife and bitterness before it could achieve recovery. It may be that, as Party Chairman, I was then unduly influenced by my desire to win the 1959 election. But looking at it as impartially as I can, I still think that we were right.

When the Labour Government was elected in 1964, it became necessary for us to consider the matter afresh. Mr Wilson clearly thought that some action in regard to the unions was necessary because he took great credit for setting up, soon after he took office, the Donovan Commission. Indeed, he made great play of our failure to do the like. It therefore became necessary for us to think out our own position. Quite clearly, trade union law was, and it has become again, something of a mess. For this, Parliament, and the parties, have been partly to blame, but the trade unions even more so. At the beginning of the nineteenth century two new types of economic association began to evolve. Both were frowned on by the Common Law as it had developed during the eighteenth century. The first was the Limited Liability Company. The second was the Trade Union. The first the Common Law declared to be an impossibility, unless it was first sanctioned by Royal Charter or by Parliament, because it infringed the principle that traders in partnership with one another should be liable for the debts of the partnership to the full extent of their resources. The second it declared in effect to be an illegal conspiracy in restraint of trade. Owing to the prevailing economic and political climate of the times, successive Parliaments took a different view, but in so doing made a sharp distinction in the attitude they took to the two types of body. Despite its obvious possibilities as an instrument of commercial fraud, successive Parliaments smiled on the limited liability company because of its capacity to promote trade. During the century, successive Parliaments gave it a general corporate status, provided it with regulations declaring the legal relationships between its members, its board and the public, gave it a code of practice in Table 'A', established a Companies Court (now part of the Chancery Division) to regulate its affairs and preside over its obsequies in winding-up, and a Registry to regulate and certify its birth, and enforce the formal rules of incorporation. After more than a century, the Companies Act 1862, amended and re-amended, consolidated and codified from time to time, remains at the heart of company law. The limited liability company has thus come wholly within the rule of law and, although there have been successive scandals from time to time, Parliament and the courts have, on the whole, been willing and eager to intervene when necessary.

The history of trade unions has been different, and markedly less happy. Though Parliament, rather grudgingly, remitted the criminal sanctions of conspiracy, it withheld its smiles. It gave no guidance for the conduct of a trade union's affairs. It established no court and no code of practice. No doubt a trade union is less obviously a potential instrument of fraud than a limited company. But it can more easily become an instrument of oppression if its powers are misused. Experience has shown that serious questions of right and wrong arise between its members or between the leadership at branch, district and national level and individual members or groups of members, between members and non-members in the same trade, between rival unions, between unions and employers, or associations of each, between unions and individual members of the public or between unions and the public at large. If such problems arise, it is clear that they will be solved either by reason or by force, and since reason is better than force, one could have hoped that reason would be the rule. Unhappily, in human affairs, reason can only rule if force is seen not to pay, and if reason is articulated into formal rules which are known in advance, and which in the absence of agreement are capable of enforcement. This is the basis of the rule of law in every field. Without it, and without resort to impartial tribunals to ascertain the true facts and apply the rules, there can be neither peace nor order in society. There is no reason to suppose that trade unions, or that trade unionists, are an exception to this generalization. Nevertheless, Parliament has repeatedly declined to give what has been accorded freely to companies and what trade unions and trade unionists so manifestly need. The tragedy has been that only a minority of trade unions and trade unionists has ever been perspicacious enough to see the value of the requirement or to co-operate in satisfying it.

The reason for this tragedy is that Parliament having refused to intervene on a comprehensive scale, the courts were left to work out their own salvation on the basis of inherited legal principles. Law does not permit a vacuum, and disputes have to be solved in one way or another and, if Parliament gives no guidance, the courts resort to precedent and tradition. In many fields of law, this is perfectly adequate, though as a matter of history, Parliament is always compelled in the end to legislate, to formulate principles, to iron out anomalies and to establish new institutions, when old principles cannot by themselves answer the questions. But in the field of trade union law, established principles were more than usually inadequate, since both Parliament and lawyers, looking as they always have done, in the absence of legislation, to precedent, were compelled to hark back to memories based on wholly different social conditions, some going back as far as the Black Death and its aftermath. This they did against a background of Manchester School economics, and Benthamite political philosophy to which much of legitimate trade union practice was antagonistic.

The result was that, throughout the nineteenth and early twentieth century, trade unions and trade unionists came to regard the law and lawyers as their enemies, which in truth they are not, and to look to Parliament, not as the source of benevolent legislation in the style of the Companies Act, but as the source of remedy against what, rightly or wrongly, trade unionists regarded as the injustices of the law enforced by the courts. Thus successive Acts of Parliament, from 1871 to 1945, legislated *ad hoc* to get rid of particular court decisions or, in one case, a particular Act of Parliament imposed (in my view rightly) in the aftermath of the General Strike. This tradition is deep seated. Nevertheless, I had myself hoped that the Donovan Commission, presided over by a humane High Court judge and Lord of Appeal, who had himself been a Labour Member of Parliament, would produce a rational end to this unhappy story. It was soon clear that this was not to be the case since the Trades Union Congress dragged its feet over its evidence and, when the evidence ultimately appeared, showed that it had no understanding either of the problem or of the way out. In the meantime, a purely negative attitude on the part of the Conservative Party was no longer tenable. We had to consider what to do in advance of the report and, after the report, which was far from unanimous, to decide what to do about it in the light not only of the report but of the Labour Government's decision first to go beyond it and then largely to shelve it. My own legal practice prevented me from taking an active part in the preparatory work in opposition which ultimately led to the Industrial Relations Act. I criticized it in private on several grounds, but felt myself able to support the package in public. Without betraying confidences, I cannot elaborate on this. What I can do, however, is to state what I now think without disclosing whether any and if so what part of my conclusions are hindsight.

Both the Conservative package and the Donovan Commission seem to me to have got things right in so far as each would have created a legal structure of a modern kind within which the rule of law could have grown up within the industrial field. Where the Conservative package went wrong was in confusing this basic necessity with a potential role of the courts in 'preventing' or 'postponing' strikes. If the Conservative planners were wrong they nevertheless had ample precedent in the legislation of other countries, some of which was not wholly unsuccessful, and the Labour Government, until they were driven out of their conviction by their trade union masters, provided a blueprint which was at least as objectionable, and in important respects less liberal and constitutional, than the Conservatives'. My view has always been that, although the law has a part to play in the prevention of strikes, and in making trade unions and trade unionists compensate innocent third parties for the wrongs they sometimes do in the course of industrial action, no attempt either to enforce trade union bargains as contracts, or to prevent strikes against employers by court order is likely to be successful except in the wholly unlikely event, which sometimes but very rarely happens, of the fomenters of a strike misjudging the real feeling of their rank and file. For various reasons, this view prevailed during the Macmillan government, and in particular the view, with which I also agree, was taken that compulsory ballots about strike action were likely to be ineffective as a means of preventing strikes even though no objection could be taken to them on constitutional or moral grounds.

As Lord Chancellor, I was at pains to remove, and I think I did successfully remove, from the Bill any provisions which imposed on any court any issue which was not in principle justiciable, either because it involved legal principles not found and formulated in the Bill or because it involved facts or opinions not required to be proved by evidence, either orally or by affidavit. In some ways the Industrial Relations Court was an advance from the point of view of the jurist on ordinary High Court procedure and current practices. Like the Restrictive Practices Court, the Industrial Court crossed the border into Scotland, although the professional judicial element in each country was severally provided by the two judiciaries. Like the Restrictive Practices Court, it had lay members who, if the trade unions had co-operated, would always have included a trade unionist. I do not myself admire the practice of dispensing with wigs and gowns, and the absence of formal procedures. I had practised myself in the Restrictive Practices Court, and my experience led me to believe that informality often actually leads to increased expense and the very complication it is intended to avoid. The absence of formal uniform on the Bench and formal behaviour in court sometimes creates the impression that the court has not quite the right to exact obedience which the High Court is able to expect. I now even think it possible that this absence of outward form may have rendered less unacceptable to moderate opinion some of the extravagances of disobedience to which some individual militants resorted and that it would in the circumstances have been better to give the jurisdiction to the High Court or Court of Sessions.

Having said all this, the Act was a genuine and honest attempt to handle a real difficulty which various governments had too long failed to tackle. I can still see nothing in it which justified either boycott of its remedies or resistance to its orders. By their campaign against it, the unions were doing a poor service to their country and ultimately to their membership, and though there was much about it from the first which I personally thought ill-advised, I regard its almost total repeal, and the return to *ad hoc* legislation without the adoption of rule of law, as an unmitigated misfortune. As to the idea, so sedulously fostered in political debate, that it created industrial unrest, this is plainly nonsense. In an inflationary situation in which striking can be seen to pay, industrial unrest is inevitable. Since the return of a Labour Government, pledged not only to repeal the Act but to impose no sanctions on industrial action, industrial unrest has increased, and predictably increased with serious economic effects. Far worse, economic misfortunes on a scale hitherto unimagined may be in the offing and, if so, the unions and the Labour movement will be largely to blame, and in particular will be largely responsible for the massive unemployment which is likely to result from excessive wage demands and irresponsible industrial action.

43

The 1974 Elections and After

I felt the last chapter was a necessary introduction to what I feel disposed to say about politics since the fall of the Heath administration. It is not appropriate for me to disclose what took place prior to the dissolution of Parliament in February 1974. But one or two things can be said without betraying any confidences. The first is that, in retrospect, we were very obviously badly informed about the earlier dispute with the miners in 1972. If we had been correctly advised, the Wilberforce enquiry should have been unnecessary. But we acted in good faith because we believed that what was being then demanded was in excess of what was being given to others, and in excess of what the country could afford.

We had fought the 1970 election in the hope that, if we seriously tackled the unemployment which was the deliberate result of the surplus budgeting of the Jenkins Chancellorship, the unions would be prepared to co-operate with us in a policy of wage restraint. This in the event turned out to be an illusion. The unemployment proved more resistant to reflationary measures far longer than I personally had anticipated. But even so, I would have hoped for more co-operation in the national interest than we actually received from the unions. There came a time when it was clear that a new policy would have to be devised, and this was provided, within the ambit of our 1970 manifesto, by the CBI initiative. This, in fact, worked on a voluntary and one-sided basis for twelve months. It was quite clear, however, that this voluntary act of self-denial could not last without trade union co-operation and, despite long and protracted talks, this was not forthcoming. I was never under any illusions about the difficulty of enforcing a statutory policy, or the impossibility of doing so over a prolonged period. However, I equally had no doubts about the necessity for a statutory policy at least on a temporary basis if voluntary restriction failed, and I did not regard this so much as a U-turn as the necessary corollary of the rejection of our conciliatory action. I accepted then, and accept now, that if both policies failed, what will happen in the end is a period of prolonged and massive unemployment coupled with a deflationary policy imposed, ultimately, by pressures from without. I believe that should this happen, and we are nearer to it now than then, the prolonged misery that this will impose on the peoples of our island will cause such a revulsion of feeling that both trade unionists and other members of the public will ultimately submit to almost any hardships rather than return to the vicious circle which inflation of the currency imposes. This is what has happened in other countries. But in the autumn of 1973 we were sufficiently far off from a calamity of that nature to make one think it preferable to impose statutory controls on free negotiation, to which I have been, and am opposed, as a permanent policy. This could have provided a respite during which the situation might be retrieved. The alternative, as I saw it then, and see it now, is for the public, including the unions, to learn the hard way, and if this happens, as I believe it will, society may well suffer irreversible damage in the process. I do not feel ashamed of this train of reasoning. I admit that we probably overdid the reflation in 1970 to 1971. But this is a matter of judgement and degree rather than principle. I would have felt ashamed had I supported the policy of deliberately induced unemployment favoured, for instance, by Mr Powell, as an alternative to what we did. This may be due to a difference in our ages, for I am old enough to remember, perhaps with too strong a sense of revulsion, the moral unhappiness of the 1930s which led so many of my contemporaries to socialist, fascist, or even communist ideas and, in some cases, to betray their country to dictatorships of the right or left.

At all events that is what we did, and to some extent at least we were succeeding until the second miners' dispute of 1973-4. As I have said, the Labour Party and the trade union movement can never make up their minds whether their object is to destroy the capitalist system by exposing its contradictions, or to rescue it from its faults and at the same time secure a bigger share of benefits for their members. When both forces operate in the same direction, the result is calamitous, and this is what happened in the autumn of 1973. We were again informed that the offer that was being made to the miners was generous, and this time we were told that the unions were more likely to accept it than reject it. The public opinion polls were favourable to our decision to stand on the offer, and in the later months of 1973 and early in 1974 there was more pressure on us to advise a dissolution of Parliament and to secure a new mandate and a larger majority, than there was to give way to the miners' demands. I was personally against this pressure. Unless we were to see matters through to the end we could be accused of abdicating our responsibilities and running away. I did not think that our popularity was solidly based or would survive the three necessary weeks of the election campaign conducted in conditions of darkness, cold and, possibly, demonstrations, violence and crisis. No one, of course, can say for certain what would have happened if Mr Heath had appealed to the country in January or early February. My hunch was, and is, that we should have been beaten, and that we should have deserved to lose.

This however is, of course, pure speculation. What in fact happened was quite different. We won, and we continued winning, the unpleasant battle of the three-day week. I believe the public was on our side. The loss to industry was very largely compensated by collaboration between employees and management in the industries most affected. Our very success precipitated, as I had expected, a miners' strike. I had always believed that the objective of the extremists on the miners' executive was to run down stocks by a go-slow and then, when they had reached a critical level, to precipitate a crisis by a short, sharp and effective strike. This is not what happened, because the stocks of coal above ground proved unexpectedly resilient. But the result was the same. Faced with the dilemma of coming to terms (which would not in fact have been ungenerous) and declaring a total strike, the miners went in for a total strike.

The question then arose as to whether we could go on without an election. My own conviction was that the ideal answer was to do so. But to do so successfully would have involved two conditions. The first was that our majority in the Commons should remain staunch, not only on the principal issue but on any other question of confidence which might arise until the crisis was behind us. The second was that if the country really had to suffer the kind of hardship which might be expected when the stocks ran out, we could continue to govern until a settlement was made. It would not be right to disclose what happened, and since I was principally present only at the meetings of the full Cabinet, I am, in any event, not in a position to know the whole story. But it is important to recall that, when the decision was made to go to the country it was unanimous, and any critics of Mr Heath's generalship must take due account of the fact. A Prime Minister need not go to his Cabinet for support before he advises the Queen to dissolve Parliament. But Mr Heath did so and got the support. There were respectable reasons for the decision. Clearly, if there was any danger of the Commons majority faltering, the decision was right. It must be preferable to call an election than to be turned out and then let your opponents call one. Moreover, there was every reason to believe, and I do believe, that, had we been successful, the Relativities Board would have come up with proposals which the miners would not have rejected if put forward by a newly-elected government, though they might well have done so if put forward by a government whose mandate was three-quarters expired.

I always had cold feet about the result of the election, despite the polls which, until the end, remained favourable. But even in the light of hindsight, I still think we would have won had it not been for three unpredictable events which turned a narrow victory into a narrow defeat. The first was the wholly incorrect briefing given by a member of the Relativities Board to the Press which led them to report inaccurately that the offer to the miners had been based on an arithmetical miscalculation. We never really recovered from this, and I believe that the briefing was a calculated act on the part of the person responsible. But whether it was a calculated act or sheer incompetence, the effect was to mislead the nation, and the result was disastrous. This was the most important factor. The second was the action of Mr Enoch Powell in advising voters to vote Labour. The effect of this can be exaggerated, but it was significant in the industrial parts of the Midlands. I understand, though I do not agree with, Mr Powell's dislike of a compulsory incomes policy, even as a temporary expedient, and am prepared to make allowances for his declared, but to my mind incomprehensible, attitude on the Common Market. However Mr Powell did real and possibly irreparable damage to his country by this action which it is impossible to defend in a convinced anti-Socialist, and as an ex-constituency member myself, I find it impossible to condone his treatment of his constituency association which had put up so loyally with his idiosyncrasies for so long. The third, and the least important, of the three factors was the speech by Mr Campbell Adamson, about forty-eight hours before the poll, condemning the Industrial Relations Act. This was widely, and not unnaturally, represented as the considered view of the Confederation of British Industries and did us a good deal of harm at a moment at which it was too late to mount any effective rejoinder. These factors brought down the Heath government, together with our best chance of avoiding a major political and constitutional crisis in the near future. Once Mr Wilson had accepted office on what was essentially a caretaker basis and without any kind of majority, I regarded it as inevitable that there would be a second election in a matter of months returning an overall Labour majority. My only surprise was that the majority was not larger when it came.

I now look forward to the future of my country with considerable misgiving, although it is no part of my intention here to play Cassandra's role. I have no faith in the so-called Social Contract as the means of containing inflation or securing industrial peace. In fact, it has done neither, and it can do neither. You might as well try to control a rutting elephant with a pea-shooter, moreover a pea-shooter not loaded with peas. This, however, is in the future. What I believe the future holds in store for us is disagreeable in the extreme, but it will be so disagreeable as to shake the people of Britain, trade unionists not least, wholly out of the euphoria of sentimental escapism which has been their dominant characteristic since 1945. My only fear is that events will prove so unpleasant that irreversible changes may take place in our national character and even in the nature of our civilization. I need not say that in this I hope and pray I may be mistaken. What my fears mean for me in practice is that I can no longer look forward to the honourable retirement interspersed with occasional judicial duties for which I had planned. Instead I foresee for myself an indefinite period of political activity. I do not feel that I can honourably bow myself out when so much that I have loved and worked for seems to be in jeopardy.

44

The Same Door as in I went

The time has come to bring this untidy account of my opinions to an end. When I set out upon this enterprise I had intended to place on record at the end of my life a reasoned defence of my intellectual and philosophical opinions and my religious allegiance viewed not as a series of unalterable dogmas received on trust, but as a working hypothesis about life, constantly under revision and review. I had wished to show that these views are entitled to be judged as intellectually respectable. I know they have brought me infinite comfort and serenity in times of disappointment, difficulty and distress. I had intended to leave out of account any personal reminiscences which were not directly required in order to present the framework and context in which my opinions were moulded and formed. In the first chapters I was able, more or less rigidly, to conform to this prescription. When I began, however, to set out my opinions about politics, I found the frame and the picture melting more and more into one since, inevitably, it is impossible to give an account of my views without disclosing some of my political background and experience. In so far as this has involved me in inconsistency, I suppose I should now apologize.

On reflection, I do not feel disposed to do so. I have, I believe, adhered to my original resolve to betray no confidences, to injure no friends, to confess no intimate indiscretions, and to claim no particular credit for thinking or acting as I have done. It has been a matter of supreme regret to me that my public life has taken place in a period of national humiliation and decline, the like of which I do not know that the British nation has ever experienced in recent history. When one has played even so modest a part as I in public life, one can take no credit for oneself, for a career which has been played out against this background, and one can well ask oneself whether by greater sagacity, insight, courage, or virtue one could not have achieved more or at least allowed less that was of value to be sacrificed.

These are doubts I cannot answer, and I shall not attempt to do so. In the nature of things I cannot look forward now to many more years of life, and I should be ungrateful if I did not express at the end of it my profound gratitude for all the blessings I have received. The Christian religion, which I profess, would be nothing were it not for its belief that death is not the end. But if I were to be wrong, if my separate existence were to turn out after all to be concluded with my decease, as I once certainly believed, I would have no cause whatever to complain. I could not feel cheated. I have enjoyed all, or most, of the real pleasures of body and soul. I have seen and enjoyed the beauty of nature, in the mountains, and at sea, in the desert and in the air and in the gentleness of a closely-cropped and cultivated landscape. I have known the love of parents and wife and children and friends of all kinds, and almost all degrees of intimacy. I have had the privilege of serving my country under arms and in positions of authority in the state. I have loved flowers and books, and birds, and dogs and cats, and I have derived great pleasure from good food and good wine. I have visited many parts of this astonishing planet. I have never lost my zest for living, and I do not now wish to leave the scene of so much beauty and so much enthralling interest. But if my existence were to terminate tomorrow I could not say that I had been cheated, and I do not believe that the basic causes of my contentment have been more than marginally enhanced by the fact, for it is a fact, that from the point of view of money and material wealth, I have always had sufficient, although never as much as I could have liked to possess. I believe that many a man with less wealth than I possess has lived a life no less satisfying than mine; and I know that many wealthier men have failed to achieve happiness at all.

On the other hand, I do recognize that many other folk have been less fortunate than I. I do not necessarily rank the poor among them except in so far as poverty leads to ill health, or the denial of the relationships of love and affection for which we all crave, or to ignorance of the pleasures of the intellect or the spirit. But there are those for whom I would feel a sense of injustice if this life and the joys of it were all there were to hope for. They include all those who suffer without fault, whether from need or injustice, the lack of health, or love and wonder at the beauty of the world. Whilst I could not regard myself as cheated were my life all that there is for me to enjoy, I could not regard the ultimate justice of things in the way I do were it not for my Christian faith that death is not the end of the individual. I am not alone in this, nor are Christians alone in looking for something more. Eastern religions too have their origin in meditation about the degree of apparently undeserved suffering and unremedied injustice in this life, and find their relief in the doctrine of reincarnation and Karma, and ultimate identification with the absolute. I do not think that Western man, or any man who has once found the solace of the Christian religion convincing, can be wholly content with this system of belief. The difference between the religions of the East and their Western counterparts is that the symbol of the East is the revolving wheel of life, for ever turning on its axis without end, without beginning and, as I would say, without meaning or justice, while the great religions of the West, Judaism, Christianity and Islam, regard history as linear in character, the time sequence irreversible. The individual, and the race, and the planet, and the universe are set on a course, no doubt from a beginning immeasurably old, and to a destiny not seen, but on a course in time, and this postulates, to those who are not content to regard our wanderings as purposeless, an end, a purpose and a justice based on a theism which I have sought to justify. To Christians, the individual destiny is guaranteed, and the particular justice promised, by the life and resumed life after death of its Founder. Thus, though I cannot in honour claim more for myself than I have received, for in truth I have received happiness in good measure far beyond my deserts, I cannot reconcile myself to a world in which others prove less fortunate, whilst at the same time being more worthy of good fortune, and I see no reason to believe that the universe in its ultimate order and purpose is less just than I. It would be surprising if it were.

I therefore turn on the critics of Christianity with their own arguments. You ask, I say, how a just God can permit cancer, and motor accidents, and wars, and Belsen, and oppression. I reply that he does so because he wished to create a race of spiritual beings with free will, doing good for its own sake of their own free choice and because it is logically impossible to do this without evil co-existing with good, it is so ordered and decreed both that the just shall suffer and that they shall be rewarded, both that evil should exist and that it should be defeated in the end. As a guarantee and earnest of the good that there shall be we have been given a curious and unique insight into the nature of the Godhead itself. For it has been disclosed to us both that God loves, and that he suffers with, his creatures. The figure on the Cross is one reminder in time of suffering that we are not alone and that, though there is evil and hatred and bitterness in the world, the principle of reason and goodness, which lies at the root of reality, the logos of God, is neither indifferent to it nor will permit it to triumph in the end.

Index

/